The Futurists, the Formalists, and the Marxist Critique

The Futurists,
the Formalists,
and the Marxist Critique

Edited and introduced by
Christopher Pike

Translated by
Christopher Pike and Joe Andrew

Prefaces, notes and afterword provided by
Gérard Conio and translated by Rupert Swyer

INK
LINKS

The Russian journal from which each of these articles has been translated is signalled at the start of each piece. This edition first published in 1979 by
Ink Links Ltd,
271 Kentish Town Road,
London NW5 2JS

© English translation rights Ink Links Ltd., 1979.

The prefaces and afterword by Gérard Conio, as well as his notes to several of the articles, are taken, with permission, from the book, *Le Formalisme et le futurisme russes devant le marxisme*, published by Editions l'Age d'Homme, Lausanne, 1975.

© Editions l'Age d'Homme, 1975.

The translation of the Gérard Conio contributions by Rupert Swyer:

© English language rights Ink Links Ltd., 1979.

The introduction by Christopher Pike:
© World rights, Ink Links Ltd., 1979.

ISBN 0906133 149 cloth

Set in 10pt Garamond by Red Lion Setters,
22, Brownlow Mews, London WC1N 2LA.
Printed by Whitstable Litho,
Millstrood Road, Whitstable, Kent
and bound by Hunter and Foulis,
Bridgeside Works, McDonald Road,
Edinburgh EH7 4NP.

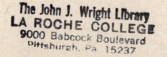

Contents

CHRISTOPHER PIKE

Introduction:
Russian Formalism and Futurism

The Beginning

The revolution which took place in Russia in 1917 was preceded and survived by similarly radical changes in the Russian cultural scene, in particular in the fields of poetry and poetics. The first of these developments in about 1910 was the reaction of a number of progressive young artist-writers (including Sergei Bobrov, David Burliuk, Vassily Kamensky, Velimir Khlebnikov, Aleksei Kruchenykh, Benedict Livshits and Vladimir Mayakovsky) against the prevailing artistic canons of traditional nineteenth-century realism on the one hand and symbolism on the other. These excited, brash, challenging writers existed in various loose and fluid groupings until about 1930; all of them, reluctantly or otherwise, came to accept the name of "futurists" to describe their attitudes and their art. Shortly after the emergence of the first kinds of futurist literature, and to a considerable extent under their influence, there were formed in Moscow and St. Petersburg between 1914 and 1916 two groups of original and energetic young linguists and students of literature who, in reaction against the traditional impressionistic, "psychological" and "biographical" academic study of literature, sought instead to apply the principles, methods and results of the newly discovered linguistic science to the phenomenon of literature. These innovative linguists, theorists and critics (headed by Boris Eykhenbaum, Roman Jakobson and Victor Shklovsky) came to be known, quite against their wishes, as the "formalists".

Both groups attempted to achieve "purity" and autonomy within their own fields: the futurists to create a pure new poetry, purged of the psychological, religious and mystical baggage of previous Russian poetic forms, a poetry which would for the first time possess a valid and completely contemporary relationship to modern reality; the formalists to develop a pure study of literature, a poetics, in which literature would be treated as an independent phenomenon in its own right, its specific features as "literature" discovered and their relationships formulated—free for the first time from the vision of literature simply as an extra dimension, a content-form for the self-expression of artist or society. With the coming of the October revolution in 1917, both the formalists and the futurists found themselves in a society to which they were naturally more sympathetic on the whole, than the old society against whose cultural attitudes and procedures they had been rebelling. At the same time, the pressure of this circumstance, together with the ensuing debate over the culture that was to be preserved and created by the new society, forced both formalists and futurists to re-examine their previous, simply adopted stances of rejection and rebellion. Both groups strove over the next decade or so to defend and further their positions in the context of Marxism and the calls for ''proletarian culture''. They thus became principal participants in this debate and, after the gradual erosion of their security, prominent victims of the debate's suppression.

The cultural environment of Russian futurism

The complex phenomenon of Russian symbolism is surprisingly similar in its essential qualities to the futurism which attempted to destroy its all-pervading influence. This similarity of essence is the explanation for the fact that many futurist poets began as imitators of symbolism and were indeed sometimes supported by elder figures in the symbolist movement; in fact, even in its later stages, futurism was viewed by several influential critics as simply a new kind of symbolism. The origins of Russian symbolism, which came into being around the 1890s, lay in the attempt to remove literature and art from the political-social dictates of civic realism (''Babylonian captivity'', as the Acmeist poets described it), which had till then dominated nineteenth-century Russian literature, and to re-discover a true aesthetic of art. The symbolists were seekers of the same purity and autonomy for art as the futurists were to be later. To this end, they attempted to develop new poetic vocabulary and to write poetry of words rather than ideas, poetry whose language would attain a reality beyond the prosaic naturalism which, they believed, characterised realist writing. As the movement developed, however, its theorists and practitioners (principally, Konstantin Balmont, Andrei Bely, Alexander Blok, Valery Bryusov and Vyacheslav Ivanov) became caught up in the tumultous religious and metaphysical revival of the turn of the century. Their attention to questions of religion and metaphysics extended ultimately into the spheres of mysticism and the occult. As a result, the poetry of the symbolists became more and more dense, super-refined, recherché and élitist: the reality, or realities, to which they directed their poetic language became increasingly abstract, remote and mysterious. Eventually, the intense rarefication of symbolist theory and practice led to the dissolution of the movement at the end of the first decade of this century, its major poets surviving as individual literary figures.[1]*

It is between these two poetic loci, the purity of the poetic word on the one hand and the nature of the referential reality on the other, that the relationship of futurism to symbolism (and, incidentally, to realism) may be constructively defined. The Russian futurist poets followed the symbolists in the extraordinary attention which they gave to the word as the foundation of poetry, but reacted against what symbolism had become in their rejection of poetry's connection with abstract, non-actual realities, the use of the word as "magic", as an entry to super-real planes of being. Instead, the futurists (in contrast to their name, perhaps) always directed their words towards a reality which was in some sense immediate, concrete, actual. To use Tynyanov's statement of their procedure (as found in his articles in this collection), they "aimed" their "word" at the "thing", and not at an idea or an ideal. The futurists almost exclusively rejected the metaphysical in favour of the physical (in all its aspects).

In the immediacy of their art, the futurists reflect their other principal origin, as described by Vladimir Markov in his definitive study *Russian Futurism*.[2] This was European and Russian avant-garde art, namely impressionism and post-impressionism (including primitivism and cubism). The closeness of the relationship between visual arts and literature is a feature of most of the European movements in art at the time in question, not just futurism, but also symbolism, impressionism and expressionism (the latter curiously absent from the foreground of Russian art, although Markov interestingly identifies in literature Pasternak and Mayakovsky as being, in their different ways, the "truest Russian representatives of this aesthetic kind"[3]). Camilla Gray in her book *The Russian Experiment in Art 1863-1922*[4] points out the way in which this universal vision of art links disparate movements in Russian art from the beginning of the twentieth century onwards. She classifies as "one of the most important innovations" of the "World of Art" movement (the dominant

---

*The notes to the introduction are to be found at its close, a procedure we have followed with each major article and preface. The notes for the group of short articles in section one are, however, all grouped together at the end of the section.

turn-of-the-century artistic movement in Russia, corresponding to "Art Nouveau" in the West) specifically "the conception of art as a unity, of a basic inter-relationship and common source of all inspiration regardless of the medium of expression". She continues:

> This spiritual affinity between the members of the "World of Art" and the Symbolist school was later realized in a physical inter-development of literature and painting which is one of the most outstanding characteristics of the Cubo-Futurist and subsequent schools of abstract painting which developed in Russia during the years 1910-1921.[6]

In the case of the Russian futurists, both the beginning of their movement in impressionist/post-impressionist ("Primitivist") painting and the symbiosis of painting and literature within the movement is shown by a number of factors. Firstly, several leading futurists (e.g., David Burliuk, Kruchenykh and Mayakovsky) began their public existence as professional painters and all of the most significant futurists at one time or another worked in both paint and ink. Secondly, there was very close collaboration, particularly at the height of "pure" futurism (1913-14), between the leading avant-garde artists (especially Mikhail Larionov and Natalia Goncharova, the chief proponents of primitivism-futurism) and the Burliuk brothers (David, Nikolai and Vladimir). Thirdly, futurist poetry itself constantly emphasised the visual aspects of its existence in its experimentation with handwriting and typography, in its use of primitivist-futurist paintings as illustrations and in the very materials of its books, e.g., the repeated printing of poetry on wallpaper. (This visual aspect of futurist publication is now excellently studied and illustrated by Susan Compton in her book *The World Backwards*.[7]) Finally, and perhaps not least significantly, the very public conduct and appearance of the futurists, the "performance" of futurism, as it were, was a continually intensive visual assault—the futurists themselves parading the streets in outrageous clothing, carrying flowers or with paintings on their cheeks, radishes or spoons in their buttonholes.[8] Moreover, they were not afraid to use film, and their poetry readings often resembled the demonstrations or "happenings" of western pop culture in the 1960s. As we shall see later, this inter-linking of the visual and the verbal is also one of the most important connections between futurism and formalism.

Russian futurism in literature

Russian futurist literature (principally poetry, but later prose as well) began to appear in representative form in 1910 in the two collections *The Studio of Impressionists* and *A Trap for Judges*,[9] and the movement identifiable from its origins as Russian futurism, or cubo-futurism, as it was later termed, continued to exist in different guises until about 1930. The history of the movement is typical, in an extreme form, of almost any avant-gardism in art, in that there existed simultaneously and consecutively between 1910 and 1930 several groups of writers who either claimed or received the title of "futurists". The most prominent of these groups was the "Hylaea" group (containing Khlebnikov, Mayakovsky, the Burliuk brothers, Livshits and Kruchenykh); it was this core group (with significant exceptions) that was to produce the Cubo-Futurists and the members of LEF in the years to come. Also of great importance (and occasionally, in their own time, more important than the Hylaeans themselves) were the movements of Ego-Futurism (1911-1914), the Mezzanine of Poetry (1913-1914), Centrifuge (1913-1917) and 41° (1917-1920). The complex variation of theory and practice among these groups, together with the itineraries of some futurists from one group to another, are discussed in detail by Markov, but are too specialised in their interest to find a place here. Markov, however, rightly warns against generalisations based on the activity of the Hylaeans alone [10] and is careful to trace his evolution of futurism through all the main groups.

Mention has already been made of futurism's struggle for the purity of the poetic word, the autonomy of poetry and the immediacy or actuality of poetry's reference. These emphases make it possible to remove a frequent confusion about the term "futurism". The futurists were not, on the whole, poets who wrote about the future. On the contrary, they saw themselves as writing about the present in terms which would enable their readers to understand the future moment that each present moment brought them to. They reacted against poetry and art which, in their view, could only see the present in terms of an invalid, discarded past, but many of the futurists themselves were imbued with an interest in the deep past and the eternal values or attributes which they saw as arising from that past. Many futurists preferred to call themselves *budetlyane*, literally "those who will be", which we might interpret as "the coming people", the heirs to the future.

The futurists, as has been seen, stood out strongly against the dominant cultural traditions which preceded them. They advocated throwing Pushkin, Tolstoy and Dostoevsky overboard from "the steamship of modernity". By adopting such an irreverent pose towards the sanctified classics of Russian literature, they incidentally aroused the dislike and suspicion of many Bolsheviks, including Lenin, whose literary and artistic upbringing was steeped in traditional realism. This, however, did not concern the futurists at the time. They were out to build a new culture of the now and the future and their first actions were deliberately destructive (of the old culture) and aggressive (towards its consumers). They had a strong urge to shock the sated and self-contented bourgeoisie (thus, the title of the first Hylaean manifesto in 1912: *A Slap in the Face for Public Taste* [11]). They challenged the refined, dense, abstractly elegant poetry of symbolism with poetic language which ranged from the simple and primitive to the vulgar and brutal. They sought to bring poetry out of the ivory tower, in which the symbolists pored over treasures only they could appreciate, into the street; they wanted to democratise poetry, to make it part of the life of the masses, an art which corresponded to their reality, but also did much more than that, in positively transforming it and aiming it towards a better future.

Characterisations of futurism are as varied as critical reaction to it and attempts to see it as a unified movement result, as Vahan Barooshian puts it in his *Russian Cubo-Futurism 1910-1930*, [12] in contemplating "the absurdity of accepting Majakovskij and Burljuk as practitioners of 'trans-sense language' and Xlebnikov and Krucenyx and Kamenskij as poets of the city". [13] Despite all the difficulties of summarisation, however, there are two coexistent, very different, but positive strands throughout Russian futurism. One (led by Khlebnikov) might be called the search for innocence in poetry, an attempt to establish the same kind of values in poetry as primitivism represented in painting. The other (led by Mayakovsky) is an attempt to cope with and transform forces which are precisely not innocent, namely the increasing complication of life in a technological, urban society, and is customarily compared to cubism in painting.

Primality is probably a better word to describe Khlebnikovian futurism than primitivism. Thematically, this primality was expressed in a preoccupation with the experience of childhood in all its aspects, with the life of prehistory and with the content and values of Russian folklore. Mayakovskian "urbanist cubism", on the other hand, showed the poet as both ordinary and extraordinary man, living the life of the city street and reacting to the technological transformation of his world.

What is more lastingly significant about futurism than these "themes", however, is the unceasing poetic experimentation and re-creation to which both Khlebnikovian and Mayakovskian futurism contributed, although it must be said that Khlebnikovian futurism (principally through the development of *zaum*, "trans-sense language") was dominant in this sphere. Futurist experimentation with the material, visual aspects of literature,—books, paper, illustrations, handwriting, typography etc.,—has already been described. More "poetic", however, is the futurist experimentation with language which took place in two areas, that of sound-creation and that of word-creation. In the area of sound, the futurists investigated new and original sound-combinations, which led them (in the person of Alexei Kruchenykh) ultimately to the basic concept of "trans-sense language" (*zaum*). "Zaum" suffers from inconsistency in the description of it by both its futurist practitioners and its scholars, but basically it meant, in the usage of Kruchenykh and others, the use of words as sound (either phonetically altered "real" words or quite newly invented "words") to convey to the reader, apart from any conventional "meaning", a meaning or meanings (connotative, emotive, even mystical) that were purely sound-based. By a different, and considerably more complex path through word-creation, the "poet-mathematician" Khlebnikov moved from an original interest in neologism to his own concept of "zaum". Typically of the poet who attempted to work out a mathematical rationale for the events of world history, Khlebnikov's ambitious "zaum" involved the creation of an entire new basis for the Russian language, through a re-discovery and a re-creation of primal verbal roots in sound, a completely new generation of meaning in words through sounds. Whatever the differences in conception, "zaum" represented the focal point in futurist concentration on the pure poetic word and, in its return to the fundamental of poetry, "zaum" might well be considered the linguistic equivalent of a crucial development in Russian avant-garde art between 1915 and 1918, that of Kasimir Malevich's "suprematism", the painting "of pure sensation".[14] (Cf. Gray's description of Malevich's culminant series of paintings, "White on White": "All colour has been eliminated, and form in the purest, most de-humanized shape of the square, has been reduced to the faintest pencilled outline").[15] On the other hand, futurist experimentation with sound and word links it not just to avant-garde painting, but also to the equally radical and progressive school of literary thought which emerged between 1914 and 1916, namely Russian formalism, to which this discussion now turns.

The motivation of Russian formalism

The philosophical, scientific and literary origins of Russian formalism are extremely complex, all the more so in that one is here attempting to trace the intellectual influences on a diverse group of original and outstanding talents who were initially based in rather different fields. The Moscow Linguistic Circle and the (Petersburg) Society for the Study of Poetic Language ("Opoyaz") gradually coalesced into a single formalist grouping which continued to attract new members. Eventually, formalism comprised theorists of literature (Victor Shklovsky, Osip Brik, Yury Tynyanov), historians of literature (Boris Eykhenbaum), linguists (Roman Jakobson, Lev Jakubinsky), verse specialists (Boris Tomashevsky), philologists (Grigory Vinokur) and at least one ethnographer (Vladimir Propp).[16] Formalism came into existence through the remarkable pooling by these men of their knowledge in different areas of language and literature, to establish common attitudes, aims and directions. This is not to say that their approach to literature and literary theory was monolithic. On the contrary, there can rarely have been a more polyphonic diversity of view among any identifiable group of scholars: not only did they argue among themselves both at any one point in time and, from changing positions, over the course of their relationship, but the individual formalists often gave the appearance of arguing with themselves, through their readiness to change their hypotheses or theories in the face of new "facts" revealed by their investigative methods. This flexibility of the formalists represented (and represents) to formalism's opponents inconsistency, non-scientism and even unprincipled opportunism, but to its followers it is a manifestation of the formalists' refreshingly honest and dynamic approach.

The basic motivation which served to unite the formalists as a whole was a positive interest in language, largely inspired by the developing science of linguistics under Jan Baudouin de Courtenay and Ferdinand de Saussure (it is striking that almost all the formalists were at one time students either of de Courtenay himself, or of his closest protégés, and one formalist, Grigory Vinokur, was one of the first scholars to propagate de Saussure's ideas in Russia).

The influence of linguistics and language studies can be traced in direct or indirect form throughout the formalists' investigation of literature. At the general level, the foundation of modern linguistics on the identification and study of the constants, and the minimum units in language (principally, the phoneme) prompted the formalists to seek the corresponding component units or the elements of literature in general, of specific kinds of texts and of identifiable aspects of the literary process (e.g., narrative).[17] A second general and related influence of linguistics was its emphasis on understanding the functioning of language in its own terms as a *system*. The transferred notion that literature, the art of language, could exist and be understood also as a *system* (or structure) was one of profound consequence for the formalists. At the general level again, this notion of system started the formalists thinking not just in terms of the system of a text, but also of the system of literature as such: by the further borrowing from Saussurian linguistics of the concepts of synchrony and diachrony, the formalists began to construct not only a system of literature as it existed for them, but also a system of history or evolution unique to literature, thus overturning the traditional view, which had glibly assimilated the history of literature to the "progress" of humanity in other spheres. The formalists were in this way capable of talking in terms of a "poetics" from their earliest ventures. One other important legacy of the systemic nature of linguistics was the stress which the formalists were to place, particularly in their conflict with Marxism, on the "scientific" nature of their work. At root, the formalist inquiry was indeed "scientific" in the broad sense that it aimed at an objective and precise study of the elements that constituted the system of literature: the "poetics" which they wished to create was to be a science, not an interpretation of literature. That there was also a pragmatic purpose to the formalist emphasis on their scientism after 1917, and particularly after 1924, is shrewdly indicated by L.T. Lemon and M.J. Reis in their comment on Eykhenbaum's "The Theory of the 'Formal Method'" (1926):[18]

'The Theory of the Formal Method' reads ... like an apologia—a defense carefully calculated to appeal to a hostile audience without distortion of the basic doctrines involved. This perhaps explains Eichenbaum's insistence upon the scientific nature of the Formal method, an insistence that is likely to annoy Western readers. Eichenbaum could not in conscience claim that Formalism was in any sense Marxist in orientation; the simplest and most logical recourse was to insist upon, perhaps even to exaggerate, the notion that the Formalists were engaged merely in a non-ideological study of data, that whatever hypotheses they used developed out of the observation of facts and were modified by those facts. The strategy, if we correctly surmise Eichenbaum's aim, was to argue that Formalism was scientific, and thus compatible with Marxism. On the other hand, it should not be forgotten that Eichenbaum's strategy is at most exaggeration, not falsification; the work of the Formalists is characterised by a desire for accuracy and concreteness that it did not always attain.[19]

Essentially, however, and more specifically, the concentration on the phoneme in linguistics as it influenced the formalists naturally focused their attention on *sound* as the fundamental element in verbal art. Moreover, the role played by sound in the contemporary futurist poetry, so strident and so breathtaking, with which certain formalists (particularly Shklovsky) were closely associated, could hardly fail to impress itself on them. Consequently, it was in sound, the meeting-place between the academic linguists and the Bohemian futurists, that the formalists gained entry to literature. Ladislav Matejka, reviewing the relationship between the formal method and linguistics as a whole, puts it as follows:

> Their [the formalists'] analytic inquisitiveness found engaging targets in the 'trans-rational' products of the linguistic alchemistry practiced by the literary avant garde, under the flag of Futurism in its Russian vintage. The Futurists' poetic games disclosed unexplored aesthetic sound texture arranged so as to fascinate by its very physiognomy, and these games served as alluring examples of a linguistic usage capable of releasing the formal means of utterance from subordination to the semantic load. It became tempting to expect that an accurate, empirically disciplined analysis of sound was the safest step in the attack on the entire complex of semantic values displayed in verbal communication.[20]

Formalist investigation of the futurists' poetic reformation of the word as sound, especially in its most extreme form of "zaum", led to the original central concept of formalism, that of the contrast between language as it appears in everyday reality ("practical" language) and language as it is constructed, organised or used in art ("poetic" language). It is to the perception of this oppositon by the early formalists, despite the criticisms and reformulations which the notion was to undergo later, that most of the significant formalist ideas about literature may be traced. Here lies the germ of the specificity of literature, of the relationship between sound and meaning, of defamiliarisation and "making strange", of the "artificiality" of art, of "form as content", of sign and referent, of the device and "laying bare", and of duality.

The formalists therefore saw the artist most significantly as a crafts-man or, in more twentieth-century terms, a technician who used his skill and the devices he commanded to transform dead materials (reality/"practical" language, paint) into a living work of art (litera-ture/"poetic" language, painting). In doing so, they emphasised the validity of the finished product as a constructed object in its own right and hence the autonomy of literary science as the study of this object's laws. The connections with futurism here are many: among the most obvious, one might refer to futurism's concern for the autonomous, "pure" poetic word, its technic transformation of poetry, Khlebni-kov's vision of the poet as "a railway engineer of language" and the atmospheric influence of Mayakovsky's urbanism.

In their efforts to establish the autonomous and "scientific" nature of proper literary study, the formalists notoriously emphasised to polemical extremes the difference between the artist and his art, the writer and the text, the poet and the poem. As already discussed, they therefore attacked traditional literary study both for its non-autonomous, writer-biased approach (studying the text as a revelation of the writer) and for its non-scientific impressionism (its lack of consistent procedures or methods).

Accordingly also, the formalists rejected the traditional division between "form" and "content" as being writer-biased. In essence, they wished to demonstrate that the boundaries between these two traditional categories were so fluid as to render the distinctness of the categories themselves meaningless. However, in the polemical manner which it was necessary to adopt in the crowded Russian literary scene (as Erlich says, "they had to shout loud to live"), the formalists moved to the opposite extreme from tradition,—from "content dictates form" to "form dictates content". This assertion, which the early formalists spent much time substantiating, notably in their study of futurist verse, particularly "zaum", still angers many critics of formal-ism. They fail to see, however, that the formalists are here playing a deliberate double game. While sincerely demonstrating that the devices and processes of construction of a work of art create the perception that may become the meaning or significance of the work, the formalists deliberately use the old, static categories of "form" and "content" which they know to be incapable of expressing this newly perceived rela-tionship, thus throwing the invalidity of these concepts back at their opponents through what appears to be a triumphant formalist slogan.

In its most positive version, formalism set out to establish an objective, complete understanding of the system of literature, through which students of literature, armed with a consistent methodology and terminology, would enable the work of literature to be used validly for the first time as a point of reference for the study of the artist or society. In this positive aspect of their endeavour, the formalists were motivated also by a vision of the unity of art as a whole which was common to all movements in Russian modernism.[21] They thus believed that their discoveries could be mutually assimilated between literature and the other arts, notably the visual arts of painting and film. In particular, both Shklovsky and Tynyanov were to produce important studies of the cinema and film theory, as well as of the relationship between literature and film (for example, in the areas of narrative and plot). In fact, formalist critical terminology is remarkable for being not only technic (e.g., "construction", "system", "material", "set"), but extremely *visual* in nature (if one may make such a statement of a movement which rejected the concept of visual imagery!). Striking examples of this "visuality" are the concepts of "foregrounding", "shift", "texture", "dominant", "laying bare the device" and "staircase construction".

Having described the principal motivation and premises of the formalist inquiry, discussion may now turn to a brief characterisation of the more significant concrete formalist pronouncements about literature.

Formalist conceptions of literature

The central endeavour of formalism, in line with its advocacy of the specificity and autonomy of both literature and literary study, is the identification of "literariness" (*literaturnost'*), the distinguishing qualities that make literature what it is. Part and parcel of this search for "literariness" is the key formalist notion of "poetic" language as language subject to a particular modality and the rejection of the term "image" in favour of the term "device" as the basis of literature's operation. The notion that literature operated with language in a "special" way not found in "real life" was certainly not new to the formalists: indeed, the term "image" was one way of indicating that speciality of language in literature. What Shklovsky principally rejected in his seminal *Art as a Device* [22] and other works was the idea that the image, which conjured up a visual representation of itself, was a distinctive feature of verbal art. To connect the functioning and efficacy of literary language to its ability to create visual images seemed invalid to Shklovsky, not only in that the image could not be necessarily visual, as he and others demonstrated, but also in that such reliance on a sense perception that was not primary to literature ignored the perceptible immanent qualities and properties of language itself.

Shklovsky's concept of "art as device" emphasised what for the formalists was the constructional nature of the work of literature and was to take the influential Shklovsky in two related directions. It provided the basis of the replacement of "form-content" by "devices-materials", in which the formalists discarded the former static and predetermined categories in favour of a formula which would show how the stuff of life was artificially worked on by literature and the fluid, dynamic relationship between the two. Most importantly, however, the notion of device was a further step away from the opposition of poetic and practical language towards the concept of defamiliarisation or "making strange" (*ostranenie*) on which Shklovsky largely proceeded to build his kind of formalism.

The view that art operates and achieves its individual existence by making strange things that are familiar to the reader in everyday life is rooted in the transformational conception of literature espoused by the formalists. As Shklovsky expresses his thought in *Art as a Device:*

> The thing rushes past us, prepacked as it were; we know that it is there by the space it takes up, but we see only its surface. This kind of perception shrivels a thing up, first of all in the way we perceive it, but later this affects the way we handle it too.... Life goes to waste as it is turned into nothingness. Automatization corrodes things, clothing, furniture, one's wife and one's fear of war ... And so that a sense of life may be restored, that things may be felt, so that stones may be made stony, there exists what we call art.[23]

The notion advanced here of "automatization" of the thing in reality is opposed in art by the quasi-original "realisation" of the thing through art's process of "making strange". As Shklovsky continues:

> The purpose of art is to transmit the sense of a thing as seeing, not as recognizing; the device of art is that of 'making things strange' and of making form difficult, increasing the difficulty and time taken to perceive since the process of perception in art is

an aim in itself and must be prolonged: *art is a way of experien-cing the making of a thing and what has already been made is of no importance.*[24]

This crucial statement of Shklovsky's illustrates a number of key concepts: the way in which "making things strange" creates a new perception ("seeing, not recognizing"); the deliberate complication of form, which emphasises perception precisely by impeding it; the "self-value" of artistic perception; the experiential nature of art; the vital dynamism of the work of art (the "making of a thing"). Additionally, "making strange" is significant of the principle of deviation and divergence from the norm perceived by the formalists throughout art. "Making strange" is, therefore, the first manifesta-tion of this principle and its direct and indirect descendants can be found at several points along the line of formalism's trajectory through literature.

The set of devices which, together with the materials, constitute the system of a work of literature were seen by the formalists as being arranged in a hierarchy which was governed by a particular device or group of devices, called the *dominant*. The dominant and other subordinated devices may emphasise or "foreground" themselves within the work, mainly through being "laid bare" or exposed to the reader of the text, in a deliberate display of the artificiality of the art. The discovery of foregrounding and the establishment of the domin-ant played an important part in the formalist analysis of literary texts, particularly of verse.

The transition between life and literature signified by the poetic-practical language contrast, with all that that meant for Shklovsky, was interpreted and developed in a related but different direction by the other most prominent early formalist, Roman Jakobson. Standing clearly on the boundary between linguistics and literary scholarship, Jakobson investigated the nature of verbal representation in literature, the relationship between the representation (the sign) and the repre-sented (the referent), a direction which developed principally from his major formalist work, *Contemporary Russian Poetry*,[25] the out-standing study of the poetry of Velimir Khlebnikov. Jakobson's interest in the dichotomy of correspondence and independence in the verbal representation of reality, the fact that there was only partial overlap of identity between the word as sign and the object signed, was the semiotic formulation of the intricate and paradoxical relation-ship between sound and meaning in futurist poetry which had first attracted the formalists and which continued to motivate much of their study of verse. The development of Jakobson's perception through later formalism, Prague School aesthetics and linguistics, and later structural linguistics places him at the fountainhead of the modern science of semiotics.

The work of formalism

The most successful investigation in totality conducted by the formalists is undoubtedly that of verse. Perhaps this is not so surprising: verse literature (where the formalists began, in futurist poetry) represents the closest and most obvious interdependence between ''form'' and ''content''. The formalists thus found poetry to be the literature in which the sets of devices used to construct the text and manipulate sound and meaning could be most systematically and ''scientifically'' studied. The evolution of the formalist theory of verse is on the whole a process whereby the more scholarly and painstaking formalists (Jakobson, Tomashevsky, Tynyanov), together with the semi-formalist Zhirmunsky, followed up the penetrating but erratic basic perceptions of Shklovsky, to produce eventually fundamental summations of verse theory, as well as complete technical studies in areas such as metrics. These have become indispensable (if often unacknowledged) equipment for subsequent Soviet and Western scholars of Russian verse.

Certain formalists, however (notably Shklovsky and Eykhenbaum), rapidly developed an apparently inexhaustible fascination with prose literature, whose major form, the novel, seemed to taunt their desire for system with its amorphous variety. The pioneering study of the short story and the novel carried out by the formalists was influenced primarily by Shklovsky's premises of art as divergence and deviation. The transition between life and literature emerged into the foreground again with the formulation and development by Shklovsky and other formalists of notions about the treatment of events and information about events in prose. Central to this study was the opposition perceived between ''fable'' (*fabula*) and ''plot'' (*syuzhet*), essentially a contrast between the ''actual'', non-fictional sequence of events in a story and the ''artistic'', fictional sequence of events as arranged in the plot of a short story or novel.[26] The formalist examination of the motivation of plot extended far into the system of prose.

Leading formalist thought (Shklovsky again notable among them) moved on to consider other aspects of the syntax of narrative

literature and soon became intrigued by the devices used by novelists
to interrupt the narration of plots. Shklovsky in particular began to
investigate the varied "digressions" and "amplifications" involved in
this process. The conclusions which Shklovsky came to in his identification of devices such as digression, repetition, parallel, retardation
and "staircase construction" in general (the latter so named because
of the notion of spiralling the narrative upwards, away from the
horizontal flow of the plot) led the formalist theoreticians of prose to
see these apparently subsidiary elements of narrative as the core of the
work. As Richard Sherwood explains it:

> ...for Shklovsky the part of the literary material which makes
> the work literary or poetic is *not* the basic 'story', but the elabora-
> tions, complications and repetitions of the story, so constructed
> that the work is truly 'perceived', the process of perception being
> heightened by 'retardation', which serves to extend and intensify
> the perceptive process.[27]

The emphasis in formalist prose theory on discovering and studying
the elements of narrative and plot gave rise to two very different
developments in the further study of types of literature.

In the field of prose again, the interest in narrative prompted
Eykhenbaum, who was perhaps the most stylistically oriented of the
formalists, to investigate the "stylization" (a key term of formalist
conventionality) of the narrative voice in literature. Eykhenbaum's
essay on Gogol's short story *The Overcoat* (*How Gogol's 'The Overcoat' is Made*[28]) introduced the narrative category of *skaz*, which
Erlich characterizes as "narrative manner which focuses on the
personal 'tone' of the fictional narrator".[29] The interest of formalists
and other scholars of literature in this speech-oriented narration
developed particularly through the sympathetic, but critical assessment of *skaz* by the pre-eminent Soviet stylistician Victor Vinogradov
and is a direct ancestor of later academic interest in the persona of the
narrator in literature. Additionally, Eykhenbaum's work points up the
way in which stylistic contrasts and parody are capable of manipulating
or even undermining the apparent "meaning" of a text.

The second, rather unpredictable consequence of Shklovsky's work
on the syntax of narrative and plot is the seminal work of the
ethnographer Vladimir Propp in his typology of the Russian folktale
(*Morphology of the Folktale* and 'Transformations of fairy-tales'[30]).
Propp was undoubtedly the most important early scholar of the
structure of the folktale, perhaps the most plot-formalised of genres,

and, in his classification of the genre structure on the basis of "functions" (constant or invariant action units), was clearly influenced by Shklovsky's writings on modern literature. Propp's contribution to the structural-semiotic study not only of folklore, but also of the text as such, is assessed by one modern scholar in the following terms:

> ... for the first time in world scholarship these works elaborated the grammar of a genre, put forward the notions of invariant and transformations, and, as the central concept for the analysis of the text, function ... The synchronic approach of the first work was supplemented by a consideration of questions of diachrony in the article 'Transformations'. This consistent application of the two types of approach showed the possibilities opened up by the concept of function as the key concept of analysis, made it possible to grasp the unity of the tale as a special kind of text, and to point out the main invariants in the process of historical development.[31]

Propp's "character-free" analysis, with its concentration on constant "actions", allowed the oppositions, choices, developments and contrasts which occur in plot-formation to be systematically examined for the first time.

Mention of Propp's contribution to the study of "the process of historical development" brings this discussion to the final general aspect of formalism to be described, namely the research into genre theory, literary history and evolution which formed such a promising later development in formalist thought. As already mentioned, the formalists consistently rejected any attitude to literary history which saw it simply as part of the traditional "progress-oriented" historical development of man. Instead, the formalists (Eykhenbaum, Tomashevsky and, principally, Tynyanov) aimed at discovering the specific history and laws of literary evolution. This aspect of the formalist inquiry might well have resulted in the most original, systematic and productive findings, had the movement not been suppressed at a relatively early stage of Tynyanov's activity in this area.

Tynyanov began by investigating the operation of parody in the literary relationship between Gogol and Dostoevsky. Most significantly, he concentrated on the transformational, negative-positive function of parody in its undermining or "debasement" of established genres and its consequent action of reformulating or replacing genres. The formalist theory of genre and literary evolution therefore concentrated on the sets of devices within established or "canonized" genres, their parody and debasement, the resulting emergence of new genres, also in their turn susceptible to change and possible replacement by previously discarded genres and forms. The illuminating picture of this intermittent cyclical evolution runs throughout Tynyanov's central work, *Archaists and Innovators*,[32] his lasting legacy to later literary history.

Russian formalism, futurism and the revolution

The confrontation between formalism and futurism on the one hand and Bolshevism on the other in the intensifying rigidity of the debate over Marxist proletarian culture between 1917 and 1930 is illustrated by the texts translated in this collection and described by the relevant prefaces and the afterword of G. Conio. It therefore requires only brief elaboration in this introduction.

As Markov affirms, united Hylaean futurism had largely ceased to exist by the time of the revolution in 1917. Markov again dates the beginning of the break-up to the visit to Russia of the Italian futurist leader, Marinetti. The division of response to the pronouncements and performance of the Italian had exposed the lack of Russian futurist unity too blatantly for the flowering of that movement to continue. In the subsequent period of decline, the two major poets of Russian futurism, Khlebnikov and Mayakovsky, distanced themselves from the original Hylaean grouping, both of them having developed a super-individuality.

Khlebnikov's Russian and Oriental wanderings, akin to the life of a "holy fool", took him further and further away from the polemical intensity of the Russian literary scene. Nevertheless, the five remaining years of his life which Khlebnikov spent in Russia under the Bolsheviks (1917-1922) were his most prolific. In these last five years, Khlebnikov culminated his activity as a "pure" futurist. His early death in 1922 at least spared him the trauma of facing the pressure to conform with the doctrinalism that was increasingly to characterize. Russian literature of the later 1920s onwards.

It was in war and revolution, however, that Mayakovsky truly found his footing. Mayakovskyan urbanist and revolutionary futurism became, at least in ideal, a "communist futurism", ready and willing to put its art to the service of the revolution. The swing to the left of the futurists under Mayakovsky meant a departure from the "purity" and "autonomy" of pre-revolutionary futurism to a new futurism which loudly proclaimed the artist's civil and class commitments. It also came to mean a retreat from the breath-taking extremes of abrasion and tenderness that had before characterised and distinguished Mayakovsky's poetry. Instead, Mayakovsky chose to put his talent into top gear in a vainly idealistic, super-futurist attempt to create directly the future, the new reality of transfigured socialist community. His communist futurism, however, with its highly original application of futurist art to propaganda and advertising, its revolutionary poetry of the mass-meeting and its attempt to establish new futurist cultural influence and leadership through the journal LEF (1923-1925), could not be reconciled with the increasing traditionalism of post-revolutionary cultural policy and its reaction against the undertones of rebellious independence, anarchy and excess of the futurists. Even Mayakovsky's muting in the eleventh-hour NOVY LEF (1927-1928) failed in its attempted self-persuasion. The courage that Mayakovsky had proclaimed, to make a void of the cultural past and to lay the path of a new culture into the future, was rejected by the solidifying Bolshevik acceptance of the security of traditional ''content-art''. A few days before Mayakovsky's suicide in 1930, he indicated at a public meeting the collapse of the ideals of futurism and LEF:

> ...twenty years ago we Futurists raised the subject of a new beauty. We said that the marble beauty of museums, all those Venuses of Milo with their lopped-off arms, all that Greek classical beauty, could never satisfy the millions who were entering into a new life in our noisy cities, and who would soon be treading the path of revolution. Just now ... our chairwoman offered me a sweet with Mossel'prom on it; and above that there was the same old Venus. So, the thing you've been fighting against for twenty years has now won. And now this lopsided old beauty is being circulated among the masses, even on sweetpapers, poisoning our brains and our whole idea of beauty all over again.[33]

To the Bolsheviks, the futurist ''barbarians'', who had so intrigued and excited bourgeois Europe, never lost that mistrusted connotation of pre-revolutionary decadence and disorder, even when they showed themselves willing to discard their futurist orange jackets for the civil service suits of the new cultural establishment.

It was probably inevitable that the school of thought which had begun by polemically emphasising the dichotomy between literature and life would rapidly come into conflict even with the relative liberality of cultural policy in early Soviet Russia. However, the accusations that the formalists had attempted to disrupt the correlation between society and history on the one hand and literature on the other were based on the polemics of formalism, rather than its reality. Serious formalism, even before it was under pressure, had not denied the existence of the "social connection" of literature: it had simply said that this was not the object of study for a student of literature, who must concern himself firstly with the study of literature itself, for which alone he was qualified. In other words, whatever their excited claims, the formalists were essentially prepared to accept the status of technical experts (as Eykhenbaum put it, "specifiers").[34] Erlich quotes Shklovsky in illustration of this technical approach as follows:

> In my theoretical work I have been concerned with the internal laws of literature. To use an industrial metaphor, I am not interested in the condition of the world cotton market or in the policies of the trusts, but solely in the count of yarn and the weaving techniques.[35]

Soon, however, the formalists naturally found that such a purely technical position in literary science was untenable and unsatisfying in their search for a genuine "poetics". To move further meant considering more closely and less dismissively the non-fictional environment of literature, that which had been dubbed rather disparagingly by early formalism "the motivation of the device".

It seems to be the case that, in Shklovsky at least, the movement outwards again from literature to life in the early 1920s coincided with the initial impact of pressures which would ultimately have brought about such a reorientation anyway. Shklovsky's new direction might well be a sign of arrogance on his part—the belief that, having "cleared the decks", formalism had now completed the required study of literature and could therefore address itself to the spheres of human activity contiguous with literature. But such a belief would at least indicate a certain sincerity of motive, rather than the pragmatic abjuring of formalism of which he is often accused. For the accepted view of Shklovsky is that, from the time of the foreign publication of his *Zoo, or letters not about love* (1923), and notably in his book, *The Third Factory* (1926) and his article, "Monument to a scientific mistake" (1930),[36] he "surrendered" to Marxism, rejected his formalist past and thus deprived the movement as a whole of any impetus to withstand its suppression. Richard Sheldon, in his recent introduction to the first English translation of *The Third Factory*,[37] conducts a passionate and strikingly well argued defence of Shklovsky

against the charge of surrender. He carefully details Shklovsky's
"political" life from the revolution onwards and, by presenting the
wider context of Shklovsky's apparently conciliatory statements in *The
Third Factory* and other works, shows that they are always juxtaposed
by other, ambiguous or even hostile comments. He thus seeks to prove
that Shklovsky was utilising "the device of ostensible surrender", and
in fact remained true after 1930 to many of his old formalist positions,
continuing to be attacked for "formalism" even in his writings after
that date. Sheldon succeeds in the persuasion that Shklovsky was not
panicked into surrender, but he fails to make clear the purpose of this
subtle device of "ostensible surrender". Was it simply that Shklovsky
wanted to survive as a formalist fifth column or was he positively
seeking a new literary method, while performing this elaborate tactical
dance? The refinement and elusiveness of Shklovsky's discourse means
that we shall probably never know the answer.

Whatever the circumstances and motives, Shklovsky moved from
1925 onwards towards the creation of a new "formo-sociological"
method of investigating literature, which continued to use much of
the "old" formalism for technical purposes, but attempted to
produce a poetics into which the material of life, principally the
society contemporary to the literature in question, would be fully
integrated. The new "formo-sociological" Shklovsky allied himself
with the concept of "factographic literature" espoused by Brik and
Mayakovsky in their painful transition from LEF to NOVY LEF. But
for every step of adaptation Shklovsky took, his increasingly aggressive
Marxist critics required two more.

Also worthy of genuine consideration, although no less subject to
critical attack at the time, was Eykhenbaum's attempt to embody the
relationship between literature and society in the concept of "literary
mores" (*literaturny byt*). Here Eykhenbaum sought to take his first
"sociological" step beyond literature, not as far as the determining
forces of the means of production, but to that sphere of life directly
adjacent to literature, the conditions of the writer's profession and
milieu. Eykhenbaum's example was that, whereas Pushkin's iambic
tetrameter bore no relation to the contemporary mode of production,
his shift to prose and to journalism could be rationally attributed to
the growing professionalisation of Russian letters, the emergence of
great literary reviews, etc.[38] Erlich describes this conception as "a
curious attempt at an 'immanent' sociology" and continues:

Instead of literary scholarship becoming a sub-division of social history, as was the case with some Marxist theoreticians, sociology was injected here into literature.... Literature was considered not so much an integral part of the social fabric, a resultant of external social forces, but as a social institution, an economic system in its own right. The writer appeared not as a member of a certain social class in the Marxian sense of this term ... but first and foremost as a representative of the literary profession.[39]

Despite the original sympathetic response to Eykhenbaum's new departure and the obvious validity of including the professional world in an assessment of literature, Eykhenbaum's version of "society" proved too narrow and too arbitrarily delimited for him and his critics. The "literary mores" of Eykhenbaum's own time could not tolerate such a possible "compromise" any more than it could Shklovsky's.

Russian futurism: past and present in Russia and Europe

Russian futurism (like formalism) did not live and die within Russia in spatial or temporal isolation. It is therefore possible to identify within Russian futurism important connections with developments in its own culture and in that of other nations. Until recently, critical and academic attention has been devoted largely to the understanding of Russian futurism, and formalism, in themselves, but one might well say that the full investigation of their Russian and European contiguities has yet to be taken beyond its initial stages. And undoubtedly, in the familiar retroactive process, this investigation will shed new light on the movements in question at their source.

Strangely enough, the connection which seems most obvious, that between Russian and Italian futurism, is one of the most obscure. The link between Russian futurism in the visual arts and the dissemination of Italian futurism which was working its way through European avant-garde art is not a matter of question. There is remarkably little detailed discussion, however, of the relationship between the two great futurist movements in their literary manifestations. It seems to have been the accepted view for some time that there could not be any substantial relationship between them, in view of their extreme political and ideological differences. Markov, however, concluded: "I distinctly saw that Marinetti's futurism was much more of an influence in Russia than is customarily thought, and more than the Russian futurists wanted to acknowledge."[40] So there is a connection to be considered and, indeed, closer examination of the evidence available provides some interesting comparisons.

The principal question is that of the influence exerted by Italian futurism through the Russians' direct contact with the leader of the Italian movement, Filippo Tommaso Marinetti, and his ideas as revealed in poetry and manifestoes. The Russian futurists were certainly aware of Italian futurism from a very early date, as the Moscow newspaper *Evening* (*Vecher*) had published an article containing translated excerpts from Marinetti's *Foundation Manifesto* soon after its appearance in *Le Figaro* in 1909. During the years that followed, the Russian intelligentsia was kept well-informed about the development of Marinetti's futurism through foreign reports and discussions, most of them quite critical, in the literary and artistic press.[41] Throughout this period, however, the practising Russian futurists showed themselves both unwilling to discuss Marinetti's ideas in detail and determined (often in ridiculous claims about which movement had appeared earlier) to assert their complete independence of Italian futurist thinking.

The collision of the two movements occurred in 1914, with Marinetti's visit to Russia. Markov describes how it was the literary establishment in Russia which fêted the self-important Italian.[42] The futurists, however, suddenly found themselves at odds with each other in their response to Marinetti and manifested a bewildering mixture of respect and contempt, acceptance and rejection towards him, both in personal contact and at the public lectures, meetings and soirées which Marinetti participated in or attended.[43] The timing of Marinetti's visit was undoubtedly of great significance for the Russian futurists, in that their divided response to this embodiment of the European movement (a difference of opinion which was not, in fact, serious in personal terms) threw into focus the increasing distance between "Hylaean" futurism and the Mayakovskyan futurism of war and revolution, the machine and the city. This critical division is indirectly reflected in the Russian futurist response to Marinetti, caught as it is between reluctant admiration for the man, with his extravagant self-assertion, his extraordinary public conduct and his noisy recitals, all redolent of original "pure" futurism, and emphatic rejection of his ideas (the cult of the machine, of war and of his own nationality). On the positive side, however, the tension between polite reception and scandalous furore which characterised Marinetti's visit to Russia resulted in a series of critical reactions to his ideas, together with increased publication of Italian futurist texts, which may well have had considerable influence on the Russian futurists in the years following

1914. But Markov, in alluding to the principal potential relationship here, that between Marinetti and Mayakovsky, points out both the difficulty of substantiating direct "influence" and the need for much more work in this comparative area before any firm statements can be made.

Nevertheless, at a general level it is possible to distinguish an intersection between Russian and Italian futurism in the following terms: a similarity, if not in some instances a parallelism, in atmosphere and poetic practice, countered by a fundamental difference, even antipathy, in ideology.

The atmosphere, or public stance, of the two futurisms reveals their greatest degree of closeness. The desire to shock bourgeois sensibilities in the name of the present and the future, to attack the traditional culture of dead poets, libraries, museums and art-galleries and to take poetry into the streets (in the sense of making poetry impinge on the life of the masses) precisely by making the street come into poetry (through thematic modernity, verbal innovation and experimentation and the introduction of "real noise" into art forms) links Russian and Italian futurism together, as, indeed, it assimilates them to other movements in European modernism of the period.[44]

There is also a great deal of similarity, although not without important differences of degree and emphasis, between the poetic practice of the two movements. It is interesting to note, incidentally, that Marinetti is generally considered to have been a poor, if not unreadable, poet, whereas Russian literary futurism contained poets not just of distinction, but of genius (Khlebnikov). There is, therefore, a contrast in dimension between the two movements, with the artistic predominating over the literary in Italian futurism (literary futurism in Italy was very much a one-man band), but both attaining equal levels of originality and distinction in Russian futurism.

At the thematic level, the Italian futurist demand for modern subject-matter in poetry and abandonment of "... the primitive and the savage, the sylvan and the rustic; ... the adoration of the gloomy, the mouldy, the filthy and decrepit; ... the exaltation of decay, disease, failure and suicide"[45] as content corresponded to Russian futurism's striving for the immediate relevance of their art. Italian concentration on the assimilation of technology and the life of machine and matter into poetry is also obviously similar to Mayakovskyan urbanist futurism. In the construction of poetry, the Italian revolt against "logic" and their advocacy of "analogy" resulted in experiments such as the abandonment of traditional syntax and metre, the use of mathematical and musical symbols, the remodelling of words and the use of typography which have been seen to characterise Russian futurism. There is, in addition, a certain correspondence between the Italian concept of "free words" ("parole in libertà") and the Russian development of "zaum".

In all of these respects, however, the Italian vision appears both superficial and narrow by comparison with the profundity and the extremity (even excess) which is evident in the Russian realisation of these conceptions. (This contrast may be explained by some critics in terms of the traditionally polar characteristics of "the Russian soul", but is more objectively and reliably attributable to Marinetti's inferior status as a poet.) The more profound Russian concept of "contemporary relevance" is seen in the primitivist "Hylaean" futurism, which feels entitled to use precisely those aspects of "the primitive" which Marinetti rejected, without losing any of its "reality". Russian futurism, in other words, may be seen as being imbued from the start with "eternal values" which Marinetti arbitrarily rejected. Similarly, the wholehearted admiration of Italian futurism for the machine and "the life of matter" (which was taken to the extent of demands that poetry be written about machines, not about men) contrasts with the Russian attitude: Mayakovsky and others were deeply impressed by technology and its transformation (especially, in potential) of human life, but evinced a much more "humane", even ambiguous reaction to it, as seen in their desire for the transformation of the negative capitalist "machine" and "city" into the positive socialist "engine" and "community". In their poetic experimentation also, the Russians took things to much greater extremes than the Italians: for example, in their revolutionary attitude to syntax, punctuation, typography etc., they were not only more radical than Marinetti, but also more profound. Thus, whereas the Russian futurists regarded such work as a *sine qua non* of futurism and attempted to press on beyond it, Marinetti (as Livshits' memoirs reveal) tended to regard these innovations statically, as a poetic achievement on which he could rest. In particular, the Russian development of "zaum", especially in Khlebnikov's all-encompassing vision of it, was a far more extensive reformation of language than the experiments with orthography and sound-words which were part of Marinetti's "free words" doctrine.

The basic opposition between Italian and Russian futurism, however, lies in their ideological and political contrasts. These are dealt with at some length by Nikolai Gorlov in his stimulating *Futurism and Revolution*, which forms part of this collection. Gorlov demonstrates

most effectively the way in which the pure revolutionary essence of
Italian futurism, which in his view unites it with Russian futurism, was
overlaid (in Gorlov's terms, distorted) by the espousal by Marinetti
and others of aggressive nationalism and fascism as the embodiment of
that revolutionism. Gorlov's understandable and quite valid attempt
to ensure that Russian futurism is not viewed by Marxist critics as a
similarly reactionary force is most cogently phrased in his observation
that Bolshevik Marxism is not invalidated by the existence of Menshevik Marxism. His attempt to identify a "pure", non-political Italian
futurism (similar in a way to Marinetti's persistent, but vague efforts
to distinguish between "artistic" and "political" futurism) is not,
however, substantiated by the facts. From the beginning (e.g., its
early propaganda for Italy's entry into the First World War), Italian
futurism constituted a nationalist, anti-socialist movement which
irrevocably distanced it from the Russian school, whose adherents were
neither concerned with the problems of a national inferiority complex,
nor ever likely to adopt a reactionary political stance. Livshits' memoirs
reflect the hostility of all Russian futurists (whatever their other
differences) to the nationalist imperialism of Italian futurism:

> How little did the political programme which Marinetti was
> expounding to his audience resemble our declarations! ... Marin-
> etti's ecstatic screaming was nothing more than the passionate
> inclination, the frenzied thirst of the propertied classes of a semi-
> agricultural country to possess, at whatever the cost, their own
> industry, their own export markets and their own colonial
> policy.[46]

Consideration of the historical and contemporary connections of
Russian futurism almost brings the topic to a close. For there has been
no resurrection from the demise of LEF and constructivism, the end-
point of futurism's development in Russian art, within the Soviet
Union. Traces of futurist-style poetic practice and principle are to be
found in the work of such poets as Pasternak and Tsvetaeva on the one
hand, and of Yevtushenko and Voznesensky on the other, but they
are, in the former, so refined and, in the latter, so generalised, as to
constitute only the most distant and partial echo of the futurist assault
on life and literature.[47] The future of Soviet poetry may still,
however, witness a thorough reawakening and reworking of the
futurist forces buried in the past.

Russian formalism: development and evolution

The historical position of Russian formalism is very different from that of Russian futurism. Formalism in its time was unique—there was no comparable movement in the theory of literature, nor had there been. More significantly, however, formalism has not suffered the fate of almost total extinction that descended upon futurism, even in Russia, although it has seemed from time to time that the formalists would not survive in their own land. Instead, the direct influence of Russian formalism has spread through Europe, while its efforts have to some extent been paralleled in English and American schools of literary criticism.

Before moving on to consider the developments made on the basis of Russian formalism after its practical end in 1930, reference must be made to the activities of a most significant school of thought known as the "Bakhtin school", which was in existence in Russia from the latter half of the 1920s to the middle of the 1930s. The principal members of this school were the literary scholar M.M. Bakhtin, the literary historian and theorist P.N. Medvedev and the linguist V.N. Voloshinov. These three, with followers and students, embarked in the 1920s on the creation of a science of ideologies based upon Marxism (although, to their cost, not the Marxism approved by Stalin). Within the fields of linguistics and literature, their work constituted an attempt to elaborate what they termed a "sociological poetics" which in essence represented the treatment of literature as one of many sign-systems susceptible to examination by a new Marxist semiology. This enormous, and doomed enterprise was approached chiefly through three significant works, Bakhtin's *Problems of Dostoevsky's Work* (1929), Medvedev's *The Formal Method in Literary Scholarship* (1928) and Voloshinov's *Marxism and the Philosophy of Language* (1930)[48]

To do full justice to the complexity of Bakhtinian theory and to its problematical relationship with formalism would require far more space than is available here. In addition, extended consideration of the Bakhtin school would not be strictly relevant to the concern of this introduction, which is intended in part to characterise formalism and thereby the differences between that movement and the developing Party line on literary study. Bakhtin's theory was not formalism and did not attempt to stand as a compromise between formalism and the Party. On the contrary, Bakhtin and his colleagues were concerned throughout to challenge and contradict the basic principles of formalism. This said, however, it may well be judged that historically the

Bakhtin school could have occupied what middle ground there was between formalism and its adversaries.[49] It must, therefore, be accorded some attention here.

In brief, the Bakhtinists, while acknowledging in courageously complimentary terms the "technical" achievements and discoveries which the formalists had made in basing their study of literature on literature's specificity, rejected the formalist interpretation of that specificity, which had led to the isolation of literature as a system divorced from any other "ideological" product or system (thus, the Bakhtinists, severally and together, reacted critically to what they saw as the negatives of formalist specificity, such as the contrast through defamiliarisation of "poetic" as opposed to "practical" language and the "self-valuability" of the word, the sign and the perception in art). In their predominantly semiotic approach to literature, they emphasised instead the social nature of the sign in art, as in everything else.

On the other hand, the Bakhtinists rejected just as strongly the crude sociology of literature, prevalent since the mid-nineteenth century, which ignored the complexity of the relationship between the life of society and literature by its failure to recognise the specificity of literature, the need to be able to explain verbal art in its own (here, artistic-semiotic) terms.

Medvedev's vision, counter to formalism and crude sociology, of the universe of ideologies, including literature, is described by I.R. Titunik as follows:

> ... an elaborate and dynamic "system of systems" ... wherein each ideological domain is an autonomous system of a specific kind in a complex (mediated) interrelationship and interaction with all other systems and in an equally complex, ultimate dependence on the one common "socio-economic basis". Literature is to be regarded as just such a member-system. It is composed of works of literature—ideological productions with a structure peculiar and distinctive to themselves—operating within the immediate milieu of literary culture at some particular stage in the development (generative process) of some particular literature, the milieu of which is only one of a whole atmosphere of milieus, so to speak, governed by the unitary socio-economic basis ... [50]

At a significant basic level, therefore, and in line with this particular version of literature's "specificity", the Bakhtin school concentrated on the way in which the language common to all the verbal ideological domains within the "system of systems" was integrated into the system of literature. What interested the Bakhtinists most, therefore, was the *affinities* between language in "life" and language in literature, rather than the *differences* on which the formalists had concentrated.

It was through this orientation towards rather than away from "ordinary" language that Bakhtin reached his central perception, namely that of the *dialogical* nature of literature. Bakhtin and Voloshinov together studied the modes and functions of dialogue within speech, noting particularly the duality of discourse which directs a speech-sign not only towards its referent but also to the signed speech of another listener/speaker. Their resulting study of different forms of discourse and the role of the "other speaker" in the literary process was embodied in its most revolutionary form in Bakhtin's *Problems of Dostoevsky's Work* (later, *Poetics*).

In Dostoevsky's novels Bakhtin identified the extreme development of "dialogue" in their polyphonic speech structure. Not only did Bakhtin perceive the speech structures whereby Dostoevsky's characters entered into dialogue within and between themselves, but he also indicated the consistently disruptive dialogue which thus took place between text and reader. In Bakhtin's view, Dostoevsky's novels had forever put an end to the false security of the monophonic novel, with its stable, reliable world-view. Essentially, this concept of dialogue came to permeate all aspects of Bakhtin's thinking, not only his conceptions of language and literature, but also of such spheres as the relationship between literature and society (his notion of "carnival" literature which inverted the accepted social hierarchy of values) and the development of literary science (thus, his attribution of formalist errors to the fact that the "other voice" opposing formalism was too weak and Medvedev's urging of the Marxists to measure and discover themselves against worthy adversaries, the formalists.)

The last courageous call, however, fell on deaf ears. Both Medvedev and Voloshinov vanished into oblivion during the 1930s, their fate still unknown, and only Bakhtin survived through an extended period of silence, to see eventually some of his works republished in his own country and in translation abroad. They are now receiving increasing recognition and exerting considerable influence on modern literary structuralism and neo-structuralism.

The emigration of Roman Jakobson to Czechoslovakia in 1920 coincided with the development of a new school of linguistic-literary studies there, strongly influenced by the writings of Ferdinand de

Saussure. Needless to say, the work of the Czech linguists and literary scholars was given considerable impetus by the advent of Jakobson, the herald of Russian formalism. Erlich describes the formation in 1926 of the Prague Linguistic Circle (thereafter often known as the "Prague school"). Its principal original participants were Jakobson, B. Havranek, Jan Rypka and B. Trnka. They were soon to be joined by the Slavic folklorist Petr Bogatyrev, D. Chizhevsky, Jan Mukařovsky, N.S. Trubetskoy and René Wellek; Boris Tomashevsky also participated occasionally.[51]

In many ways, the Prague School critical examination and development of Russian formalism bears close similarity to the initial aspects of the Bakhtin school just discussed. Prague School work was principally semiotic in nature, although lacking the Marxist coefficient of Bakhtinism. This semiotic emphasis had the effect of reformulating poetics, in the Prague school view, as part of the science of signs, rather than language. Between Russian formalism and Prague structuralism, language lost its position of unique signary, although it retained its central importance.

The other principal direction taken by the Prague school (again, in parallel with that of Bakhtin) was to develop on the later formalist realisation that their initial emphasis on "literariness" could not encompass the specificity of literature and that only a theory of literature which could account for the transformative integration of extra-literary material (or factors) into the aesthetic structure that literature represented could claim to be a "poetics" in the total sense desired by both formalism and the Prague school. Through this reorientation of aesthetic inquiry from the "devices" to the "materials", formalism took its most significant step towards structuralism.

These important reformulations of formalist attitude and emphasis were the principal legacies of the Prague school to later literary theory. Jakobson and others left Czechoslovakia in 1939 and the work of the Prague school declined into inactivity after 1945. Its most distinguished scholar of literature, Jan Mukařovsky, in Erlich's phrase, "renounced his initial stand and put his considerable ratiocinative powers at the service of the official creed."[52]

In England, the island fortress of traditional, impressionistic, "literary" criticism, where poetic analysis has usually been a polite gesture, there emerged in the 1920s the figure of I.A. Richards. Richards might well be called the English Shklovsky for his proudly amateur, radical, iconoclastic and widely eclectic approach both to literature and to the establishment of literary criticism. His desire to scientifise literary studies, based on his readings in the new psychology, and his use of poems as experiments in communication are in some way reminiscent of similar "ulterior motives" in formalism.

Richards' "psychological" emphasis, his attempt to discover the effect of poetry on its audience through its appeal to the feelings and emotions, as revealed in his (with C.K. Ogden and James Wood) *The Foundation of Aesthetics* (1922) and (with C.K. Ogden) *The Meaning of Meaning* (1923), certainly place him in a very different category from the Russian formalists. As René Wellek states it: "Form is totally dispensed with, dissolved into impulses and attitudes".[53] However, the comparison with formalism cannot be denied that simply. There is, at the least, a correspondence of principle, a similar perception of opposition between Richards' conception (in *The Meaning of Meaning*) of the "symbolic" use of language in science and the "emotive" use in poetry and the formalist notion of "practical", as opposed to "poetic" language. Furthermore, and more importantly, the methods adopted by Richards in his *The Principles of Literary Criticism* (1924) and *Practical Criticism* (1929) to investigate the "emotive" use of language in poetry are of interest here. Richards would distribute to his classes of Cambridge undergraduates for critical comment the modernised texts of poems, with no evidence of authorship, and then analyse the results of this communication. Richards' similarity to Russian formalism here lies in his reaction against the "biographical" criticism of the Victorian period and in his willingness to "clear the decks", to violate the connections between the author and his reader through the text, in order to develop a "scientific" appraisal of literature.

There are similar general, but distinctly superficial correspondences between Russian formalism and American New Criticism, a school which has been obliged to acknowledge I.A. Richards as its founder. [54] The term "New Criticism" is unsatisfactory, in that it tends to ignore the continuing strands of social, historical and political orientation which are evident in the approach of many of its adherents. However, its "newness' in the 1930s to 1950s lay in the principles of unhistorical "close reading" of texts which are revealed in the work of its principal critics, John Crowe Ransom, Allen Tate, Robert Penn Warren, W.K. Wimsatt and Cleanth Brooks. As George Watson comments:

> [The] unhistorical reading ... encouraged by Richards as an "experiment" though never recommended as an ideal, is

promoted to the ultimate ideal of analysis in the "New Criticism" which arose in England in the late twenties, spread to the
United States before the Second World War, and showed signs of
dominating academic criticism, especially in America, after
1945.[55]

The New Critics, however, inherited from I.A. Richards not only this
"lemon-squeezer school of criticism" (as T.S. Eliot came to term it),
but also a general "psychological" orientation, which they combined
with their own considerable idealism. Thus, their verbal analysis,
increasingly conducted in terms of paradoxes, ironies and tensions,
bears little relation to the "specific" verbal analysis of the formalists.
Ewa M. Thompson in her profound study of the relationship between
the two movements sees "a criss-crossing of tendencies" in both
Russian formalism and New Criticism. The gradual fading away of an
original idealistic (symbolistic) trend in formalism, to be replaced by a
positivistic (linguistic) scientism, is contrasted with a growing idealism
and anti-scientism in the New Criticism. She concludes:

> The New Critics have asserted that literature provides a kind of
> knowledge (Ransom) or the most complete kind of knowledge
> (Tate). This knowledge is said to be independent of human
> attitudes and appetencies; it points at the objects themselves, not
> at our attitudes towards these objects. It is inseparable from lang-
> uage. The New Critics have tried to indicate this cognitive value
> of literature through textual analyses which aimed at the explica-
> tion of individual facts rather than at establishing the laws of
> literary evolution.[56]

Only in the "minor heresy" of Chicago neo-Aristotelianism under
R.S. Crane, with its greater rigorousness of methodology and attention
to the grammatical aspects of poetry, does New Criticism approach
slightly closer to formalism.[57]

The work of the above movements in Anglo-American criticism
stood out clearly (and perhaps still do) against the impressionism,
moralism and value-orientation long prevalent in the Western world.
The individualistic, almost anarchic position of the literary critic is best
portrayed in recent times by F.R. Leavis. This most influential critic,
possessed of his own discreet private morality, conducts a passionate
re-examination of English literature in the name of 'values', without
feeling any necessity to develop his examination through verbal
analysis or even to clarify his critical procedure.[58]

No "traditional" western criticism can now, however, exist in ignorance of the formalist and structuralist tendencies which have come so strongly to the fore since the Second World War. The influence of the republication and translation of original formalist works is very considerable in this evolution, particularly in its mediation through the turbulent and chaotic growth of French structuralism and semiotics.[59] The critical reworking of Propp's functional analyses of the folktale has been a vital element in the work of Claude Levi-Strauss and has also been undertaken by the French structuralist, A.J. Greimas. The anthology of formalists texts published by Tzvetan Todorov in *Théorie de la littérature* (1965) served to introduce key statements and examples of formalist work for the first time to French students of literature. The influence of formalism has since that time been prominent, although subject to much criticism and re-examination in the writings of such notable French critics as Julia Kristeva and Roland Barthes. Just as significant, if not more so, has been the effect of the translation and republication of Bakhtin's work, with its conceptions of polyphony and dialogue, and its close attention to the relationship between text and reader.

The Soviet Union has also seen, in the 1960s and 1970s, the republication of important formalist works by Propp, Tynyanov and Eykhenbaum, together with those of Bakhtin, although many formalist productions, particularly those of Shklovsky, still lie buried. This gradual reopening of the topic has had a considerable effect. It has led, firstly, to a somewhat more reasoned and uninhibited attitude towards the formalists in literary debate (although they are still far from being accorded their full merit) and, most importantly, it has acted as one of the major incentives to the emergence of a new school of Russian structuralism, based mainly in Tartu, under the leadership of Yury Lotman.[60] The Tartu school comprises structural folklorists, semioticians, cyberneticians and specialists in information theory, who are engaged in the historical and theoretical scientific study of literature. Their attitude toward the formalists is far from enthusiastic, and has already gone through one period of revolt, but the debt which they owe to the formalist inquiry has never been denied and the development of this school of Russian structuralism, particularly in the influence exerted by Lotman's work in many fields, may well come to be viewed as the most important consequence of Russian formalism, at least within the Soviet Union.[61]

The English-speaking world has also witnessed since the War a considerable activity in the translation and examination of Russian formalism, the full effects of which have undoubtedly yet to be perceived.[62] The steady development of this interest in England and America and, most importantly, its gradual extension beyond the Slavic field could yet bring about, in the context of structuralism, lasting changes in the principles and methods of Anglo-American literary criticism.

Conclusion

Russian formalism and futurism had many failings and, especially in the case of formalism, they have not lacked criticism in subsequent history.

That the world seems more accepting of futurism is explained simply by the fact that no school of Russian poetry has yet arisen in explicit, but positive reaction to it, a result of the movement's premature and unnatural termination. Critics of futurism, however, attach themselves to its failure to develop in more refined form the large-outline concepts with which it began, a failure to move sufficiently far beyond its polemical beginnings, as well as the "philosophical" weakness of the movement in its unresolved division between primitivism and urbanism.

Many of the criticisms made of Russian formalism, on the other hand, have been integral to the various reworkings and redevelopments of formalism discussed above. General criticisms of the movement are also understandably similar to those of futurism: the formalists are reproached for the incompleteness and the considerable impressionism of their supposedly "scientific" poetics (particularly in Shklovsky's version), as well as the failure to move far enough (or fast enough) beyond their original conceptions, formulated as they often were under the pressures of the literary battlefield. René Wellek provides a typical critical review on the following basis:

> I am thinking ... of what, from the point of view of a literary critic, must appear as the major deficiency of the Formalist point of view: the attempt to divorce literary analysis and history from value and value judgement. The Formalists essentially chose a technical, scientific approach to literature which may appeal to our time but ultimately would de-humanize art and destroy criticism.[63]

From another standpoint, it is encouraging to see in a recent article by Galvano Della Volpe a remarkably sympathetic and constructive critical re-examination of formalism by Marxism. This concludes both with a similar reproach of formalism's inability to deal with "value" and with a call for a properly cognitive-gnoseological remodelling of the formalist inquiry on the basis of a transformed practical-poetic language opposition.[64]

On the whole, however, the critics of Russian formalism and futurism have at least a grudging admiration for the exaggerated aspects in both schools which they criticise. In addition, they, as much as any modern audience, continue to be impressed by the freshness, originality, colour and dynamism which formalism and futurism injected into their own age and which has reached out to us through the years of silence.

The existence of this book and other publications, which deal with these schools of poetic practice and theory which ran their brief course in Russia half a century ago, testifies to the originality and enduring meaning of the two movements, as well as to the sympathetic critical interest in them. It is to be hoped that this age may see a true meeting of minds over formalism and futurism.

Keele, Staffs. May 1979

1 For a good account of Russian symbolism and its aesthetic, see James West, *Russian Symbolism* (London, 1970).
2 Vladimir Markov, *Russian Futurism: A History* (London, 1969). Markov's book remains the only full-length study of the movement in English. It concentrates almost entirely on pre-revolutionary futurism.
3 *Ibid.*, p.238.
4 Camilla Gray, *The Russian Experiment in Art 1863-1922* (London, 1962).
5 *Ibid.*, p.65.
6 *Ibid.*
7 Susan P. Compton, *The World Backwards. Russian futurist books* 1912-16 (The British Library, 1978).
8 Gray, *The Russian Experiment*, p.115.
9 *The Studio of Impressionists* ("Studiya impressionistov"), Petersburg, 1910 and *A Trap for Judges* ("Sadok sudey"), Petersburg, 1910.
10 "Russian futurism, however, was flexible, varied, and contradictory, and any effort to reduce it to the aspirations or achievements of only one group or of a single person are bound to end in the worst possible simplifications and distortions". Markov, *Russian Futurism*, pp.269-270.
11 *A Slap in the Face for Public Taste* ("Poshchechina obshchestvennomu vkusu"), Moscow, 1912.
12 Vahan D. Barooshian, *Russian Cubo-Futurism 1910-1930* (Mouton, 1974).
13 *Ibid.*, p.108.
14 The futurist Benedict Livshits also makes this comparison in his book of memoirs: Benedikt Livshits, *The One and a Half-Eyed Archer* ("Polutoraglaziy strelets"), Leningrad, 1933. Now in English translation, with introduction and annotation, by John E. Bowlt, Oriental Research Partners, 1977, from which this reference is taken

(p.164). Livshits' book is the best, although not unbiased account of Russian futurism by one of its participants.

15 Gray, *The Russian Experiment*, pp.166-167.

16 The principal account of Russian formalism is Victor Erlich's *Russian Formalism* (3rd edition, The Hague, 1969), a pioneering study of the movement, which has been supplemented and critically developed in other works since its first appearance in 1955. There have also been a number of collections of essays by and about the formalists, e.g., S. Bann and J.E. Bowlt (eds.), *Russian Formalism* (Edinburgh, 1973). A collection of formalist texts has been published in Russian, with German facing translation, in *Texte der Russischen Formalisten*, Band I and II (Munich 1969 and 1972). Significant collections of formalist work in English translation are L.T. Lemon and M.J. Reis (Trans. and intro.), *Russian Formalist Criticism* (Nebraska, 1965); L. Matejka and K. Pomorska (eds.), *Readings in Russian Poetics* (MIT, 1971); and (in part) Victor Erlich (ed.), *Twentieth-Century Russian Literary Criticism* (Yale, 1975) which also includes essays by early Soviet Marxists. Otherwise, translations of individual formalist works are scattered through many books and periodicals. Most recently, an important collection of formalist texts and information about formalism has been published in the journal *Russian Poetics in Translation* (Holdan Books Ltd., Oxford) 1977-1978, Nos. 4 and 5. Articles on formalism are also to be found in the journal *Essays in Poetics* (University of Keele, 1976-), edited by the translators of the present collection.

17 In this search, the formalists were also influenced by the nineteenth-century comparative literary historian, Aleksandr Veselovsky, who attempted to study the "motif" as the elementary narrative unit. See Erlich, *Russian Formalism*, pp.26-31.

18 First published in Ukrainian in 1926. The Lemon and Reis translation is from the Russian text "Teoriya 'formal'nogo metoda'" in *Literature: Theory, Criticism, Polemics* ("Literatura: Teoriya, kritika, polemika"), Leningrad, 1927.

19 Lemon and Reis, *Russian Formalist Criticism*, p.101.

20 L. Matejka, "The Formal Method and Linguistics" in Matejka and Pomorska, *Readings in Russian Poetics*, p.281.

21 See note 5 above.

22 "Iskusstvo kak priem" originally published in *Collections of the Theory of Poetic Language* ("Sborniki po teorii poeticheskogo yazyka") issue II, Petrograd, 1917. Available in English translation in Lemon and Reis, *Russian Formalist Criticism*, pp.5-24 (under the title of "Art as Technique").

23 This translation is taken from "A Contextual Glossary of Formalist Terminology" in *Russian Poetics in Translation*, 1977 No. 4, p.35.

24 *Ibid.*

25 *Noveishaia russkaia poeziia. Nabrosok pervy*, (Prague, 1921). Available in almost complete English translation under the title of "Modern Russian Poetry: Velimir Khlebnikov" in E.J. Brown (ed.), *Major Soviet Writers* (Oxford, 1973), pp.58-82. There is also an excellent summary of this work, demonstrating connections between Russian futurism and formalism, in G.M. Hyde, "Russian Futurism" in M. Bradbury and J. McFarlane (eds.), *Modernism* (Penguin Books, 1978), pp.259-273. In addition, there is an important basic work on these connections: K. Pomorska, *Russian Formalist Theory and its Poetic Ambiance* (The Hague, 1968).

26 This is necessarily a very simplified version of the opposition, which was in any case differently interpreted within formalism. See T. Todorov, "Some approaches to Russian Formalism" in Bann and Bowlt, *Russian Formalism*, pp.6-19.

27 Richard Sherwood, "Viktor Shklovsky and the development of early Formalist Theory on Prose Literature", *ibid.*, p.36.

28 "Kak sdelana 'Shinel' Gogolya" in *Poetika* (Petrograd, 1919).

29 See Erlich, *Russian Formalism*, p.75, n.29.

30 *Morfologiya skazki* (Leningrad 1928, Moscow 1969) and "Transformatsii volsheb-nykh skazok" in *Poetika* IV (Leningrad, 1928). In English: *The Morphology of the Folktale* (Texas, 1968) and "Fairy tale transformations" in Matejka and Pomorska, *Readings in Russian Poetics*, pp.94-114.

31 "Biographical Notes" in *Russian Poetics in Translation* 1977 No. 4, p.5.

32 *Arkhaisty i novatory* (Leningrad, 1929).

33 Quoted in Boris Thomson, *Lot's Wife and the Venus of Milo* (Cambridge, 1978), p.73. A very stimulating discussion of conflicts over the Russian cultural heritage since the revolution.

34 This technical status was proposed as a compromise solution which would allow the formalists to continue by the Marxist critic, A. Zeitlin (see Erlich, *Russian Formalism*, pp.110-111). The proposition was not taken up, however, and Zeitlin himself turned much more severely against the formalists.

35 Erlich, *Russian Formalism*, p.119.

36 The latter in "Literaturnaya gazeta", 27.1.1930.

37 Victor Shklovsky, *The Third Factory* (ed. & trans. Richard Sheldon), Ann Arbor 1977.

38 This is the paraphrase given in Erlich, *Russian Formalism*, p.126.

39 *Ibid.*

40 Markov, *Russian Futurism*, p.382.

41 *Ibid.*, p.148-149.

42 See also the description of Marinetti's reception given by Livshits in *The One and a Half-Eyed Archer*, p.182.

43 See the description in Markov, *Russian Futurism*, p.149-155.

44 There are apparent similarities, at a superficial level, between both Italian and Russian futurism on the one hand and such movements as French surrealism, German expressionism, Dadaism and English vorticism. It is impossible to go into these relationships here, but there are brief comments on them in Jane Rye, *Futurism* (London, 1972)—an excellent short work on futurism as a whole.

45 Quotation given *ibid.*, p.111.

46 Livshits, *The One and a Half-Eyed Archer*, p.186.

47 I am grateful to my colleague, Valentina Polukhina, for pointing out to me the instances of this vestigial survival of futurism.

48 These works are now fortunately available in English translation. Bakhtin's *Problems of Dostoevsky's Work* was republished in significantly expanded form (principally, with the addition of the section on carnivalesque literature) as *Problems of Dostoevsky's Poetics* (Moscow, 1963); it was translated under this title by R.W. Rotsel (Ann Arbor, 1973). The other two works are: P.N. Medvedev/M.M. Bakhtin, *The Formal Method in Literary Scholarship* (trans. A.J. Wehrle), Baltimore and London, 1978 and V.N. Voloshinov, *Marxism and the Philosophy of Language* (trans. L. Matejka and I.R. Titunik), New York and London, 1973. The debate over the authorship of these publications, together with original information about the work of the Bakhtin group, is presented in A.J. Wehrle's introduction to his translation of Medvedev/Bakhtin.

49 I.R. Titunik sees formalism and Bakhtinism as "ultimately completely reconcilable methods" in his "The Formal Method and the Sociological Method (M.M. Baxtin, P.N. Medvedev, V.N. Vološinov) in Russian Theory and Study of Literature", in Matejka and Titunik's translation of Voloshinov (see preceding note). It must be said, however, that by no means all students of the two movements would agree with this.

50 *Ibid.*, p.180.

51 Erlich gives a good account of the Prague School redefinitions of formalism in *Russian Formalism*, p.154-163, and follows it with a survey of formalism in Poland under Manfred Kridl in the late 1920s and 1930s (p.163-168). The Prague school is

also reviewed in René Wellek, "The Literary Theory and Aesthetics of the Prague
School", in his *Discriminations* (New Haven and London, 1970), p. 275-303.
Representative texts of the Prague School are available in English in P.L. Garvin, *A
Prague School Reader on Esthetics, Literary Structure, and Style* (Washington,
1964).

52 Erlich, *Russian Formalism*, p.163.
53 René Wellek, "Concepts of Form and Structure in Twentieth-Century Criticism"
in his *Concepts of Criticism* (New Haven and London, 1963), p.59.
54 These connections are examined in a thorough comparison of the two movements
in Ewa M. Thompson, *Russian Formalism and Anglo-American New Criticism*
(The Hague, 1971).
55 George Watson, *The Literary Critics* (Penguin Books, 1968), p.201.
56 Thompson, *Russian Formalism and Anglo-American New Criticism*, p. 109.
57 See, for example, the statements of R.S. Crane in his *The Languages of Criticism
and the Structure of Poetry* (Toronto, 1953) and the comment of René Wellek in
"The Main Trends of Twentieth-Century Literary Criticism", in his *Concepts of
Criticism*, p.360.
58 "There is remarkably little evidence ... for this very substantial legend that Leavis
was a verbal analyst"; Watson, *The Literary Critics*, p.209. Also, "Leavis decepti-
vely emphasizes linguistic, verbal values, but he leaves the verbal surface very
quickly in order to discuss the particular emotion or ethos an author conveys";
Wellek, *Concepts of Criticism*, p.59.
59 See J. Culler, *Structuralist Poetics* (London, 1975).
60 The best authority on Lotman is the English scholar Ann Shukman, who has
written widely and illuminatingly on the subject of Soviet structuralism. Her principal work on Lotman to date is *Literature and Semiotics: A Study of the Writings
of Ju. M. Lotman* (Amsterdam, 1976).
61 It is regretted that it is not possible to discuss the movements of French and
Russian structuralism, as well as their connections with Russian formalism more
fully here. Reasons of space, the complexity of the subject and the distance overall
between them and formalism are added to by the relative inaccessibility until
recently to the English-speaking reader of the basic texts. There have now
appeared, however, a number of translations of the work of Roland Barthes and
Russian structuralist texts are available in English in the journals *Russian Poetics in
Translation* (see note 16) and *PTL: A Journal for Descriptive Poetics and Theory of
Literature* (Amsterdam, 1976-).
62 Examples of the growing Anglo-American interest are, of course, the works mentioned in note 16. The journal *Essays in Poetics*, referred to there, presents the work
of the British Neo-Formalist Circle, which studies Russian formalism and related
structuralism, attempts to apply and develop its theory and critical methods and to
extend knowledge of formalism to specialists in other areas.
63 René Wellek, "Russian Formalism", in George Gibian and H.W. Tjalsma (eds.),
Russian Modernism (Ithaca and London, 1976), p.47.
64 Galvano Della Volpe, 'Settling Accounts with the Russian Formalists'', in *New Left
Review*, No.113-114 (January-April 1979), p.133-145.

SECTION I

Debate on the Formal Method

G. CONIO

Preface

The following articles have been translated from a special issue of the journal *Pechat i Revolutsia* (Press and Revolution),[1] 1924, n.5, devoted to formalism. The very fact that a revolutionary and Marxist journal should have agreed at that time to hold an objective and open debate about a movement that was sharply disapproved of by those responsible for Soviet cultural policy is noteworthy in itself. But this document does more than merely bear witness to the state and spirit of Soviet culture before the 1932 decree put an end to its awkward, teeming diversity.[2]

The discussion of formalism raises a certain number of problems that are now of more immediate concern than ever before and in it we find two opposing conceptions of literary criticism and of literature which still have their followers to this day. It is hardly necessary to recall structuralism's debt to formalism (and vice versa); as for the position of Sakulin[3] and of Piksanov[4] it represents a sociological approach to literature that is still being enriched and stimulated by a great many fresh studies. Formalism was undoubtedly the centre of attraction of that varied and fascinating period of Soviet Letters in the 1920s, the impassioned vitality of which so contrasted with the rigidly monolithic character of the period that followed; indeed, its coordinated research efforts seemed to create a sort of unity. But even it was not immune from dissension. Thus Eykhenbaum,[5] in his statement, at the same time as denouncing the label 'formal method' as an inexact definition of his ideas, excluded the future academician Zhirmunsky [6] who was generally regarded at the time (and who still is regarded) as one of the leading representatives of the formalist movement.

It is true that by his theoretical rigour, his intransigence even, Eykhenbaum stood up as the leader, as the guardian of orthodoxy, eschewing all attempts at compromise.

Shklovsky [7] has drawn the following portrait of his friend in a recent book: ''I first met Boris Mikhailovich Eykhenbaum in 1916. A highly promising young scholar, he was lucky to boot and was writing some able articles. He was poor, but poverty did not seem to bother him; a musician who had given up the violin though without losing his love for music; a poet who had set aside verse, though continuing to translate other people's poetry, (Blok greatly appreciated his translations), Boris Mikhailovich was already by that time an accomplished philologist ... This polite quiet-spoken and articulate man was not one to be distracted from his course; he was polite, but unyielding. He was a man of politely extreme convictions."[8]

Eykhenbaum at that time was already the author of a certain number of works; but he owed his celebrity to his analysis of Gogol's *The Overcoat*, which had earned him the sarcasm of Marxist criticism. The very title of the work was significant: "How Gogol's *The Overcoat* was made?" and Eykhenbaum's study, published in *Poetica* in 1919, was an exemplary demonstration of the formalists' essential principle, namely that, as with Valéry: "literature was an application and an extension of certain properties of language", no piece of writing having any other secret than a certain "doing", certain techniques, and various processes employed in its production. Excluding all other types of approach, they focused attention on the specific organisation inherent in and interior to literature: "Not a single phrase of a literary work can at any time be the expression of the personal sentiments of the author, it is always construction and play." (Eykhenbaum). This conception of literature coincided with a conception of language that was no longer verbal or literal but symbolic.

Hence their demands for a more scientific approach to literature and the proscription of 'eclecticism' in the name of these demands, their certitude of possessing the truth, and their categorical rejection of any other type of explanation which they assimilated to a different and hence false and unacceptable conception of literature.

Formalism is not a method but a principle, Eykhenbaum points out. This principle states the absolute specificity of the literary fact and the senselessness of any references to spheres other than that of language: life, social background, society, history, etc.

The most important persons to respond to the formalists were the representatives of the sociological school: Sakulin and Piksanov, who have produced some interesting work, and who were concerned to reconcile or even to merge their views with those of the formal school. Though condemned by Eykhenbaum for their "eclecticism", later, bizarrely, official criticism was to assimilate them to the formalists. In fact, Eykhenbaum's article seems largely to be centred around the notion of eclecticism, which he applies to most of his opponents (or supposed opponents) in order to refute them. But it is true that at that time one was always more or less somebody else's eclectic. We may compare his "principled" position to the attitude of today's structuralists, who have adopted the main points of his argument. Conversely, we may compare Sakulin's idea with "historical" and diachronic tendency of "sociologist" critics, often driven by the same desire for synthesis and for the search for a history of forms through a history of societies (and vice versa).[9]

This connection between literature and society lies at the very heart of the debate, and is violently denounced by those who favour an autonomy, a "sovereignty" of the science of literature, while it is accepted by certain "sociologists" vainly seeking to reconcile the two terms; it is this connection between literary creation and social demands, between art and revolution, which lies at the heart of, and determines official Marxist criticism and its conception of a directed, committed "party" literature.

This was the subject of the only important book ever to have been written by a leader of the Soviet Union on cultural problems: *Literature and Revolution*, by Trotsky, which had just been published (1924). In fact, there is reason to believe that Eykhenbaum's principle concern was to reply to the very severe criticisms of formalism which Trotsky had just made in the name of Marxism.

Not that Trotsky entirely rejected its achievements; in his view, "the methods of formal analysis are necessary but not sufficient", but formalism remained for him "an insolent freak of idealism", one that could only lead "to the fetishism of the word". We touch here upon a problem which is central to our times, that of the relations between art, thought, and politics, that of the possibility or otherwise of creating an autonomous science of literature, one that is independent of the philosophy of history which cannot resist encompassing it, explaining it and integrating it like any other social product, for fear of losing its raison d'être, of denying itself and of ultimately destroying itself. And yet the formalists had set out to accomplish, in aesthetics and literature, the same revolution as the Marxists had made in society, the economy and politics. This was a revival of the old dream of attuning words to action so that they would march together in step, breathing the same breath; the old dream of totality, of unity of progress in every direction and in every sense; the old dream that we find at the heart of every major crisis that was to occur in revolutionary thought throughout the twentieth century.

Consequently, the "formalists" only oppose themselves to the Marxists in so far as the latter seemed to them to be mistaken in retreading the beaten path of bourgeois academism, and to be damaging themselves by acting counter to the vital interests of the revolution, a revolution that could only be conceived as total. Presenting the work of literature as an organic whole, as a reality that is distorted if criteria other than those that it secretes itself are applied to it, they intended to open up new and authentic paths to understanding of means of expression, paths which, according to their vision, were to lead to the conditions of a true culture. This was what being a revolutionary meant to them; consequently, in their view, their work could have no meaning other than in and through revolution. In their ambition to wipe out the old, false and traditional dichotomy between form and content, moreover, they were more concerned to create a science that would be the auxiliary of Marxism than to refute it.

Their scientific ambitions, their concern to avoid subjective principles of explanation, to look beyond the individual and the particular in order to attain objective truth seemed to bring them close to the positions of those who were criticising them. It is for this that Eykhenbaum's statement and the discussion to which it gave rise are of vital interest to us not only from the standpoint of the history of literature and ideas, but also from a more contemporary point of view: that of the burning question as to whether or not it is possible, or feasible, to reconcile the imperatives of revolutionary Marxism with the demands of free thought, and, above all, whether there is not a risk of Marxism denying itself the moment it denies this freedom; the question as to whether a revolution in social structures that is not accompanied by a revolution in mental structures does not run a very great risk of thereby condemning itself.[10]

Jean Laude was almost certainly correct in writing:

"In the USSR, with Zhdanov's report (1934), the defeat of LEF and the state takeover of ideology were to mark the moment from which the term 'Formalism', which had in the first place been polemical, came to designate counter-revolutionary designs. There was a tragic confusion between 'the theory of art for art sake' (in as much as this theory saw art both as a phenomenon isolated from social life and as the focal point for the crystallization of religious attitudes) and the specificity of artistic facts— the search for which was concerned on the contrary with a 'demystification' (by rejecting both idealism and illusionism) and stipulated a concrete form of insertion of art into everyday and social life.''[11]

At the very best we are entitled to wonder whether this mistake, this confusion was not deliberate, and at any rate at what moment it became so. The subsequent history of the USSR, moreover, has tragically confirmed Eykhenbaum's remarks, the bureaucracy coming to apply his *reductio ad absurdum* method of reasoning to the letter and subordinating the objectives and the interests of science to those of dogmatism in the Stalinist era.[12]

All this already existed in embryonic form, though in a latent state, in a controversy between formalism and Marxism in 1924, which was to lead to the 1929 crisis, and then later to the decision to reduce all tendencies to a single one and to institutionalize the truth. Thus formalism, born of futurism, or at least from a reflexion on the latter, was to share its destiny, its ambitions, its hopes and its final misfortunes. This should be enough for us to view it as an essential current of avant-garde revolutionary thought and art, rather than as the progeny of decadent bourgeois thought.[13]

1   *Press and Revolution* was a highly influential literary journal in the 1920s. It was edited by Vyacheslav Pavlovich Polonsky (1886-1932), a Marxist critic and historian closely connected with official circles. He campaigned vigorously in the columns of his journal against Averbach and the Proletarian writers on the question of the "social command", to which these writers wished to bend Soviet literature, and which Polonsky rejected in the name of Marxism.

2   A decree issued by the Central Committee in 1932 pronounced the dissolution of all literary groups. In principle this was aimed at extremism and at the monopoly then enjoyed by the Rappist Averbach, but in fact it was inspired by Stalin's determination to bring all literature under party control. This is an important date, marking the end of an era of tolerance, of relative freedom and of that absence of direct Party interference in cultural affairs, the first, fairly rich period of Soviet literature dominated by the achievements of Lunacharsky. The colourful profusion of schools and groups gave way to a single organisation: the Soviet Writers' Union, responsible for seeing to it that the dogma of socialist realism was respected.

3   Pavel Nikich Sakulin (1868-1930). Literary historian, left a voluminous body of work (*Russian Literature. Sociologico-Synthetic Summary of Literary Styles, Russian Literature and Socialism*). He was the chief representative of the sociological method. Both formalists and Marxists criticised him for his "eclecticism", for he sought to reconcile the study of forms and styles with a sociological approach to literature which neither was prepared to countenance.
    Sakulin was a member of the Academy of Sciences, and Lunacharsky held him in high esteem.

4   Nicolas Piksanov (born in 1878). Another representative of the sociological school. His "Creative history" of literature aroused a storm of controversy. In particular,

he dealt with Griboyedov (*Histoire créative du 'Malheur d'avoir de l'esprit'*). He was co-director, with Lunacharsky, of the "Russian and World Classics" series.

5   Boris Eykhenbaum (1886-1959). Literary critic, professor at the Institute of Art History, author of several works on Lermontov, Gogol and Tolstoy. He was regarded as the leader of the formalist school. He belonged to *Opoyaz*, and then to the LEF.

6   Victor Maximovich Zhirmunsky (1891-1971) belongs to the history of the formalist movement. Academician and corresponding member of most of the universities and academies of Europe. Eminent scholar in the fields of linguistics, philology, and folklore. Great friend and admirer of Akhmatova, to whom he devoted several studies.

7   Victor Shklovsky (1893-) He was one of the founders of *Opoyaz*. Member of the LEF. This prodigiously active man was one of the outstanding figures in the world of criticism, the novel and the cinema in the 1920s. Friend and associate of Mayakovsky, Eisenstein and D. Vertov. His writings are as varied as they are abundant, and they include a number of classics of Soviet literature: *Theory of Prose, Zoo, The Sentimental Journal.*

8   Victor Shklovsky, "Tetiva", *Sovetsky Pisatel*, Moscow 1970, p.15.

9   Compare the following statement by Sakulin: "So, at the risk of being taken for an eclectic by B.M. Eykhenbaum, I believe that the sociological method in literary history is not only possible but indispensable and that, in resorting to it, we do not give up an inch of this autonomous sphere which belongs as of rights to the science of literature." (*Press and Revolution*, 1924, no.5) with this recent statement by a literary critic: "In its present twofold aim, the most *advanced* literary research, that of the 'sociologists' and that of the 'formalists', ought to enable the school of literary history to make decisive progress. The historical study of literary forms undeniably opens up a vast, virtually unexplored, field of investigation for future students; but these investigations cannot be separated from all those that may contribute to the construction of a more complete history of mentalities. There is nothing to suggest that there need be incompatibility or conflict between these two orders of investigations", (Roger Fayolles, *Scolies* 1972, n.2).

10 Cf. J.P. Sartre, *The Problem of Method*, London 1963, p.22: "Marxism stopped. Precisely because this philosophy wants to change the world, because its aim is 'philosophy-becoming-the-world', because it is a veritable schism which rejected theory on one side and *praxis* on the other. From the moment the USSR, encircled and alone, undertook its gigantic effort at industrialization, Marxism found itself unable to bear the shock of these new struggles, the practical necessities and the mistakes which are always inseparable from them. At this period of withdrawal (for the USSR) and of ebb tide (for the revolutionary proletariats), the ideology itself was subordinated to a double need: security (that is, unity) and the construction of socialism *inside* the USSR. Concrete thought must be born from *praxis* and must turn back upon it in order to clarify it, not by chance and without rules, but—as in all sciences and all techniques—in conformity with principles. Now, the Party leaders, bent on pushing the integration of the group to the limit, feared that the free process of truth, with all the discussions and all the conflicts which it involves, would break the unity of combat; they reserved for themselves the right to define the line and to interpret the event. In addition, out of fear that the experience might not provide its own clarities, that it might put into question certain of their guiding ideas and might contribute to 'weakening the ideological struggle', they put the doctrine out of reach. The separation of theory and practice resulted in transforming the latter into an empiricism without principles; the former into a pure, fixed knowledge."

11 Jean Laude in *L'année 1913*, (Klincksieck, 1971) p.205.

12 Cf. Medvedev. *The Rise and Fall of T.D. Lysenko*, New York/London 1969.

13 It is worth referring here to Osip Brik's manifesto, in which the "formal method" is unambiguously situated within the framework of revolutionary and avant-garde ideas as opposed to bourgeois conservatism and academicism. We are grateful to Ann Shukman for having given us permission to use her translation of the following passage which appeared in *Russian Poetics in Translation*, Vol.4, Oxford 1977 (O. Brik's *The So-Called Formal Method* originally appeared in LEF, 1, 1923):

Opoyaz (Society for the study of poetic language) and its so-called 'formal method' has become the bugbear of the priests and high priests of literature. Our bold attempt to approach the holy images of poetry from a scientific point of view has roused their vociferous displeasure. A 'league for the struggle against the formal method' has been formed, or rather a 'league for the struggle against the removal of poetic values'.

Opoyaz proposes that *there are no poets or literary figures, there is poetry and literature*. Everything that a poet writes is significant as part of his work in the common good—and quite insignificant as a manifestation of his 'I'. If the poetic work is understood as a 'human document', as a diary entry, then it is interesting to the author, to his wife, his relatives, friends, and to maniacs such as those passionately seeking the answer to the question 'did Pushkin smoke?'—and to no one else.

The poet is an expert at his job. And that's all. But in order to be a good craftsman, he must know the needs of those for whom he works, he has to live the same life as they do. Otherwise the work won't do, won't be any use.

The social role of the poet cannot be understood by an analysis of his individual qualities and habits. *It is essential to study on a mass scale the devices of poetic craft*, what distinguishes them from adjacent domains of human labour, and to study the laws of their historical development. Pushkin was not the creator of a school, but only its chief. Had Pushkin not existed *Evgeny Onegin* would all the same have been written. America would have been discovered even without Columbus.

We have no history of literature. There is the history of the 'generals' of literature. *Opoyaz* makes it possible to write a real history.

The poet is master of the word, language-maker, who serves his class, his social group. What he writes about is suggested to him by the consumer. *Poets do not invent themes, they take them from their environment*.

The poet begins by working over the theme, finding the suitable verbal forms for it.

To study poetry is to study the laws of this verbal work-over. *The history of poetry is the history of the development of the devices of verbal formation*.

Why poets took just these and not other themes can be explained by the fact of their belonging to a particular social group and has no relationship at all to their poetic work. This question is important for the biography of the poet, but the history of poetry is not the 'life of saint so and so' and should not be one.

Why poets used just these devices and not others in working over their themes, and what caused the appearance of a new device, why an old one dies out, this is what scientific poetics has to subject to careful research.

Opoyaz demarcates its work from the work of adjacent scientific disciplines, not in order to withdraw from 'this world' but in order in all clarity to pose and extend the most essential problems about man's literary activity.

Opoyaz studies the laws of poetic production. Who dares stop us?

What is Opoyaz contributing to the building of proletarian culture?

1. A scientific system instead of a chaotic conglomeration of facts and personal names.

2. The social evaluation of creative personalities instead of the idolatrous inter-pretation of the 'language of the gods.'

3. Knowledge of the laws of production instead of some 'mystical' penetration into the 'mysteries' of creation.

Opoyaz is the best teacher for our young proletarian writers.

Our proletarian poets are still sick with yearning for 'self-revelation'. They are breaking away from their class every minute. They do not want to be simply proletarian poets. They look for 'cosmic', 'planetary' and 'deep' themes. They think that, as regards theme, the poet must leap out of his milieu, that only then will he reveal himself and create something 'eternal'.

Opoyaz will show them that everything great was created in answer to current questions, that 'the eternal' today and in the past was a matter of current affairs, and that a great poet does not reveal himself, but only fulfils a social demand.

Opoyaz will help our comrades the proletarian poets to overcome the traditions of bourgeois literature, by showing scientifically its lack of vitality and its counter-revolutionary nature.

Opoyaz will come to the aid of proletarian creation not with misty talk of the 'proletarian spirit', and 'communist consciousness' but with precise technical knowledge of the devices of modern poetic creation.

Opoyaz is the grave-digger of poetic idealism. It's no good fighting against it. And so much the worse for the Marxists.

Concerning the Question of the "Formalists"

(A survey and a reply)

1

During the past two years, the authors of literary articles, prefaces, reviews and critical pamphlets have devoted a great deal of attention to the question of the so-called "formal method". There is not a single literary journal in which this question, which seems almost to have become one of immediate urgency, has not been discussed with some degree of passionate involvement, even though it would seem to be far removed from problems of the "first priority". Not only the journals (*Red Virgin Soil*, *Press and Revolution*, *Book and Revolution*, *Literary Notes*, *The Life of Art*, *Thought*, *Beginnings*, *Literary Thought*, *Art* and so on) but even the newspapers are constantly bringing up the question of the "formal method", the "formalists" and "Opoyaz".[2] All kinds of writers, from the most respected littérateurs and academics to venturesome young ladies, have been exercising their wit or displaying the profundity of their thought in criticism or discussion of the "formal method". The question has spilled over from the sphere of literature into pedagogics, engaging the interest of wide circles of students and their teachers and thus becoming a question of methodology. And finally, L. Trotsky himself has spoken out about it quite recently (in the Moscow *Pravda*, 1923, No. 166 and in *The Life of Art*, 1923, nos. 30 and 31; see also L. Trotsky's book, *Literature and Revolution*, Moscow 1923, Publishers "Red Virgin Soil"), and has thus attracted to the question the attention of new circles of people who were probably quite unaware that any such creatures as "formalists" existed.

The history of this varied literature about the formal method (please note that I am writing without quotation marks, but assuming them) can be divided into two stages: that of philistine mockery and that of academic discussion. At first, the formal method, as it was defined in the works of members of "Opoyaz", seemed to be a daring escapade, and every pamphlet writer, accustomed as he was to writing about the topic of the day, considered himself quite justified and qualified to poke a bit of fun at the vulgarity of the formalists. But after a short time the position changed. The pamphlet writers wrote nothing except their pamphlets, while the formalists produced a series of works of which serious account had to be taken. Experienced critics and well-versed professors began to be aroused. Silent contempt became impossible, if only for tactical reasons. Positions had to be taken up as quickly as possible, the old had to be combined with the new, if only nominally. Self-determination and stratification began. As has been the case in the history of every movement, revisionist eclectics began to emerge, devoting themselves to interpretations, corrections, reconciliation etc. Everyone started to talk about "methods" and "approaches", —even those who had never given them a thought before. This process, of course, has still to go further and deeper, but the initial grouping has evidently come to an end. We have already seen the appearance of the "for-soc" [3] who, without realising the comical role they are playing in the hands of History, take the line of least resistance and suggest the unification of the two "methods"—the formal and the sociological. Next, it will be the turn of the young generation, who are already emerging onto the stage. However they conduct themselves, they must be helped to make sense of all this confused "history".

2

First of all, there is, of course, no such thing as a "*formal method*". It is difficult to establish now who thought up this name, but it was definitely not a success. It may have been convenient as a simplified battle slogan but it serves no purpose as an objective term to define the activity of the "Society for the Study of Poetic Language" ("Opoyaz") and the Linguistic Section of the Institute of Art History.[4] A name by itself is, of course, of secondary importance, but if it leads to misunderstandings and absurd quarrels, then it must be taken seriously.

The question at issue concerns not the methods used in the study of literature, but the principles of the construction of literary science—its content, the basic subject of study and the problems which give it its structure as a special science. It has at last been made clear that the science of literature, not being simply part of the history of culture, must be an independent and specific science, one which possesses its own sphere of concrete problems. It has also been made clear that the conversion of the historical parallelism of different categories of culture (their "correspondences") into a functional (cause-and-effect) connection is a forced transformation, which for that reason does not produce any positive results. In addition, the selection which is made in this process of one category as the progenitor of all the others is dictated by the demands not of science, but of a world-view. Such selection thereby introduces a tendentious premise into science. As a result, phenomena become over-simplified, schematised and thus lose the very qualities which distinguish them from each other.

The impulse towards the *specification* of literary science has been expressed above all in the declaration of *"form"* as the basic problem for study, form as something deliberately specific—something without which there is no art. The word "form" has many meanings and, as always happens in such cases, this has led to a whole series of misunderstandings. It must be understood that we attach an especial significance to this word. We use it not as something corresponding to the concept of "content" (a correspondence which is, incidentally, false, since the concept of "content" [5] in fact corresponds to that of "extent", and not to that of "form"), but as something which is basic to the artistic phenomenon, something which acts as its organising principle. What is important to us is not the word "form", simply its particular connotation. We are not "formalists", but rather, if you like, specifiers.

That's what I have to say about the word "formal". Now, to turn to the word "method". The recognition that the basic problem of literary science is the specific form of works of literature and that all the elements of which that form is constructed have formal functions as constructional elements, is, of course, a *principle* and not a method. The concept of "method" over recent years has broadened out of all proportion—everything has begun to be called a "method". (The "formal *method*" is just as meaningless a combination of words as the expression "historico-materialist *method*". We have reached a situation where "methodology has swallowed up science itself",—an impasse to which we have been brought by the old history of literature.) The word "method" must be reinvested with its previous modest meaning of a device used for the study of any concrete problem. The methods of study of form may be as varied as is wished, while holding to a single principle, depending on the theme, the material and the way the question is put. Methods of study of the text, methods of study of verse, methods of study of a particular author or period, and so on,—these are the natural uses of the word "method". The biographical method, the sociological method, the psychological or the aesthetic method,—none of these are methods, but different view-points on science, or even different sciences. It is clear that real "methodology" (i.e. the methodology of the study of concrete problems) may exist and develop normally only when science itself exists and develops normally, otherwise one is faced with "methodology of methodology". The question of the "formal method" became one of pressing urgency precisely because the formalists started talking about principles. If it had really been a matter simply of methods, then such excitement would have been strange, at the very least. One would have been drawn to the conclusion that Russia had become a predominantly "methodological" country and this, of course, is not so.

So we are not formalists and do not constitute a "method". By saying this, I free myself immediately from polemics with those who reproach us for being narrow, intolerant, etc. If the formal method is indeed useful, they say, then why exclude other methods, which are no less useful? Why must there always be only *one* method in science? These peace-loving or unprincipled eclectics begin their discussion of the question *in medias res*. Dear and respected colleagues, please understand that we are dealing not with methods, but with a principle. You can think up as many methods as you like, but the best method will be the one which can be relied upon most to lead to the goal. We ourselves have an infinite number of methods. But there can be no question of peaceful coexistence between ten different principles, there cannot even be two principles. The principle which establishes the content or the object of a specific science must stand alone. Our principle is the study of literature as a specific category of phenomena. It goes without saying that no other principle can stand beside it, for instance, that literature should be studied as a psychological or biographical document, as the emanation of the soul of the poet or that literature is a "reflection of life" etc. (I am speaking, of course, not about the ancillary use of literature in other sciences, but about the content of literary science as such). If it were possible for such principles as these to coexist peacefully, then we would have to say that Russia is predominantly an unprincipled country, which evidently is also not quite true.

3

But, anyway, what has been written about the formal method? A great deal has been written, but I shall deal only with what is most typical. Until 1922 there was almost nothing, despite the fact that the first "Opoyaz" collection appeared in 1916. The revolution drove many writers and scholars from their work. The formalists spent these years in active and intensive work. During the years between 1917 and 1921 the founders of "Opoyaz" (Victor Shklovsky, Osip Brik,[6] Lev Jakubinsky[7] and others) produced several books and articles. There was a great deal of talk about them in society: lectures and debates took place in the "House of Arts" and the "House of Writers". In 1919 Victor Zhirmunsky published in *Life of Art* an article called "The Aims of Poetics", in which he gave an exposition of the basic principles of the authors of "Poetica" (the collection of essays published by *Opoyaz*) and defended his middle-of-the-road position. This article was symptomatic, as an attempt to gloss over the acuteness of the problems. And from the beginning of 1922, with the partial reanimation of the periodical press, articles and reviews about the formalists began to appear. Various points of view were expressed by people of different traditions and generations, including the follower of Potebnya,[8] A. Gornfeld,[9] the Marxist P. Kogan,[10] the centrifugist and pupil of Andrei Bely, S. Bobrov[11] and the Pushkinist M. Gofman (I am leaving aside pamphlet writers, like V. Iretsky). The majority of the authors were ill-informed about the actual situation and their articles were therefore full of misunderstandings and curious statements. Bobrov and Kogan consider Victor Zhirmunsky to be the main formalist and his article on "The Aims of Poetics" (*Beginnings*, No. 1)—the codex of the formal method, whilst in fact this article, as is indicated above, is a reply to the works of the formalists and in its essence rejects their basic principles. Bobrov calls Victor Shklovsky "Zhirmunsky's fellow-thinker", Kogan considers that the formal method "is scientifically established by V. Zhirmunsky and his fellow-thinkers". As well as being ill-informed, Bobrov also displays a tendency towards over-simplification of the whole question; he adopts the haughty pose of an arbiter and turns the formalists into simpletons: "The members of the "Poetica" circle are realists of extreme naiveté, and the general course of their reasoning may be reduced to a play on words: a poem is a series of concretely interrelated words and there is no more than that to it" (*Red Virgin Soil*, 1922, No. 1). He condemns Zhirmunsky, but immediately afterwards adopts the same stance as him against Shklovsky and Jakobson,[12] agreeing that the "laying-bare of the device" is a mere trick. P. Kogan is even less well-informed. He is so aroused and indignant (although it is difficult to understand why), that in his outrage he proclaims K. Chukovsky[13] a great scholar and the founder of formalism: "Chukovsky is older than the other modern "formalist" scholars. His critical sense and artistic taste have helped him to anticipate many of the conclusions(?) to which the different linguistic circles and "Opoyaz" are now coming. In practice, he applied to the poets(?) the same critical method which is at the present time being scientifically established by V. Zhirmunsky and his fellow-thinkers. But he is not only older than they are—he is also broader" (*Press and Revolution*, 1922, book 2). In another article ("The News of the All-Union Central Executive Committee", 1922, No. 166) he takes up a revolutionary-dictatorial pose and hurls down an angry phrase, pointing his finger at us: "Poor, naive specialists, who have lost the last remnants of their sense of modernity", and so on. There is no need to dwell on this—it is all over and done with now. Gofman also appears curiously ill-informed and flippant. In his words it emerges that the formalists are destroying "historico-comparative poetics and the history of literature ... How can one conceive of the construction of a poetics without taking into account the study of the changes and development of literary schools and traditions, or the resolution of the question as to how the *given* of an existent poetic school and tradition, the *given* which results from preceding poetic experience, prompts the construction of a creatively new form and a creatively new poetic tradition?" (the book *Pushkin*, Athenaeum, 1922). Once he had begun to protest and got carried away with his own rhetoric, Gofman failed to notice that he had begun to repeat the words of the formalists, distorted only by the aura of bad taste peculiar to himself.

Different in nature is the article by A. Gornfeld ("The Formalists and their opponents", *Literary Notes*, 1922, No. 3), which constitutes an editorial correction to V. Iretsky's ridiculous feuilleton ("The Maximalists", *ibid.*). About Iretsky there is nothing to say—he was sufficiently "corrected" by Gornfeld himself when he declared that "science can permit itself the luxury of taking no account of the irritation of V.Ya. Iretsky". But, having taken up the position of an arbitrator between Iretsky and the formalists, Gornfeld decided to exploit this pretext and, standing on his rights as an old, experienced man of letters, read the formalists a sermon. He makes three accusations against them: 1) "they have made questions of purely scientific method into topics of raucous journalism"; 2) "they have represented techniques long known to Western science as the discovery of bold Russian Newtons"; 3) "they have treated the jargon of their own circle as scientific terminology". The first point I have answered above—we

are concerned not with "purely scientific method", but with principle. Our "stepping out onto the street" seemed as elemental and as
natural as the stepping out onto the street of the futurists. Gornfeld is
obliged to agree that questions about the existence of science or art go
beyond the boundaries of those academic questions which are restricted to the professor's study; after all, he himself has spent his whole
life writing not in academic "Communications", but in journals and
newspapers. The second point is simply untrue. I suggest that
Gornfeld examine the articles in the *Collection on the theory of poetic
language* on the works of Nyrop, Grammont and Sivers and in *Poetica*
the bibliography of foreign works on verse (previously unmentioned
by him, by Bely and by Bryusov) etc. The names of Sivers, Saran,
Dibelius and others were introduced into Russian science by the
formalists. The facts speak for themselves, therefore I continue. It is
strange to hear talk of "circle jargon" from Gornfeld, who himself
wrote a book about new words. What is one supposed to do—invent
terms individually or seek the blessing of the Paris Academy of
Sciences for them? This is all due to the fact that Gornfeld is used to
the position of "war on two fronts" (these are his own words about
himself in the foreword to his collection of articles, *The paths of
creativity*, 1922). The content of what he says changes, depending on
whom Gornfeld thinks he is addressing. In his foreword to the above-
mentioned collection, directed not to the formalists, but to the public,
Gornfeld has something different to say: "*At one time* it may have
seemed that this study (i.e. the study of poetic form) at best should
not extend beyond the workshop of the artist or the study of some
narrow specialist on stylistics, the history of the text or linguistics. *Now*
it is quite obvious that the new poetics—quite independently of its
self-sufficing scientific interest—is one of the sciences of greatest
educational interest", and so on. What do these words "at one time"
and "now" mean? The signature of the foreword is dated 31 August
1922, while *Literary Notes* came out on 1 August of the same year. As
we can see, Gornfeld has got over-excited and, despite his know-
ledgeability (he was the first to declare that the formalists were all very
different, and to identify V. Zhirmunsky as a "cautious eclectic"), has
turned out in the end to be an unsuitable arbitrator. He undoubtedly
came to regret this later, when A. Tinyakov started his hysterical howling about how the formalists "with the arrogance of ignoramuses and
the harsh vulgarity of dimwits raise their voices, attempt to seduce
wide circles of our young people, and calculate and mutter and pile up
their computations, their 'indisputable' conclusions, sowing around

themselves aridity, decay, self-opinion, graphomania, pedantry and narrowness' (*Latest News*, 1923, No. 1) and, in uttering this tirade, declared his "warm sympathy" with Gornfeld's article ("The artistic word and the scientific number". *Literary Thought*, No. 1). Yes, history sometimes produces unexpected combinations of names: Kogan-Chukovsky—Gornfeld-Tinyakov…

4

I move on to the literature of 1923. We are now faced with something new: Professor A. Beletsky (in his foreword to the translation of R. Muller-Freüienfels' "Poetics"), Professor A. Smirnov ("The paths and tasks of the science of literature". *Literary Thought*), Professor P. Sakulin ("On the question of the construction of a poetics". *Art*, No. 1). Professor N. Piksanov ("The new path of literary science", *ibid*.) and so on. As we can see, real scholars have now begun to tackle the question of the formal method. When "Opoyaz" acquires its own journal, then we will have our say about these articles (if they have not become an anachronism by then) in detail, as they deserve—here I am limited to talking only about the most important points, and that cautiously, because I find myself in strange company.

The basic aim of these articles is to smooth over the pointedness of the questions. Persuaded that the formalists could not be ignored, these respected scholars decided to eliminate the domination of "Opoyaz" by another means: that of declaring themselves also to be "formalists" or, at least, profoundly in sympathy with this young movement, but at the same time to turn the whole thing round so that nothing of the "formal method" will be left. It is a subtly diplomatic device, well known to us from the history of other kinds of movement. Every historian of literature has had, even if only occasionally, to deal with "form"—why then should he not call himself a "formalist", if that is the whim of the time? One can keep all one's old habits and principles, but call it all "poetics". And then it'll turn out that "Opoyaz" were shouting and getting excited to no effect—scholars had known it all for ages and see much more deeply into the very heart of things.

Beletsky, for example, had always sympathised with "formal-stylistic studies", but had never striven, as the members of "Opoyaz" did, "at whatever cost to obtain the patent of the pioneer in unexplored thickets or to create his own systems, not suspecting or not wishing to suspect the existence of other, often quite substantial systems'', and so on. A model is supplied by R. Muller-Freuïenfels' book, hopelessly eclectic but written with complete German thoroughness, which is recommended to the reader instead of ''the lively and provocative articles of V. Shklovsky''. Smirnov is quite well-disposed towards the formal method but, apparently, it is necessary to distinguish literature from poetry. Jules Verne or Dumas is literature, Shakespeare is poetry. The science of literature is one thing, the science of poetry another. Good, truth and beauty are to be found only in poetry; this wondrous trinity does not exist in literature. The formal method is quite lawful in the study of literature, but intuition is needed for the study of poetry. This is the kind of naively generous form that ''Gershenzon's[14] wisdom'' took, translated into the language of university learning. Sakulin is also in full support of poetics, the study of style, composition, devices—all that needs to be added to that is a little sociology, a little aesthetics, a little biography etc. Then everything will be remarkably good and fine: ''The organism of the work will stir with life, for the soul of the poet is alive''. It is with this unusually rhetorical phrase that the article ends. Piksanov, it turns out, spends all his time dealing with ''poetics'', but in a more profound form—not that which aims at ''the description of the definitive text'' (this is what rank-and-file formalists are concerned with), but another kind, whose main task is the establishment of ''the creative history of chefs d'oeuvre''. By this is meant the study of draft manuscripts on the basis of material drawn from biography, sociology, psychology and, when it is necessary, psychopathology. This used to be called simply the study of the text, but now it can be called ''poetics'' or ''formal method''. It turns out that Piksanov (and not Chukovsky, as Kogan asserted) is the real founder of formalism. Referring to the argument about the teleological status of the device, Piksanov declares: ''it pleases me to note that this young and energetic group of theorists of poetry supports the idea and the formulation of poetic teleology which I made the basis of my analysis of the creative history of *Trouble from Wit*''. We, for our part, are pleased to note that Professor Piksanov is so delighted at this coincidence (which, by the way, is quite irrelevant to the formal method); the final judgment on the question we shall postpone until the appearance of the works he has promised, in which all the positions he has adopted are to be developed in detail and, to use his language, backed up by ''exemplifications''.

As far as V. Zhirmunsky is concerned, his foreword to O. Walzel's book (*The problem of form in poetry*) shows quite clearly that it is, of course, impossible to consider him the founder of the formal method and its principal theorist. Of course, Zhirmunsky is a man of our generation and formal questions interest him deeply. On his lips the word "poetics" sounds not like a fashionable label, but like a real term. But as soon as he goes beyond the province of individual themes into the area of the general principles of construction of the history and theory of literature, then we have before us the typical eclectic, the reconciler of extremes. It emerges that there is absolutely nothing to quarrel about—one only has "to ask the question about the boundaries of application of the 'formal method', about the interrelationship of formal-aesthetic problems with other possible problems of the science of literature". The formula of "Opoyaz" (art as a device) can, it seems, coexist peacefully with other "equally legitimate formulae, for example, art as the product of spiritual activity, art as a social fact and as a social factor, art as a moral fact, a religious fact, a cognitive fact etc.". It turns out that it is not only "legitimate", but also correct "in studying the poet Nekrasov to depart from the influence of the ideas of Belinsky and his circle". The evolution of style is closely connected(?) with the "world-perception of the age", and so on. As we see, there is no enthusiasm in Zhirmunsky for the intensification and the elucidation of such problems. He languidly repeats old academic "truths", and it is still not quite understandable why he is talking about these questions, when he simply doesn't have enough theoretical temperament to put them. It is no wonder that he (like Gornfeld) condemns the formalists for "insufficiently thought-out speeches at debates and meetings". Well, we condemn Zhirmunsky for his too well thought-out foreword, which is therefore bereft of any principles. Let history choose which of us acted more correctly.

Finally, the article by L. Trotsky, entitled "The formal school of poetry and Marxism", which I mentioned at the beginning. This article has played a serious role in connection with the strengthening of the social-pedagogical position of the formal method, inasmuch as Trotsky, in contrast to many other people, recognised that "a certain part of the investigative work of the formalists [was] most useful". But, if we leave aside the question of usefulness or harmfulness and approach Trotsky's article simply from the point of view of scientific truth, then it gives rise to a number of puzzling questions. Usually precise and lucid, Trotsky here expresses himself sometimes vaguely and indecisively, sometimes too decisively and mistakenly.

Let us begin with the fact that, in Trotsky's opinion, "formalism opposes Marxism with all its strength". This is not quite so—the matter is both simpler and more complicated than that. Simpler, because formalism and Marxism cannot be "opposed" to each other: formalism is a system of an individual science, Marxism is a philosophical-historical doctrine. It is impossible for Marxism to be opposed by the theory of relativity, because these are incommensurable things. More complicated, because there are points of contact between formalism and Marxism, inasmuch as both these systems have to do with the fact of evolution. The formal school studies literature as a category of specific phenomena and constructs a history of literature as the specific, concrete evolution of literary forms and traditions. The question of the genesis of literary phenomena (their connection with the facts of everyday life and economics, with the individual psychology or physiology of the author, and so on, ad infinitum) is consciously put aside, not because it is generally unimportant, but because it clarifies nothing within the limits of this single category. To indicate the genesis means to recognise and identify the connection between phenomena but not the *causality* which explains them. The connection of everything with everything else is a fact both of life and of culture, but there are various different connections. Trotsky is quite right when he says: "One must suppose that curly hair and lumps are in fact connected in some way with character, but it is not a direct link and the human character is in no way exhausted by that". It is necessary to distinguish the concept of *evolution* from the concept of *genesis* not only as separate problems, but as problems pertaining to different sciences. Marxists, in studying politics, study evolution and not genesis, and for this very reason they, as we, allocate to personality and the accidental factors connected with it a secondary place; this is why they regard every war not as a fact of pure politics with all its attendant "links" (in genetic terms), but as a socio-economic fact (in evolutionary terms). Here is the point of our organic contact. When Plekhanov writes that "if some mechanical or physiological causes, unconnected with the general course of the socio-political and spiritual development of Italy, had killed Raphael, Michelangelo and Leonardo da Vinci as children, then Italian art would have been less complete, but the general direction of its development in the period of the Renaissance would have remained the same", we agree with him, because he is talking about evolution and the laws of development. But here lies the very question, in that, in approaching the study of art, and especially literature, the Marxists are beginning to talk not about evolution, but about genesis. The specific and the concrete is discarded because it does not fit into the system. Literature becomes either an "illustration", or an aesthetic appendage (hence the unique "aestheticism" of many Marxists).

Formalism does not "oppose" itself to Marxism, but simply protests against the simple transfer of socio-economic problems into the sphere of the study of art. The material resists this, because it has its own specific sociology. And if it is forced, then evolution is replaced by genesis, and instead of concrete causality we have distant "links". The transfer of general schemes from one scientific sphere to another leads inevitably to scholasticism.

It is characteristic that Trotsky, in objecting to the formalists, is diverging not only from the evolutionary point of view, but also from Marxist principles. Restraining himself from so-called "vulgar Marxism", he ends up by force of circumstances with something no longer resembling any Marxism. For example, he suggests that we study "the world-sensation of the artist", i.e. the same subject that "idealistic" science stubbornly continued to study, and against which not only Trotsky, but we ourselves rebel. After all, "world-sensation" cannot be studied objectively, as we study verse or style, but can only be attained "intuitively". Is this what Trotsky wants of us? It is also characteristic, on the other hand, that in several instances he has to give way to formalism—again, in order not to fall into "vulgar Marxism". But here he has to take up what for him is the highly uncongenial position of the eclectic. For example, in making use of a formula already considerably soiled in the old science and thoroughly genetic—"new form for the new content of life", he is at the same time compelled to admit that "verbal form is not the passive imprint of a preconceived artistic idea, but an active element which has an impact on the plan itself". In another article ("The art of revolution and socialist art"), he even admits that form "within known limits develops according to its own laws, like any technique" and that every new literary school "derives from the whole preceding development, from the existing mastery of the word and colours" etc. This is a big concession to formalism. Surely this is the very problem, that the eclectics' so-called "known limits" are in fact unknown. But what if the answer to everything lies within them?

The basic cause of all this vagueness, all this indecisive decisiveness lies in the fact that Trotsky has an inaccurate idea of what formalism is. In his opinion, the formal school (not in poetry, of course, as is signified for some reason in the title, but in science) reduces its basic task to "the analysis (actually descriptive and semi-statistical) of the etymological and syntactical features of poetic works, the calculation of repeated vowels and consonants, syllables and epithets". Such, indeed, is the widespread image of formalism among readers, which is very convenient for criticism and polemics, but extremely remote from reality. The efforts of the formalists are directed not towards the description of individual works (this is what A. Bely and S. Bobrov were once concerned with), but towards the construction of the theory and history of literature as an independent science. Trotsky obviously bases his judgment on transitory impressions drawn from various kinds of books and articles which are perhaps not at all characteristic of formalism—otherwise he would not be talking about the analysis of some "etymological features" (whatever does this mean?) or about the calculation of syllables and epithets (in which works does this take place?), he would not ascribe to us the definition of a poem as a "combination of sounds", he would not juxtapose V. Zhirmunsky with V. Shklovsky and R. Jakobson, etc. And as far as statistics are concerned, then it is well known that no science is averse to them.

It is natural, given such a notion, that formalism appears to Trotsky as something like a microscope—not a scientific principle which liberates science and makes it concrete and specific, not even a method, but simply a useful technical tool. It is also natural that his main reproach is that the formalists "do not want to be reconciled on the ancillary, auxiliary-technical significance of their devices". This reproach is most familiar to us—we have heard it from "Volfila"[15] and from a whole series of respected scholars and readers, disturbed by the formal method. Also well known to us is Trotsky's overall assessment: a certain portion of the research work of the formalists is "most useful", but their methodological devices must be brought within "acceptable limits". Oh, these "known" and "acceptable" limits! Trotsky turns out to be a fellow-thinker of the eclectics and revisionists, and this is no accidental coincidence. Revolution encompasses all culture as a whole, but its concrete manifestations are unique in every sphere. Marxism by itself does not guarantee a revolutionary position in astronomy or in art. Within the limits of literary science, formalism is a revolutionary movement, in that it liberates literary science from old, outworn traditions and compels a renewed examination of all basic concepts and schemes. Not reckoning with the uniqueness of literary science and basing himself on ready-made prejudices, Trotsky turns out to be a defender of old science and a fellow-thinker of the peace-makers. Such is the force of things.

The revolutionary nature of the formal method is expressed in the intensification and specification of the basic problems of literary science and in the attempt to endow it with a scientific nature and to rid it of vapid conversations "concerning ..". I therefore think that the generally severe sentence pronounced by Trotsky at the end of the article, which is somehow not quite in keeping with its beginning ("the formal school is a premature child, of idealism, nurtured by academic dogmatists and applied to the questions of art"), is deeply mistaken and unjust. If we are "idealists", then only in the sense that we have some sort of "ideas" of our own, but then in this sense Trotsky, if you like, is also an "idealist" to a certain extent. And as regards the "premature child" (in another place—"an extremely haughty premature child"), this is an oratorical gesture, to which it is best not to react at all.

5

They talk about the "victory" of the formalists. It is not a matter of who is victorious—it is not the formalists who win, but science. And from this point of view the position of literary science is now more dangerous than it was in the years of the initial struggle. The illusion is created of academic equilibrium. There is a growing pressure from eclectics, canonisers, appeasers and epigones. At times, the struggle seems to become not so much scientific as moral-social in character. The obscuration of the basic questions is facilitated by the misunderstandings which have accumulated over these years—such as that by which the struggle for the construction of a science is understood as a struggle for a "method", and hence follow all manner of recipes for the reconciliation and uniting of the various different methods. I wanted by this article simply to clarify the actual position of the question.

From First Source

Two circumstances annoy B.M. Eykhenbaum. Firstly, the continuing false reports about the formal method, which on examination turns out to be not at all formal and not even a method. Secondly, the threat to literary science that lies in "the pressure from eclectics, canonisers, appeasers and epigones".

One cannot help thinking that this talented scholar is greatly exaggerating the position. He is under the impression that the so-called formal method is the centre of the whole science of literature. As soon as "Opoyaz" appeared, then "everyone began to talk about 'methods' and 'approaches'—even those who had never thought about them". Yes, the pronouncements of the Opoyaz members greatly enlivened our science; their work has imparted much that is of value. But it is laughable to assert, as unfortunately B.M. Eykhenbaum does, that scholars, having decided to destroy the domination of "Opoyaz", took to "subtly diplomatic" ruses in order to do so: they pretended to be supporters of "the formalists" and insidiously began to distort matters in such a way that nothing would be left of the formal method. What amazing politicians they were, you might well think! Would it not be more realistic to consider that the academics suspected of such treachery also have their own views, and that the development of methodology need not simply follow the path laid down by the members of Opoyaz? It is just not worth trying to make calculations on this basis. B.M. Eykhenbaum also devotes several lines to my article "Towards the question of the construction of a poetics", but I shall not say anything *pro domo sua*. What I am interested in is the essence of the question.

B.M. Eykhenbaum complains that the "formal" method is judged wrongly and indiscriminately. Uninformed people consider V.M. Zhirmunsky a representative of the "formal" school and frivolously place him "in the same category as V. Shklovsky and R. Jakobson", while Zhirmunsky is, in fact, a "typical eclectic". "Let history choose which of us acted more properly'', concludes B.M. Eykhenbaum modestly. However, without awaiting the judgment of history, he assures us that the true spokesman of Opoyaz ideology is not Zhirmunsky, but himself, Eykhenbaum. I must admit, this ''domestic quarrel'' does not seem to me particularly important. We judge each writer by his printed works; we see in the representatives of one school a certain difference in their scientific devices, against the background of a similar understanding of the principal tasks facing them; we can even see how some of them evolve (V.M. Zhirmunsky and B.M. Eykhenbaum himself);* we consider all this to be quite natural in any scientific movement and we assess the results achieved. For me, V.M. Zhirmunsky is associated, in this respect, not with V. Shklovsky, but with B.M. Eykhenbaum. One cannot talk about Zhirmunsky without special emphasis: not only has he given us several talented pieces of research in the style of the ''formal'' school, but, besides that, he has scientifically systematised his own theoretical views. But now, B.M. Eykhenbaum speaks on behalf of ''Opoyaz'' and the ''Linguistic Section of the Institute of History of the Arts'', whilst in the Institute's collection of essays, *The aims and methods of the study of art* (1924), the leading article on poetics is written by the same V.M. Zhirmunsky. Here is another cause of misunderstandings. But I willingly admit that B.M. Eykhenbaum is more orthodox than V.M. Zhirmunsky, and I therefore turn to his article. It is always nice to get information from the primary source. I am only sorry that this article is polemical and that the author does not develop even his own more responsible thoughts.

What do we discover that is new about the ''formal'' method? ''First of all—thinks B.M. Eykhenbaum—there is of course no such thing as a 'formal method'. It is difficult to establish now who thought up this name, but it was definitely not a success... The question at issue concerns not the methods used in the study of literature, but the principles of literary science—its content, the basic subject of study, the problems which give it its structure as a special science... The word 'method' must be reinvested with its previous modest meaning of a device used for the study of any concrete problem... The best method is that which can be relied upon most to lead to the goal. We ourselves have an infinite number of methods''. I do not know how B.M. Eykhenbaum will react to my announcement, but

*B.M. Eykhenbaum himself indicates his own evolution, see the foreword of the collection *Through Literature* (1924).

basically I fully agree with his view. Quite independently of B.M. Eykhenbaum or anybody else, during a recent Moscow discussion about sociological method I put forward and defended my *long-held* thesis, which I formulated thus: ''Method is the totality of devices of scientific research, which are based on defined principles deriving from the understanding of the nature of the studied object and, accordingly, of the aims of the research. The classification of methods must be built on the classification of aims, given the existence, however, of a common understanding of the nature of the object''.

I shall not now start to develop my thesis (I hope to produce a book on methodology in the autumn): B.M. Eykhenbaum will be able to see where the similarity and the difference of our views lies. I shall say only that for me the whole question rests on the understanding both of the nature of the studied object and the aims of the research.

To go further, I must again point out my solidarity in all essentials with B.M. Eykhenbaum. I am afraid of causing him some unpleasantness, but I do not perceive anything at all new in his ''principles'' of literary science.

Calling himself and his fellow-thinkers ''specifiers'' (a technical term used by publishers), B.M. Eykhenbaum attempts to show that the science of literature ''must be an independent and specific science, one which possesses its own sphere of concrete problems'' and that ''the basic problem of study'' is constituted by so-called form, understood ''as something basic to the artistic phenomenon, as its organising principle''. In this B.M. Eykhenbaum posits ''the revolutionary nature of the formal method'': ''within the limits of literary science formalism is a revolutionary movement, in that it liberates literary science from old, outworn traditions and compels a renewed examination of all basic concepts and schemes''. I am not inclined to belittle the indubitable merits of the ''formal'' school, but how can we fail to remember that, long before the appearance of the first issue of the *Collections on the theory of poetic language* (1916), these very specific aims of literary science were already the subject of much discussion. Let me refer just to the first volume of A.M. Evlakhov's book, *Introduction to the philosophy of artistic creation* (1910), with its conclusions that ''the history of literature is the history of poetry'', but the history of poetry is ''the history of forms''. I also note, by the way, that the First All-Russian Congress of Linguists (1916-1917) had already seen heated debates on this very subject.

Of course, beyond all this there remains the question of what meaning should be given to the concept of form. Here begin our divergences, because the problem of form has still not been fully studied. B.M. Eykhenbaum makes fleeting reference to his understanding of the problem. Knowing his scientific works, we have the right, apparently, to assert that if some members of "Opoyaz" have not yet outlived the concept of form which was prompted to them by early futurism and based itself in formal-linguistic poetics, then B.M. Eykhenbaum and several others (including—if I am allowed to say it— V.M. Zhirmunsky) have significantly broadened the content of the concept of "form". However that might be, this problem still demands further scientific definition.

But perhaps the most essential point, where, in fact, there remains a considerable difference of opinion between us, is the question of the social nature of the literary process. B.M. Eykhenbaum protests against the subordination of literary science to the history of culture. In this respect, it is not difficult for him to find allies amongst scholars of literature. Not satisfied with this, B.M. Eykhenbaum attempts, as it were, to separate literature from the general process of social life, rejecting all that relates to the sphere of the "genetics" (in my terminology, causality) of literary phenomena. He is right, in so far as he is struggling against unilateral determinism. It seems to me, however, that here also the position is not so hopeless, that a sociological treatment of literary facts is possible without any infringement of the independence of literary science and the specificity of literature as an art. If we linguists renounce this task, no one else will take it on, and indeed no one else will be fit to carry it out.

Again without going into detailed discussions, I shall allow myself to put forward one more thesis from my work, namely: "The sociological method in literary study presupposes *the special resolution of several problems* in their application to the specific properties of literature, in particular the delimitation of the evolutionary and the causal factors in the dialectical development of phenomena". I attach great importance to the last statement.

The fact that it is extremely difficult for us to do without "sociology" is felt, I think, by B.M. Eykhenbaum himself. For example, in characterising the style of Nekrasov, he saw the poet as "a historically inevitable and necessary phenomenon": "Nekrasov, like Béranger, understood that at that moment the voice of the crowd, and not that of the "chosen", was the voice of history... It was necessary to seek new devices, new methods both in the sphere of verse and in the sphere of genre. It was necessary to create a new poetic

language and new poetic forms, because art lives by its perception''.*
Is it not true that one more small step will bring us into the domain of
sociology? We will be carried there by the very same ''crowd'' as that
which so powerfully determined the poet's style by the demands of its
taste. Why has the ''crowd'' acquired so decisive a significance? and
what kind of crowd is it? how has the relationship between the poet
and this crowd come about? These and all similar *pourquois* cannot be
answered within the limits of literary phenomena alone: an excursion
into the sphere of ''sociology'' is inevitable. If we attempt to shirk the
solution of the questions outlined, then, of course, they will remain
unanswered: a competent reply can be given only by someone with
specialist knowledge of literature. This, in the present case, is B.M.
Eykhenbaum.

And so, at the risk of appearing an eclectic in the eyes of B.M.
Eykhenbaum, I hold to the opinion that the sociological method in
the history of literature is not only possible but necessary, and that, in
operating by it, we do not yield a single inch of the autonomous
sphere which by right belongs to the science of literature. These
thoughts I have also developed in my promised book. Perhaps this will
be that ''specific sociology'' which, it seems, B.M. Eykhenbaum is
prepared to allow.

---

*The collection of articles, *Through Literature* 1924; the cited article dates from 1922. I
also deal with an analogous problem in the book *Nekrasov* (''Zemlya'', Moscow 1922),
which was printed before the jubilee, but, as a result of the bankruptcy of the
publishers, went on sale only in a very small number of copies. (P.N. Sakulin)

The Method and the Apologist

It would be a strange notion to demand from a man who was select-
ing a profession for himself the exact basis of his interests, not to
mention the essentials of the subject which he proposed to study. All
this is so; however, the philosophical murk and the terminological
bickering surrounding the formal method must be dispersed one day
and it would seem that this should be done by the formalist comrades
themselves, and no one else. But instead of this, B.M. Eykhenbaum
displays the pretentiousness of a first-year student and makes a series
of patronising gestures to his critics in the manner peculiar to the
person of His Formalistic Majesty B.M. Eykhenbaum. I once had the
pleasure (1922, *Red Virgin Soil*, No. 1) of writing about the synthetic
(at least, it was intended to be such) work of Zhirmunsky, and I
suppose that Zhirmunsky has no idea how to give sensible answers to
my comments—and at the time I wondered: what is it, comrades, that
you call your method or principle (call it what you like) and what is it
really all about?—I have not received any reply to this from
Zhirmunsky and, in all probability, it would be impossible for him to
reply to this, as he does not know the answer. It is clear from Eykhenbaum's article that he does not know either—and this is extremely
annoying. Nobody, I repeat, is demanding from Eykhenbaum the
complete philosophy of his scientific doctrine, but even in the simplest
terms one has a right to demand something concrete, not just this
endless beating about the bush. It is indeed pleasant to learn that the
worthy Gornfeld has fallen into the same company as that time-
serving pornographer Tinyakov, no less piquant is the misalliance
between Kogan and Chukovsky. But this is nonsense and rubbish, we
have no time to spend on this sniggering and winking. So far as anything fundamental in Eykhenbaum's work is concerned, it's completely empty.

It is not the "method" that is important, says Eykhenbaum, but
the principle, the new principle from which viewpoint literature is

studied. What kind of principle this is, is not stated exactly; from the reasonings, interrupted by polemical escapades, it seems to become clear (although I do not guarantee it) that this principle may be reduced to the fact "that *form* has been declared the basic problem of study". Or: form is a formalist's principle. Evidently (one has to draw several conclusions from unfinished statements, although it would be difficult to answer for them), it is presupposed that the method stems directly from this principle. If this is so, then it is obvious that comrade Eykhenbaum is preaching to us some purely deductive worldview which by that very fact cannot be a science. When it comes to philosophy, then speculation and dialectics are pertinent: in that the subjects entering the circle of Eykhenbaum's doctrine are pure phenomena, the method is the criterion and the sole criterion of the entire whole. The principle (an intellectual one, cognoscenti) is the primary basis—period. However, the method, completely independently of the principle, may be comparative and genetic and descriptive and whatever you like. Further, it is said that the formalists study the evolution of form; this is said in a completely different place and independently of the statement adduced previously—but if the evolution of form also comes into the principle, then it is not a principle but a philosophical system, and if that is so, then what sort of a system is it? Eykhenbaum strenuously attempts to shrug off method, saying they have no method and that's not what it's about and that "the efforts of the formalists are directed towards the construction of the theory and history of literature as an independent science". Absolutely nothing follows from all this, and if the formalists still want to emerge from behind their polemical gestures and talk seriously about their business, then it must be they who do it, and not their critics. Swearing at a critic is one thing, but the theory of formalism is another; we have seen more than enough swearing and bumptiousness, but there is nothing to be heard of theory... Are the critics responsible for this?

The whole of B.M. Eykhenbaum's article is filled with various coquettish poses: some have the appearance of profundity, others show restrained silence, while yet others put on a display of solemn indignation, but about the matter in hand there is not a whisper. It is said, for example, that the historical parallelism of literature and other branches of culture points to correspondences (the correlative connection), and not to causality (the functional connection), to which one may object that in practice a correlative connection is a causal connection, and that it is not yet proven that the historical process is in false

correlation with literary evolution. This, of course, says nothing about
the quarrel between the formalists and "sociologists", but it does
show the kind of nonsensical phrases with which Eykhenbaum thinks
to rid himself of serious problems. It is later announced that content[18] is correspondent not to form but to "the concept of extent",
but the extent of concepts is the sum of those concepts whose predicate is the total concept, while form is the connectedness of correla-
tions defining the object—inasmuch as form also constitutes the
contraposition to content, while the content in relation to the extent
of the concept is simply its determinant: the greater the extent, the
lesser the content and vice versa. It would not be a bad idea for B.M.
Eykhenbaum to explain what he means.

Further: "all the elements of which the specific form of works of
literature is constructed have formal functions as constructional
elements". This position is also a principle. Apparently, this enigma-
tic phrase is intended to illuminate the following position: there exists
a linguistic construction or scheme, arbitrary operations on which also
produce as a result a work of literature (Heraclitus is simply a tear-off
calendar in comparison with the philosophy of Eykhenbaum!); what
"formal function" means, Eykhenbaum does not say, and it is not
recorded in any encyclopedia, the subject not having been covered
there. We know that the ordinate of a curve is a function of its
abscissa, i.e. that any position of the abscissa corresponds to a completely determined and uniquely possible position (the point) of the
ordinate. To talk of the content and form of the function is therefore a
little strange ("we call a given variable y a simple function of given
variable x, if there exists a law by which to each value of x which can be
considered there corresponds one, and only one, value of y". Max
Rose: *Introduction to the theory of functions*). After this it is
announced that soon, apparently, methodology will engulf science ...
nothing remains except to add that it is impossible to encompass the
unencompassable, and to quote Aksyonov:

> Benefactors, call the fire-fighters—
> Begins the grief of the world ...

There follows a list of outcasts, those who have raised their unclean
hands against the temple of the formal function; of the modest author
of these lines it is said that, in taking up the "haughty pose of an
arbiter", he has transformed "the formalists into simpletons". This
author is extremely sorry; he had no idea that his modest attitude and
inquisitiveness were marked by such destructive features, moreover he

had no way of knowing that he was dealing with such unstable material, which loses its meaning immediately after direct contact with another's (so to speak) arrogance. Now, reading through Eykhenbaum's article, one cannot help being convinced of this, in which connection it is most surprising that the effect of my attitude has not worn off even after a full two years; I must admit, I did not count on such breath-taking success. It is a pity, by the way, that Eykhenbaum has not seen my other articles about the formalists, one of them written individually about his person (or is he again passing over things in silence?). I have insulted Eykhenbaum, by copying in Russian his phrase about constructional elements and by confusing Zhirmunsky with Shklovsky, when, it turns out, they are quite different, belonging as they do to different parishes. Delicate family matters—from Moscow one can make nothing of all this; however, by juxtaposing my reviews of Zhirmunsky's and Eykhenbaum's books, it would have been possible to discover that even I had noticed this, despite the fact that many of Zhirmunsky's feelings are shared by other formalists. But here is Gornfeld (he lives in Petersburg, it's easier for him) singling out Zhirmunsky and still he is no good, as he cursed the inventors of formal function for their free-and-easy writing, their pretence of being geniuses and their circle jargon. Whence the whole story may be reduced to a fairy tale about the way in which the poor orphans were insulted by their terrible uncles, but they, the orphans, still did not fear them. Let's make sandcastles, let's run off and play tag, Mummy's said we'll have ice-cream today—all this is meant to be the principles of a great science. By the way, about one of these orphans, Zhirmunsky: Eykhenbaum's article says for the first time exactly and clearly that ''he's not one of us''. So we shall know in future.

This small article shows with great clarity that the formalists don't know what they're doing or what they want and it should also serve as a definite indication to some of them that it is time for them to get to grips with this. The fact that they were castigated by Tinyakov does not mean that they are right. Neither does this follow from the fact that they do not know the meaning of function or historical materialism, but in fact quite the reverse. Nor can anything sensible be gained from their affected babbling. If the academic specialists can find nothing better to do than pat them on the head with all the awkwardness peculiar to them, then again this is no demonstration of the formalists' right to occupy the territory which they covet.

Formalism in the Science of Art

We Marxists should in no way reject the existence of purely formal art.

Such purely formal art has long had a plain but expressive and exact nomenclature, in the vernacular: art without content.

I'll make my reservations at once, since I cannot imagine any more pedantic and carping people than formalists, of whatever sort. The Becmessers who note the mistakes of poetic inspiration with grating chalk on the blackboard, the Bridoissons who constantly harp on about "f-o-o-rm", or the Eykhenbaums who prove brilliantly that Gogol made his "Overcoat" in exactly the same way as any fashionable designer cuts his cloth to the taste of a fastidious customer.

To pre-empt the carpings of these Bridoissons, I'll say directly that not every form of art without content is lacking in value, far from it.

Tolstoy, one of the most rigorous exponents of content in art, when confronted with such a phenomenon as a pure ornament, and wondering which feelings, according to his own theory, the reader would be "infected" with, replied that the feeling aroused was "pure admiration".

And one would be quite correct in pointing out to Tolstoy that in such a case one could include in the category of objects arousing "pure admiration" a whole host of statues and paintings, pieces of music and even poetry which he dismissed outright because they lacked emotional and ideological content.

The whole point is that form in art, or, to put it another way, the method of combining the constituent elements of a work of art, is based on certain psycho-physiological peculiarities of our perception, which are partly rooted in the structure and functioning of our sensory organs and partly in the tendencies which are peculiar to the central perceptual apparatus.

Everyone knows that if we put a blot of ink on a sheet of paper, fold it in two, press it and then open it out, then, thanks to the exact duplication of the formless stain on each half of the sheet (symmetrically) there appears something like a design, an ornament; that is, something which has a certain potential for evoking admiration.

To look at the essence of the matter, all the formal work of the artist is analogous to this very simple method. An artist either simplifies the mass of elements he has organised by arranging his material in space, time, in the realm of thought or feeling; or else, on the contrary, complicates this basic material, in such a way, however (by lending it interest, piquancy or picturesque disorder), that he does not in any way exceed the boundary beyond which real disorder would have gone.

When we are dealing with elementary art which merely makes use of colours, lines, sounds and the like then precisely these elements as such, as pure sensations, are combined and composed by the artist to achieve admiration.

But if we are dealing with an artist who is rich in complex and powerful ideological and emotional experiences, then the task alters. Such an artist has before him two types of material: on the one hand, the experience which has matured in his consciousness, on the other, the matter (be it stone or words) into which he must inject his experience and to which, as a result of this, he must "give form". Giving form for such an artist means, on the one hand, acting like the Enteleche of Aristotle, that is, for a certain time he relates to the formless matter as though he were animating it by breathing into it all his creative inner experience.

There are powerful artists of the prophetic type for whom this is quite sufficient. Their inner agitation will give their work its rhythm, while the power of their experience, reflected in the work, will touch the hearts of those to whom it is addressed.

However, it is quite obvious that an artist, in the proper sense of the word, a master and the bearer of a particular social function, is first and foremost a master of expressiveness.

Expressiveness is a very extensive phenomenon and this term cannot fully convey what is involved. In the end, it is a matter of the artist's attainment of the most extensive and most profound psychic reach in his work, which is usually aimed at a specific circle of people (one's own people, one's own class etc.).

From this point of view the artist bears in mind both the specifics of the material in which he is working and the specifics of the milieu he is perceiving.

Let us imagine for a moment that an artist has no particular experience, that he has in his head no thought which is worthy of being publicly expressed, that there burns in him no feeling with which it would be worth "infecting" his neighbours, that he takes on something that is not his own, or is banal; but he is able to express this, putting to beautiful use the material that he has thoroughly studied and mastered, and equally, by his ability he produces an optimally entertaining impression on his public. What results is a purely formal art which, perhaps, will preserve a certain charm even beyond the bounds of a specific public.

From this results another conclusion: formal work pertains to all art, in certain instances art may be entirely reduced to formal work.

But when does this occur?

As I have already said, this occurs firstly when art has an elementary character, in other words, when it is restricted to the sphere of sensations and their organisation. This phenomenon is perfectly normal and has found widespread application at all stages in the development of art, and mainly in the field which is called applied art or industrial art.

By analogy one can imagine sound compositions which are naive and beautiful in their own way, but which express absolutely nothing. In this category one might include all kinds of word play: ritornelli, refrains and *zaum*. [20]

In essence, however, real art goes far beyond this stage: it grasps, in its own way, the organisation of things (it organises them so that the perception of them will be the easiest, and, at the same time, the richest in impressions). Moreover, it grasps the world of the highest and most complex emotions, their intricacies, their ideas and their systems.

In this instance art belongs entirely to the sphere of ideology. It ceases to be that part of human industry which is directed to the attainment of the admiration of things, and becomes a real, powerful instrument which acts on all of the human consciousness, on man's "psyche": it becomes an educative and agitational device of immense power.

Inasmuch as any society needs prophets, tribunes, publicists, and in as far as they emerge to answer this need, so they, often unconsciously, find that art, in particular poetry, is the most natural and powerful expression of their educative tendencies.

For the prophet Jeremiah, for Solon in his hexameters, for Tolstoy in the most strikingly prophetic period of his creativity (and I deliberately choose examples which are separated by thousands of years) the artistic form is secondary in comparison with the message they bear to the world.

But it is obvious that Tolstoy was not alone in understanding the acute infectiousness of a message organised by artistic devices, for an artistic message—which at times fully becomes a parable in which the attraction of the story and the art of the narrator seem to obscure completely the original conception, for the greater advantage, however, of the story's "infectiousness"—such artistic messages confront us in all courageous, progressive and powerful epochs or, what is the same thing, in all classes which are the leaders of society in such epochs.

There is a whole series of gradations in this ideological art. The message may dominate and its artistic expression be reduced to a fanciful design of metaphors and the musical organisation of its sentences (in Cicero, for example). Of course, this is not really art, but the more a feeling possesses the prophet, the more the centre of gravity in the living message is shifted to intonation, timbres and gestures.

The more the prophet seeks to act not on the reason, but on the whole organism, by exciting it, the more the words themselves lose their precise meaning, the more the prophet, in the very sound of the words and their orchestration, seeks forces which at first sight seem magical, both to subjugate the listeners, independently of the real sense of the words, and to bewitch them. It is here that we finally enter the realm of poetry and, at the same time, we note the tendency towards artistic synthesis: on the one hand, the poetic word tends towards an expressiveness which is both pictorial and plastic, and, on the other, the word strives for musical expressiveness. The word, of itself, seeks to create vivid and visually tactile illustrations, as it were, and, at the same time, to act upon the nervous system by the power of rhythm, tone, timbre, which at times aspire to the level of melody.

(I deal here only with literature but it would be easy to extend all I have said to the other arts).

In order to have a real work of ideological art and not merely a simple art of individual creativity on the part of the artist, but rather a social phenomenon, it is obviously necessary that the artist be possessed by his experience: in other words, he should perceive it, with his whole being, as something immensely important, while his audience would be in a position to enter into this importance through its own consciousness. Only under these conditions does the experience itself naturally become a powerful complex of ideas and feelings, which are called images and music.

When people talk disapprovingly of tendentious art they unconsciously have in mind works which are based on an insufficiently powerful experience which is not capable, from its own resources, of giving birth to its own flowers and fruit, so that the music and images seem to be grafted onto dry branches. One should relegate to this order of the ''arts'' almost everything that is born of the honest desire to instruct by entertaining.

The genuine artist does not wish to entertain. Nor does he wish to instruct, rather does he desire to disturb and by means of the contact of others' souls—evoked by what we call art—with his own soul, he seeks to change them, enrich and enlighten them. Artistic value is defined by the power of the experience and by the craving to discover methods which will as fully as possible transfuse this experience into others.

The reader may think that, by the same token, I consider it absolutely essential that ideas should be present in ideological art. Such a supposition would be correct, with one important reservation.

Beethoven, for example, would say with a cunning smile: ''In our time they thought there could be no music without an idea ... now they no longer think this''. (Bekker, *Beethoven*).

Of course, Beethoven had in mind not programmatic music, not music, written to illustrate certain ideas.

It cannot be denied that there do exist ideas which are completely musical, completely pictorial, plastic or architectural. Rejoicing in the recognition of this fact, a formalist might say that a purely musical or purely architectural idea is nothing other than a compositional, formal task. This would be a complete misconception. If an idea which is dominant in a work of art is, in the very act of creation, merely a compositional task, then the given work is not ideological, but, as it were, merely part of the artist's craft. Indeed, with what could such works infect the listener, if there is nothing in them apart from elementary sounds and their formal combinations?

What should an artistic idea be, for it to be placed in the ideological realm? It is obvious that it should have the characteristics of a feeling.

One solution or another of the structural resistance of a colonnade and the pressure of a roof, cannot, in its genuine artistic essence, be translated into words or, perhaps, can only be feebly denoted by a description and noted in the thinking consciousness as an expression of peace, graceful lightness, an ominous and sombre force, etc. ... and in this situation these words are very far from expressing the feeling which possesses us at the sight of the colonnade in question, just as there are no words to express to the man born blind what blue or red looks like.

Instinctively or, more accurately, sociologically, the coming task of ideology generally consists in the need to reinforce and disseminate the consciousness of the class which creates this ideology, and in the subjugation to it of the consciousness of other classes, and in the weakening and dissolution of the principles of existence of inimical social forces.

And it is entirely evident that the task of ideology implies not only the organisation of thoughts but, perhaps even more, the organisation of feelings, and consequently of voluntary impulses.

When any tribe or military detachment enters battle to menacing howling and to a rhythmic beat, intoxicated by this music, then, obviously there is no thought in this music, but there is a very specific and powerful emotional idea: infused in this music is, perhaps, the feeling of the blood-thirsty impetuousness of the musician who is attuned to the battle, or else the consciousness of the collective might of the masses moving uniformly into battle. This ''infects''. I will sum up: all art is ideological which stems from a powerful experience, which, as it were, involuntarily stimulates the artist to expansiveness, to the reaching of other souls, to the dissemination of the power of his dominant over them.

We Marxists presume that these dominants have a class character, that they are supported, accepted and rejected by specific classes, at a specific period of their development and under specific conditions.

But what of formal art?

Perhaps it is an extra- or supra-class phenomenon? Not at all.

At legitimate stages of its development and in its legitimate place, formal art is, in essence, the organisation of forms of being. What people admire, and how, is in no way accidental: it is true that a foreign costume or ornament, especially in an international and eclectic age, can attract admiration, but originally all this was felt to be ''one's own'' and served as a unifying force for our own national or class way of life.

So when formal art becomes the dominant, it is as if a horde of masks without faces invades all spheres of art—up to and including poetry. It begins to play a completely different role: in general it entertains or, more precisely, it distracts; it acts consciously or unconsciously totally in accordance with the motto of Metternich, who was a fairly perceptive class politician, when he remarked as follows: ''Let the Viennese amuse themselves—the government is the friend of the arts but will not allow anything serious to be brought into them''.

But here again one must make reservations. Louis XIV's cook hung himself because one of his sauces did not work out. In the same way, artist-entertainers can seriously relate to their role as entertainers to the point of tragedy. In order to elevate their own value, they themselves or their theoretician-cousins declare that entertaining art is "pure" art—"sweet sounds", that it is much higher than any art which serves society. They go on to say that pure formal mastery is the most sophisticated product of culture and those who are unable to appreciate it are savages and blockheads; that, moreover, the admiration afforded by such mastery is the highest form of joy in life, and that man lives for joy, and so art which is light and smiling is endlessly higher and more necessary than sweating tendentiousness, which is yoked to the same plough as beasts of burden like thought and labour.

Others, who are unsatisfied by such a happy solution of the question, apply themselves to metaphysics and discover in their entertaining or distracting art threads which link them to the other world and to the deity. Their formal songs are "prayers".

Which class, at which time can feel the necessity for such an art and can try by any means possible to disseminate it among all other classes?

The dominant class which needs no amelioration of its own position, lacks any inner idea; a class, that is, which has ceased to believe in its own vocation and no longer seeks to impress its own experiences upon anyone. A class which fears like the plague that another class should arise alongside it, one which is full of belief in itself, and which passionately strives towards the amelioration of its own position and the transformation of the social order, and which is rich in a store of captivating ideas and feelings. To entertain and distract such a class, to deflect other classes from it, would obviously be an important task for the government concerned, for the consciousness and instinct of the masters on their way out.

Bismark was in the habit of saying: "If you're stronger than your neighbour—hit him: a professor can always be found who will prove the legitimacy of your attack, from the point of view of eternal right".

But what's worse is that this sort of professor will dedicate his whole being to this problem and tear out his guts with the conscientiousness of the dog who delivers the dairyman's milk.

The contemporary bourgeoisie can love and understand only contentless and formal art: moreover, it would dearly like to impart such art to all strata of society. In response to this demand the petty-bourgeois intelligentsia has brought forth a phalanx of formalist artists and formalist critics.

What was least expected was that separate detachments of this phalanx could have any success in Russia, which is almost without a bourgeoisie.

Let us, then, attempt to understand how it has turned out that the strongest competition to the growing revolutionary art and emergent Marxist criticism should be artistic and critical formalism. How could it happen that Mr. Eykhenbaum, for example, even speaks of its triumph, admittedly without any basis for doing so, but honestly enough, at least from his point of view?

2

Despite a certain originality in its literature of the nineteenth century, Russia, towards the end of that period, fell completely under the sway of Western European fashions and tendencies. This began with the first appearance of literary symbolism, pictorial impressionism and the like.

How are we to explain this shift from highly original literature and representational art to the glaring Europeanisation of them? This shift can be explained by the radical change in the position of the Russian intelligentsia, which has produced almost all our artists.

Recruiting its representatives initially among the progressive aristocracy and then from the ranks of the *raznochintsy* (men of no fixed class) Russian art discovered in populism its basic axis. There were no parallel populist tendencies in the West. But the populist sources, which nurtured our creativity, were sufficiently strong to give rise to Mussorgsky and his group, to the Russian novel, to Repin[21] and Surikov,[22] Antokolsky[23] and Stasov,[24] all of whom drew little support from the West.

Then, after the twilight years of the eighties, Russian capital strengthened its position and began to create new forms of social discourse. The expansion of a privately owned capitalist economy and state capitalism created a large group of affluent intellectuals who gradually fused with the capitalist bourgeoisie and drew to themselves all that was most talented from the ranks of the *raznochintsy* intelligentsia.

The main cultural axis of the intelligentsia became cadet liberalism[25] in politics, and a study of European culture and constitutionalism.

As though in a mirror, albeit a slightly distorting one, Russia began to reflect the West. Pure art raised its flag on high. All this is absolutely in the order of things.

The February Revolution, in itself, in no way threatened an over-throw of this order of things, in as much as those who guided it were precisely the leaders of the Europeanised bourgeoisie and the whole of the socialist-revolutionary and Menshevik intelligentsia which had been more or less entirely integrated into the organisation of the bourgeois intelligentsia. This, in turn, was a kind of "Young Russia" in its tendencies, although the internal dissensions in no way hindered the unity of the practical slogans.

If a social miracle had taken place and the thin film of the above-mentioned order had resisted the eruption of the revolutionary Vulcan, then one could say with assurance that in Russia, in the field of art and criticism, the pure formalists would have been triumphant.

Probably we would have had in art decorative realism, highly coloured acmeism and drum-beating futurism—all of which would have been based on the total disregard of "content"—that is, the most vacuous, the most pallid, and at times, the most worthless experience of artists, which would have been disguised by verbal trickery of the most virtuoso kind.

The October Revolution and the Civil War for a time almost completely brought to a standstill the well-springs of our culture. When the time came for a gradual re-establishment of cultural life much seemed changed. The people, that is, the proletariat and the progressive peasantry began to create its own intelligentsia. Potentially, this intelligentsia contains within itself all that is necessary to develop an art which can express its experience and which can "infect" others. On principle and instinctively this intelligentsia feels apathetic towards purely formal art. However, this extremely young intelligentsia has not as yet managed to clarify for itself its own position and tendency, nor has it managed to invent a more or less suitable form for its own artistic content. It is still experiencing its own brand of tongue-tied infancy and, perhaps, the poetry of Bezymensky will for the first time create something which will remain of value in Russian literature.

All this produces a certain helplessness and weakness in the position of the new intelligentsia which is manifested both in the powerful influence on it of the old intelligentsia, as well as in the angry gibes of the proletarian extremists in the field of literature.

On the other hand, the immense strength of the position of the proletariat is shown in the fact that parts of the intelligentsia are becoming "fellow-travellers" of this new formation. It goes without saying that I not only do not reject the possibility of the most beneficial borrowings from the old culture, but rather I insist on their inevitability and necessity. Moreover, I admit that these borrowings may come not only from the classics and populists, but in certain cases and details from the formalist artists.

One should not think, however, that the old intelligentsia will consent, like a good cow, to nurture the growing hero with its own milk. Not only is its role limited, but its right wing and centre have, with the revival of our cultural life, re-emerged with all their formally inherent tendencies. One may merely say that, before October, formalism was simply a vegetable in season, whereas now it is a living vestige of the old, it is a palladium around which is being conducted the defence of the bourgeois, Europeanised, thinking intelligentsia which, moreover, knows that attack is the best form of defence. One should not imagine an open struggle between cadetism and communism, but an open struggle between formalism and Marxism is perfectly possible, and this is very good: Marxism is still very young in this particular sphere and can only gain strength in this struggle. But Marxism does like to know the exact class underpinning of any ideology and so, before entering the battle proper, asserts quite definitely: formalism, whether in art or the criticism of it, is the child of the late maturity or early senility of the bourgeoisie, such as it is when transferred to Russia, into the milieu that is most akin to it.

The aim of the present article is mainly to give a more or less precise definition of the social place of formalism. But I would like to offer a few more judgements on particular positions held by Eykhenbaum, as he is the most militant exponent of Russian formalism.

3

In his article "Concerning the Question of the 'Formalists'". Mr. Eykhenbaum devotes a fair amount of space to proving that there is no such thing as the formal method. In so doing, it becomes clear that by the term "method" the author understands a particular device of investigation, on the basis that Formalism in art criticism (although the author only concerns himself with the science of literature) is the basic constructive principle of the science.

If the argument simply concerned words then one could ignore these deliberations of Eykhenbaum—no-one has as yet given an exact definition of what a "method" is or what a "constructive principle" is. We, Marxists, talk of the dialectical method, although it is far wider than any basic principle of any given science, as it is the constructive principle of all knowledge in general. One could adduce scores of examples from the judgements of great authorities to the effect that each science, if it wishes to become separate from the others, must isolate its own *method* which belongs to it alone.

If I wish to dwell a little on this question, then it is for two reasons.

In the first place, Mr. Eykhenbaum does not hide the fact that his "principle" is analogous, for example, to the historical materialist principle. We would like a great deal more clarity about this relationship.

At the beginning of his career in literary criticism Mr. Eykhenbaum was fond of discovering the basic philosophical dominant of each poet. If formalism is indeed analogous to historical materialism then it means that formalism encapsulates a whole world-view. Which?

But Mr. Eykhenbaum gives no answer to this question, rather he hides behind other observations. He writes: "It has at last become clear that the science of literature, in that it is not simply a part of the history of culture, must be an independent and specific science, one which possesses its own sphere of concrete problems. It has also become clear that the conversion of the historical parallelism of different categories of culture (their "correspondences") into a functional (cause-and-effect) connection is a forced transformation, which for that reason does not produce any positive results. In addition, the selection which is made in this process of one category as the progenitor of all the others is dictated not by scientific demands, but by factors arising from one's world-view. It thereby introduces a tendentious premise into science".

First of all, one involuntarily asks oneself—to whom has all this become clear? When? Why?

The science of literature is not merely a part of the history of *culture*. What, to be exact, does this assertion mean? Does Eykhenbaum mean by this that a *theory* of literature can exist outside of its *history*? Of course, one may consider grammar, stylistics, poetics and so on and so forth separately from any relationship they may have with history, but merely as a collection of rules, which always are, incidentally, exceedingly scholastic, and which are extracted from artistic works, and are considered to be exemplary, or constructed on the basis of various allegedly given axioms.

We are extremely little interested in such an approach to literature, but in any case it has long been "clear" to us that this approach stands outside the history of *culture*, since, from the very beginning, it stands outside *history*.

But Mr. Eykhenbaum wishes to prove something altogether different: it is not by chance that he talks of parallel categories and their
mutual independence. It is obvious that he wishes to prove that it is
precisely the *history* of literature which lies beyond the sphere of the
history of culture.

What evidence, then, does he offer that all this has become
"clear", apart from, in truth, a disgustingly vague assertion?

His evidence is of the following order: the history of literature has
particular concrete tasks and must therefore be a separate branch of
science, and so on.

Just imagine a biologist who reasoned in such a fashion: "as the
physiology of the brain has particular concrete tasks, so it must be
separated completely from physiology in general, and there could be
nothing more disgusting or forced than an examination of it in conjunction with the physiology of respiration or digestion".

Every biologist, as a true scientist, knows that an organism is a
totality, that the division of the study of it into separate sciences is
artificial, that it is inconceivable to imagine a histologist or an
anatomist-pathologist who would not regard his science as a branch
which in no way could be investigated except by remembering the
most profound links the particular branch has with the totality.

The histologist may have certain specific additional methods in his
own science but these are mere details by comparison with the overall
arsenal of the basic methods of biology.

But a point that any doctor, any zoologist would immediately agree
with evokes a heated protest on the part of the sociologist (a bourgeois
sociologist, of course). The bourgeois sociologist fears a unified history
of culture like the plague. It is not enough for him to distinguish
different categories which are mutually independent, he would also
like to transform the study of each of these categories into a science
with its own particular principle, which definitely cannot be applied to
related sciences. But why?

Look how cunningly Eykhenbaum constructs his assertion: "The
conversion of the historical parallelism into a functional connection is
a forced transformation".

So it appears: it is forced to consider, for example, that the law of a
given country at a given time is based on its economy—this is not
science but tendentiousness, it is too accommodating to "the
demands of a certain world-view". But to assert that the law is, from
time immemorial, autonomous and in no way depends on the
economy—that's science, this "has become clear".

But, excuse me, Mr. Eykhenbaum; let us suppose for a moment that this or that functional dependence between two categories is hypothetical. But, if you are an honest scientist, you must agree that the absence of a functional dependence between them is not only a hypothesis but a clearly nonsensical one, since what scientist, or even what literate person, could believe that there is no interdependence between separate aspects of culture?

Of course, Mr. Eykhenbaum would reply that he does not reject objective mutual dependence, but simply postulates this independence as a condition of correct scientific work.

He would be correct in as far as bourgeois sociologists place a metaphysical dismemberment of the unified social process at the basis of their lifeless science.

To destroy these partitions, to return to science a unified cultural flow, to revivify the study of each separate category, each separate fact by placing them alongside the general cultural picture—these are the tasks of genuine scientific thought. In our view, it is precisely this that has become clear.

Now a few words as to whether it is legitimate or not to introduce into a science principles stemming from a particular "world-view".

It is possible, of course, to imagine certain scientific operations, more easily than whole sciences, which are illuminated by no world-view whatsoever. One can gather scientific collections of coins or establish the nomenclature of ants without thinking of a world-view. But, as soon as we approach a real science, whatever it may be, we see immediately that at its basis lies a world-view.

Let us take the natural sciences. One can divide natural scientists into approximately three groups, of which one stems from the completely unshakeable principle of the quantitative causality of all phenomena. It not only supposes that *ex nihilo nihil*, but also establishes, or, at least, strives to establish that nowhere are there any absolutely precise laws for the transformation of one form of energy into another, for the transposition and transmogrification of matter. It rejects any form of existence outside of matter and energy, which, in the final analysis, can be reduced to the same substance. This is a realistic monism which can also be termed materialism.

The second group considers the point of view of sceptical criticism to be more scientific. This group suggests that all laws which are established by reason, right down to the final ones—that is, mathematical axioms, are in essence not obligatory for the object under examination. Rather, they argue that science's business is to build up experience and summarise it according to rubrics which are convenient for the cognition of it. Science then formulates experience as simply and precisely as possible, without attempting to construe any particular system of the world, as human reason is unable to cope with this task.

Finally, the third group admits of a spiritual causality, that is, that the origin of certain facts (such as the transposition and transformation of material particles and quanta of energy) is inexplicable from a materialist point of view, but can have an explanation if one presumes the action of forces which are analogous to so-called psychic phenomena.

Outside these three world-views any natural science is unthinkable: moreover, it is glaringly obvious that the first approach has already produced exceptionally rich results, the third approach in essence represents a rejection of a purely experiential cognition of the universe, while the second, taking refuge in a particular strictness and impartiality, opens up loop-holes for the third way. The further one goes, the more each of these world-views takes on a class character. The proletariat energetically insists on the first view, having largely taken it over from the bourgeoisie of the revolutionary period. Scientists who are conscious puppets of the ruling classes, and who long to preserve religion as a convenient weapon of defence, defend the third view with all their might.

Many representatives of the uncommitted intelligentsia cover their social and scientific faint-heartedness with the advantageous cloak of scepticism and agnosticism.

We see approximately the same thing in the field of the social sciences, as well as in the history of literature.

The time when the social sciences can be reduced to physico-chemical laws is still very distant. But the exact materialist method, which has been accepted only by the proletariat, of course, has made an enormous step forward, thanks to dialectical and economic materialism. This method, in the first place, recognises the unity of social life, in the second, the class structure of society and the conflict between the classes as the dominant social phenomenon, and in the third place, the means of production and productive relations as the force which defines the character of the class structure of society.

This inspired approach has in fact provided the key to an understanding of social life in all its manifestations. In the natural sciences, so too in the present instance, the main argument of its opponents is that not all has been done as yet, nor has everything been resolved.

This retort is misused by Eykhenbaum too, but we may simply laugh at such a retort, as Timiryazev did in his own sphere. True enough, little has yet been done by Marxists in literary history. How could it be otherwise! So far they have conquered a mere one-sixth of the earth's surface and are occupied in the resolution of the trifling task of conquering the remaining five-sixths. It is natural that they find it difficult to direct a few individuals, in fact mere fractions of mankind, to the resolution of the most serious scientific questions outside the fields of politics and economics. And all the same, if we put on one side of the scales all the prattle of the formalists together. with their few grains of various useful details, and on the other, shall we say, just the book on Gogol by comrade Pereverzev,[26] then we Marxists, at least, can be entirely satisfied by the results.

In the history of literature one may imagine completely idealistic approaches. When Mr. Eykhenbaum says that it is just as absurd to use the expression "the formal method" as it is to speak of "the historical materialist method" and then goes on to assert that historical materialism implies a world-view, then, by the same token, he recognises formalism as a world-view, but we cannot insist on this, as such opponents of Marxism as Mr. Eykhenbaum prefer a position of scepticism which is allegedly of a rigorously scientific nature.

We, so we are told, should not even think of a world-view. This merely spoils our science, we restrict the sphere of literature and rummage around in it like worms in the ground: we should move from one fact to another, one observation to another, but what significance the given work of literature has in the overall life of society—the devil knows!

But this position equally involves a world-view: it is that peculiar agnostic pluralism which is the world-view of epochs and people who lack creativity, who have lost their way, are decentralised, but who proudly present their nasty disease as the most genuine health.

Partly out of a desire to know my opponent, partly because amid the heaps of detritus you occasionally find an interesting fact or healthy thought in the formalists, I have read most of Mr. Eykhenbaum's studies. He is an excellent example for the social pathologist; indeed he is unable (or perhaps, does not wish) to see in creativity, even of the classical epoch, a living experience, which is, after all, always a social act.

You will remember the story of the man, who, when asked at a Beethoven concert "What is going to be played?" replied: "They're going to scrape a horse's hair on cat gut". In just the same fashion,

Eykhenbaum reduces every work of literature to a verbal conjuring trick, all writers to verbal jokers, jesters, who only think of how one should make *The Overcoat*, and in their works one may only look for the most immediate pleasure in a sort of clicking of the heels or, for a deeper pleasure, from the analysis of the devices by means of which this artful dodger executes his hocus-pocus.

You may imagine, for example, that *The Overcoat* is a masterpiece of humour, and has immense power to move its readers, that it is precisely that mixture of laughter and tears of which the author himself spoke of in sonorous tones, that it is something original, which has been equally experienced by other countries and which has awoken the democratic feeling of protest; how old-fashioned you are!—it's nothing of the sort. Gogol simply put words together out of the innocent desire to amuse himself and others by a well-made tale.

You may think that Tolstoy moved from writing novels to populist Christian parables, swayed by the turmoil within his own conscience, which in turn was the result of the enormous, immense clash of cultures within Russia. You're a troglodyte from before the flood! After all, it has now "become clear" that Tolstoy merely changed his manner of narration because the old one had been exhausted. No doubt he changed his frock-coat for a peasant blouse in order to freshen up fashion a little.

Incidentally, it is highly characteristic of Mr. Eykhenbaum to declare constantly "it's old, it's worn out!" Modishness and the desire for novelty are necessary companions for the formalists. Paradox, curiosities—they are what inspire the epoch of the formalists—that is, an age without content, the culture of classes which have lost their content.

I would willingly reply to Mr. Eykhenbaum, and to his seeming delight in the apparent efforts of certain half-hearted people to recognise in formalism (which is slightly propped up by their concessions) a convenient position from which to defend themselves against Marxism. But this would take me too far. The question of the grouping and regrouping of our academics and intelligentsia is too large a one to fit within the confines of this article. Nor will I reply to that part of Mr. Eykhenbaum's article in which he criticises Marxist writers, in particular, comrade Trotsky. They will answer for themselves.

On the Formal Method

When I received Boris Eykhenbaum's article from the editors of *Press and Revolution*, and read it, I immediately realised that it was useless to try to change his mind about anything. Although I am not a formalist, I have, thanks to many years' experience, grown used to defining the basic characteristics of an author according to the form of his exposition. Of all the tropes and figures of speech, Eykhenbaum is most fond of hyperbole. In his opinion, if, for example, we continue to talk of methods, and not of principles, then we will be obliged "to think that Russia has become primarily a methodological country, whereas this, of course, is not the case".

It further transpires that Russia is threatened with an even greater danger. If we place other approaches alongside the formal method, such as the sociological, the psychological and the like, then we will be obliged to say that "Russia is primarily a country without principles which, apparently, is also not quite the case". And thank goodness for that! In the eyes of Boris Eykhenbaum, Russia has not utterly perished: there is the hope that she will emerge with honour from the quarrels about formalism and will grasp all the profundity of the difference between "method" and "principle". Of course, the author's love of hyperbole also explains his declaration that the professors have become agitated by the fact that "history sometimes offers unexpected combinations of names: Kogan-Chukovsky—Gornfeld-Tinyakov ... ".

If Eykhenbaum were not so encased in his felicitous certainty he would, of course, have noticed that the formal method or principle (if he prefers) is not throwing Russia into turmoil and is not distracting Russian workers and peasants from the business of construction, and that, if Kogan—Chukovsky—Gornfeld—Tinyakov and the like happen to call the day day and night night then is it really worth seeing this combination of names as all but historically unexpected?

One remark about the author's polemical attacks against me

personally. In one of my reviews in *Press and Revolution* I did, in fact, point out that Korney Chukovsky's aesthetic sense had helped him to come to certain conclusions from his formal analysis of this or that poet, which were very valuable for the sociologist as well, and that, in this sense, he was more mature and broad-ranging than the formalists. And I still think that to see in a poem merely ''a series of words which are concretely interlinked'' (as Bobrov precisely defined formalism) is the same as seeing nothing. And now it appears that my modest thoughts about Chukovsky seemed to Eykhenbaum, carried away as usual by hyperbole, to be a howl of despair. He (that is, me) was ''so agitated and so indignant'' that ''in his despair, he declared Chukovsky to be a great scholar and founder of formalism''. Obviously, in Eykhenbaum's eyes, the grandfather of the formalists just has to be a great scholar. I am not so blinded by the Opoyaz circle, and so do not consider Chukovsky a great scholar, I am not at all interested in formalism's family tree, but I continue to think that Chukovsky's formal analysis is valuable, while a purely statistical account of rhythm is unnecessary.

Now, a few words on the heart of the matter. In the last chapter of my book, *The Literature of These Years*, I explained why from my point of view the formal method is doomed to sterility, so I do not need to give a detailed reply here. (I should make the reservation that I always have in mind false formalism, that is, the kind advocated by Eykhenbaum and his comrades. The approach to the study of form that we find in the work of Pereverzev or Piksanov, for example, can be considered extremely fruitful.)

I find complete confirmation of my thoughts in Eykhenbaum's article. The question is not whether one should study form or content, but *how* one should study, *how* one should analyse, *from what position* one should approach the text. Eykhenbaum contrasts ''scientific demands'' with ''the demands of a world-view''; and ''the conversion of the historical parallelism of different categories of culture (their ''correspondences'') into a functional (cause-and-effect) connection'' seems to him ''a forced transformation''.

We have here thoughts on formalism and Marxism which are amazing in their naiveté. ''One cannot compare formalism with Marxism; formalism is the system of a particular science, Marxism is the philosophical study of history'', ''one cannot compare Marxism with the theory of relativity because the two things are not commensurable'', ''the question of the genesis of literary phenomena, their links with the facts of everyday life and the economic structure ... is deliberately set to one side, not because it is an idle question in general, but because it elucidates nothing within the limits of the particular category'', and so forth.

Every attempt to compare science with a world view is itself the product of a world-view. The scholar deals with a particular group of phenomena. His interest in these phenomena and, consequently, his method as well (if we are to talk of real science and not scholasticism) is dictated by his interest in the surrounding world, which in our day means social phenomena. Every attempt to disengage the specific peculiarities of a given sphere of phenomena from the totality of phenomena is, of course, a vestige of metaphysics, from which it is high time we liberated ourselves. The scholar who performs such a disengagement and believes that one can study form, style, structure etc. without reference to social relations, undoubtedly is a representative of a specific world-view but of a world-view which is obsolete, reactionary, and moribund. The scholar who declares, ''It is essential to free the object of my science from the rest of the world in order to study this science as such (a meaningless expression), it is necessary for a while to forget that I am a man of flesh and blood, surrounded by other people, and occupy myself entirely with my own little world''— such a scholar is, of course, doomed to sterility. It does not follow from this that every branch of the social sciences does not have its own special methods of study. But it's one thing to use special techniques and methods when studying a particular phenomenon as a link in a single whole, and quite another to erect the metaphysical bugbear into which the formalists have turned literature—of the most capricious and complex kind, it's true—but it remains all the same, super-structure.

Eykhenbaum concludes: we won't touch Marxism, and you leave literary phenomena alone. There's no shortage of various categories of culture, and even some interesting ones, but why establish a ''cause-and-effect'' connection between them. How persistent this Marxism is: it pokes its nose in everywhere it has no business to be. It was so peaceful without it. Various critics are excluded from the hallows of ''the scholars'' and are assigned to the ranks of those who profess a ''world-view'' (please forgive us for using this word, at least in as far as we forgive Eykhenbaum for his ''the demands of a world-view''): yes, he excludes even such as Gornfeld who sees poetics as ''one of the most general sciences'', and Zhirmunsky, who fell into the most terrible heresies when he realised that one may regard art ''as a social fact and a social factor'', and that ''the evolution of a style is linked to the perception of the world in a particular age''. After all, if the ''traitors'' and ''apostates'' go any further along this particular path, then it's difficult to foresee where they'll end up. They'll begin to sort out what a ''general'' science is and what the ''world-view'' of an age means. And it will then emerge that work has been done on the explanation of the source of this ''world-view'' of an age by various Marxs and Plekhanovs and many minds which are no less learned than Shklovsky or Eykhenbaum.

But, perhaps, in their apostasy the ''traitors'' will go even further along the path of logic and the facts. And suddenly they will understand that Marxism is not one of many useful occupations, but, first and foremost, a monistic view of history, that it is the sole scientific approach to all social questions, to which the study of literature also belongs, and that they will flounder all over the place until they link all ''categories'' in a ''cause-and-effect'' connection. It is quite true that one should not compare Marxism with formalism (which Trotsky does not do—Eykhenbaum understood nothing of his article), just as one should not compare Marxism with the law of relativity. But Trotsky explained brilliantly both the genesis of formalism and its place in contemporary consciousness—and explained it brilliantly precisely because he approached it with the sharpened blade of Marxist analysis. Let Boris Eykhenbaum read what Marxists write about the law of relativity, and he will see the place of this law among the ''categories'' whose cause-and-effect interdependence is still not clear to him within the limits of his truly felicitous ''learnedness''. Thankfully, it has been given to Gornfeld and Zhirmunsky to go beyond these limits. Whether Eykhenbaum will manage this, I don't know. Perhaps our ''everyday life'' which is spreading ever wider and wider will influence even his consciousness.

The conclusion to which I was inclined before and of which Eykhenbaum's article fully convinced me is as follows: formalism is not a method, it is not even a principle but none other than ''the demands of a world-view'' which Eykhenbaum discovered. But these ''demands'' are akin to a particular illness of pedantic connoisseurship—an illness which has been well elucidated in Marxist literature. Yes, gentlemen formalists, it is all a matter of world-view. There can be no science without this. And this pedantic, sterile and excessive zeal—alas!— also has its own social genesis. This zeal will soon be extinguished for lack of material, as its source is not in that social psyche which is arising in the creative and developing classes of society.

V. POLYANSKY[28]

Concerning Boris Eykhenbaum

Eykhenbaum is not pleased with Zhirmunsky. The latter is the "typical eclectic, the reconciler of extremes". He, you see, "flabbily repeats old 'academic truths'" and "criticises the formalists for their insufficiently thought-out communications at discussions and public meetings".

We well understand the tendency in human nature to be displeased when under attack. That, however, is not the question. The question is more profound, more serious. If Eykhenbaum's article "How Gogol's *The Overcoat* was Made" indicates a "watershed" in the author's consciousness and direction, then Zhirmunsky's remarks indicate a "watershed" in the formalists' camp and the more intransigent and less pliant among them naturally shout about "eclecticism and reconciliation of extremes". We in no way defend Zhirmunsky by this declaration. His methodological assertions make him no more acceptable to Marxism than Eykhenbaum, Shklovsky and the others. We argue that the incipient crisis in the camp of the formalists, by removing the "extremes", will show all the theoretical weakness of formalism. What is more, it could make their preparatory, rough, statistical work, purged of all its confused theorising, more useful and sensible in a Marxist analysis of literary phenomena. We must facilitate this crisis. Not because we advocate brawls, although they rarely pass off without some gain, but with a view to purging the morphological method of all its excrescences, and with the aim of applying it more appropriately to the demands of the times.

The author of the article persistently repeats that "the question is not about the methods of studying literature, but about the principles of construction of a literary science—about the content of the latter, the basic object of study, about the problems which make it a particular science". "We are not 'formalists' and we are not a "method". We are, if you like, specification makers".

Marxism makes a clear distinction between method and principle, but it just as clearly recognises the intimate connection between a principle and this or that method when the former is actualised in real life. Instances are common where a principle stifles a method, as the method emasculates the principle. The history of the struggle of revolutionary Marxism against all sorts of opportunism could offer many striking examples. There's no need to unravel the author's semi-scholastic judgements: but it is important to point out and to emphasise that the author needs them to convince the inexperienced reader that the formal method does not contradict Marxism. If the formalists were to renounce their methodological ruminations and seriously engage in the preparatory work which Trotsky suggests for them, then they would not only cease to be enemies of Marxism but would even bring to the latter something useful. But as long as they advance absolute "scientific truth" and reduce "literary science" to the study of "*form*", whatever special meaning this word may be given, then the formal method is profoundly inimical to Marxism, it is reactionary, and its roots undoubtedly lie in the social tendencies akin to those which engendered futurism, imaginism, the theory of pure art and the vacuous idea of the Serapion Brothers[29] that art lacks ideological content. After Trotsky's article, in as much as the formalists have produced no new material, we consider ourselves correct in limiting ourselves to one decisive and firm statement concerning Marxism's hostility to formalism. There is no need to repeat ourselves since this point has already been brilliantly and comprehensively made by others.

We would like to make one minor but substantive remark with regard to method.

Eykhenbaum writes: "The method of studying a text, the methods of studying a line of poetry, the methods of studying a particular author, an epoch etc.—this is the natural use of the word "method". A biographical, sociological, psychological, or aesthetic method—all these are not methods, but different ways of looking at science or even different sciences".

It is clear from these judgements that the author moves away from the idea of a method as a living, active fundamental which inspires one's work and which is organically linked to a principle, and uses the concept of a method in such a way that it becomes an arid, soulless, formal (in the worst sense of the word) device, which is disengaged from real life, from any principle. Consequently, it becomes totally insignificant, useless and even profoundly pernicious, when it is elevated to the level of a dogma, and particularly in our time of dialectical materialism.

That this is the case is clear from the fact that the author has placed biography on the same level as the sociological, psychological and aesthetic methods. Well, who on earth, if he has any common sense, would believe that biography is a method, still less a "way of looking at science". One shouldn't place oneself in a ridiculous position. The author intolerably confuses questions and concepts which would be easily understood by any worker-student who knew nothing of Eykhenbaum or Shklovsky or the formal method in general. If biography is a method, then a novel, a story, a play and so on are also methods. Or even better: a novel is a way of looking at science. This is rubbish, Boris Eykhenbaum!

Aware that in our times any indication that an author is not a Marxist or, even worse, an antimarxist, kills the desire among the young to read and listen to him, Eykhenbaum, hiding behind the bare and spindly bushes of his ratiocinations about method, has tried to conceal the antimarxist core of his writing and nothing but confusion has resulted—and what confusion! In the literary world such attempts, with such unsuitable resources, have often ended in a scandal.

And this author, in response to Trotsky, endeavours to prove that the latter deviates from "Marxist principles" and "by the power of things, comes to a position which is unlike any sort of Marxism". We were exceedingly restrained when the author was talking of things with which he is familiar (although not fully understood by him) but when he begins to trample on Trotsky, without the slightest idea of what Marxism is about, one's pen becomes a little nervous. A limit should be set on any such audacity. We would do this, but, really, Trotsky has no need of this at all.

Eykhenbaum tries, from another angle, to reinforce this attempt to paralyse the analysis of Trotsky, who proved clearly that the formal method is incompatible with Marxism. He enters into an analysis of evolution and genesis. In this analysis, the question "of the genesis of literary phenomena (their links with the facts of everyday life, the economy, with the individual psychology or physiology of the author, and so on ad infinitum) is deliberately set to one side". According to the way Eykhenbaum understands things, evolution and genesis are "problems of different sciences". "To indicate the genesis is to establish the *links* between phenomena, and not their *causal* conditionality". According to the author, Marxists, unfortunately, only study literature from the point of view of the genesis of a particular work, and not in terms of literary evolution, and therefore, do not elucidate the causal connections. One thing is true here: Marxists are not evolutionists, they are revolutionaries. But when the author accuses them of not elucidating "causal conditionality", and thereby of converting literature into "illustrations" or an "aesthetic appendage", he is merely repeating the same turgid story he expounded when dealing with the question of method and principle. And it was Eykhenbaum who branded Trotsky as an eclectic!

The author further attempts to conceal the essence of the formal method as it was elucidated by Trotsky. He reduces this method "to the analysis (in essence descriptive and semi-statistical) of the etymological and syntactic peculiarities of poetic works, to the counting of repeated vowels and consonants, syllables, epithets". This, do you see, "is very far from reality".

"The efforts of the formalists are directed, not to the description of individual works, but to the construction of the theory and history of literature as an independent science". This declaration does not undermine Trotsky's analysis. Let us suppose that they wish to create a science, but construct this science on "the analysis of the etymological peculiarities of poetic works" etc. The difference is not one of principle or method, but of scale. Trotsky is wrong on one point. Why only poetic works: the same applies to prose. But this is an oversight, a slip which does not destroy the basic viewpoint.

Trotsky's severe verdict that "the formal school is an esoteric abortion of idealism applied to artistic questions" retains all its power even after Boris Eykhenbaum's article. This article is a striking testimony to the muddled thinking and ideological impotence of the formalists "at a watershed".

1   See note 5, p.46.
2   *Opoyaz:* "Society for the study of poetic language". Initial core of the formalist movement, this "society", which was formed in highly informal circumstances, consisted of young philologists who were pupils of Beaudouin de Courtenay at the University of Saint Petersburg and were admirers of futurist poetry: Victor Shklovsky, Osip Brik, Roman Jakobson, Yevgeny Polivanov, Lev Jakubinsky, Yury Tynyanov, Boris Kushner, Boris Eykhenbaum, Boris Tomashevsky and Victor Zhirmunsky. *Opoyaz* was founded in 1914 and survived until 1923.
3   "For-soc", abbreviation of "formalists-sociologists", name given to those critics who attempted to reconcile the formal "method" with the sociological method.
4   "State Institute for the History of the Arts", founded in 1912 by Count Zubov who handed it over to the Soviet authorities after the Revolution. It rapidly became the principal centre of Russian formalism thanks to the presence of teachers such as Tynyanov, Eykhenbaum, Shklovsky, Gukovsky, Vinogradov, Zhirmunsky, and Tomashevsky. It was this Institute which took over the publication of the journal *Poetica* (1926-1929). It carried on from *Opoyaz* to some extent.

5   The Russian language has only one word to designate the content of a work as opposed to its form and the comprehension of a concept as opposed to its extension.

6   Osip Brik (1888-1945). One of the founding members of *Opoyaz* and subsequently of the LEF. Friend of Mayakovsky, on whom he had a great deal of influence. He ardently wished to bring about a rapprochement between futurism, formalism and Marxism.

7   Lev Jakubinsky. One of the very earliest formalists; member of *Opoyaz*, which he quit fairly early on to follow Mach's theories. He worked in association with Mach for a long time before finally abandoning "Machism" and attempting to develop a Marxist linguistics. He died at the end of the war. His writings were for a long time proscribed, but they are now gradually being republished.

8   Potebnya, one of the greatest nineteenth-century Russian philologists (1835-1891).

9   Arcady Gornfeld (1867-1941) was a highly influential literary critic at that time.

10   P.S. Kogan (1872-1932). Marxist literary critic.

11   Sergei Bobrov (born in 1889). Poet, novelist, mathematician, translator of Voltaire, Stendhal, Hugo, etc. Came under the influence of Bely and was one of the founders of the "Centrifuge" group, which claimed to be futurist, and to which Pasternak belonged. ("The Forest of Diamonds", "The Lyre of Lyres", 1917, *Centrifuge* ed.).

12   Roman Jakobson (born in 1896). Linguistic scholar, founder of structuralism, one of the pioneers of modern linguistics, was a member of *Opoyaz* before emigrating to Prague, where he became involved in the activities of the Prague Circle, and finally to the U.S. (cf. *Questions de Poétique*, Le Seuil, Paris, 1973).

13   Korney Chukovsky (1882-1969). Critic, translator, publicist and principal creator of Soviet children's literature. Awarded the Lenin Prize in 1962 for his work on Nekrasov.

14   Gershenzon (1869-1925), member of the *Vekhi* Group, historian, philosopher and critic who professed a very free-ranging religious philosophy. He wrote a *History of Young Russia* and, in collaboration with Vyacheslav Ivanov, *Correspondence from One Place to Another*.

15   *Volfila*: "Association of Free Philosophy" founded by Andrei Bely and Ivanov-Razumnik in 1920.

16   See note 3, p.45.

17   See note 11, (above).

18   See note 5, (above).

19   Anatol Vasil Lunacharsky (1875-1933). Publicist and playwright. Was People's Commissar for Education (1917-1929). As a close associate of Lenin he played a leading role in the first period of the Soviet régime. His abundant works, which bear witness to his tireless curiosity and his very great broad-mindedness are now gradually being republished. He sought to promote proletarian culture while at the same time encouraging and protecting "fellow travellers". He was a friend of Romain Rolland, Henri Barbusse, Bernard Shaw, Stefan Zweig and H.G. Wells.

20   *Zaum*, transrational poetry, invented by Kruchenykh and Khlebnikov, employed an entirely new language in which words that were completely void of meaning were reduced to sound associations innocent of all semantic content.

21   I.Ye. Repin (1844-1930). Leading figure in the Wanderers Group of realist painters, who were in revolt against the Academy and sought to promote a Russian national school of painting. In 1870, with financial backing from Tretyakov, founded the "Society of Wanderers Exhibitions". In addition Repin was not without talent as a writer, as one can see from his *Memoirs*.

22   V.I. Surikov (1848-1916). Painter, also a member of the Wanderers Group. He specialised in historical paintings, his constant concern being to awaken national feeling.

23   Mark Antokolsky (1843-1902). Russian sculptor, highly popular during his lifetime.

Lived in Rome for a long time, meeting Mamontov there. He became one of the leading figures in Mamontov's group, which he followed to Abramtsevo. Like Tretyakov, Mamontov was a dealer and collector who protected the Wanderers.

24   V.V. Stasov (1824-1906). Celebrated critic and man of letters, advocate of realism and hostile to academicism. He saw in the Wanderers the national artistic movement he had been praying for and gave them his backing. He contributed greatly to their success.

25   *Cadet* liberalism: the Constitutional Democrats (K.D.'s), in power under Milyukov for a while. Favoured war with Germany. Lenin's and the Bolsheviks' sworn enemy. Cadet ideology was expressed in the joint anthology *The "Intelligentsia" in Russia* (1910) and in Struve's journal *Russian Thought*.

26   Valeryan Pereverzev (born in 1882). Marxist critic and literary historian. Became famous following publication of his book on Dostoyevsky in 1912. His literary views aroused a storm of controversy. "Pereverzevism" was denounced as a deviation from Marxism. Pereverzev arguing that one could understand authors and their writings only in the context of the process of production. He sought to apply his system in his two books on Gogol and on Lermontov, but without success.

27   See note 10, (above).

28   Lebedev-Polyansky (1881-1948). Marxist literary critic. Chief censor in the 1920s. It was from this time on that he came to embody the hard line that subsequently triumphed. In the name of "party spirit" (*partynost'*) and of ideological vigilance he denounced the futurists, the formalists, the "Serapion Brothers" as well as Sakulin's and Piksanov's sociological school.

29   "The Serapion Brothers": a group of writers heavily influenced by formalist ideas on the one hand (several of them had attended courses at the Institute for the History of the Arts) and by the works of Zamyatin on the other. Although sympathetic to the Soviet regime and opting for the status of "fellow travellers", these young writers (twelve in all, eight prose writers: Fedin, Lunts, Kaverin, Vsevolod Ivanov, Shklovsky, Nikitin, Slonimsky, Zoshchenko; three poets: Polonskaya, N. Tikhonov, Vladimir Pozner; and one critic: Gruzdev) pleaded literature's "disengagement" from reality and politics. Their views subsequently evolved and the group broke up, but Soviet literature, before submitting to the yoke of socialist realism, owed to the "Brothers" some of its finest moments and its best works.

SECTION II

Formalism and Futurism

G. CONIO

Preface

"In my opinion he is unsurpassed in his analysis of verse."
(Victor Shklovsky, *Sovietsky Pisatel*, Moscow 1970)

Among the bonds uniting futurism with formalism, we must include
the critical work of Tynyanov. While this talented novelist, author of
The Death of Wazir-Mukhtar and biographer of Pushkin, is well
known to be one of the most brilliant theoreticians of formalism, his
perceptive observation of the poetry of his time is still too often
ignored.

The two articles that follow are interesting for several reasons. They
prove that formalist criticism was not necessarily content with producing a synchronous "cross-section of history", but that it was also
capable of apprehending and expressing the very movement and
unfolding of history. "Interval" thus provides us with a good example
of what, leaving aside chronicle and anecdote, an authentic history of
literature could be: a history that would reproduce the full richness
and dynamism of the "literary fact", which was all too often reduced
to biographical, individual or social factors. Lastly, they remind us that
in poetry, knowledge is of little account if it is not accompanied by
taste; that a poem cannot be reduced to a series of algebraic formulae;
that criticism in this domain is as much a matter of intuition as intelligence, and that there can be no understanding without re-creation.[1]
This serves as a corrective to the standard, simplified, pejorative
picture of formalism.

Exemplary too in these lines is the balance, so difficult to achieve
and so rare, between sympathy and detachment, without which there
can be no critical judgment. This detachment is dictated by evolution,
by history; it is the scalpel which delimits and defines differences in
scale; it engenders a system of values: it is this which gives the picture
its light and shade, and its relief. It is, in a word, the criterion which
introduces a third dimension into the present and imparts to works of
art that final stamp which, so we imagine, posterity alone can give.

Above all, these analyses raise a question that hangs over all the
literature and the aesthetics of the age, that of the relationship

between past and future, between tradition and novelty, conservatism and modernism.

In *Sovietsky Pisatel*, which we have already quoted from, Shklovsky retraces his friend's career and analyses his importance.

At Saint Petersburg University, Tynyanov attended the lectures of Vengerov, Baudouin de Courtenay and Shcherba; together with a few fellow pupils, he formed a circle that was later to call itself the formalist school which included Polivanov and Yakubinsky, Boris Eykhenbaum, Shklovsky and Vinogradov. The futurists were becoming notorious at the time. Baudouin de Courtenay held a futurist "event" that was later to become famous. Mayakovsky had just made his appearance. The vociferous, rowdy Moscovites had dragged the better behaved St. Petersburg students along with them. Shklovsky and Jakobson called themselves futurists. Formalism was to arise from discussion of futurist poetry, but it did lend to futurism a substance it had hitherto lacked, namely scientific rigour and an historical dimension. Without Jakobson and Tynyanov, Khlebnikov would have been the poorer. Rarely had a meeting been more felicitous, rarely a merger more efficacious. Tynyanov situated Mayakovsky, Khlebnikov, and Pasternak deep in the major currents of Russian poetry. He revealed what it was in them that was unique and eternal; he revealed to them their place and their necessity, what lay behind their attitudes, poses and gestures. Only a deeply cultivated mind was capable of this: "Yury read books that others merely browsed through ... He sought to understand the connection between function and form, the purpose for which genre is often designated, and the change in the significance of genre". (Shklovsky, *Ibid*.)

From his ponderings, his reading, from the long and patient research of the scholar, a book was eventually written, *Archaists and Innovators*, which was Tynyanov's essential contribution to formalist work in the field of literary criticism:

"Tynyanov was beginning his work on the book *Archaists and Innovators*. I [Shklovsky] suggested another title, which would have expressed his thinking even more clearly: 'Archaists-Innovators'. At the time, Akhmatova agreed with me. Tynyanov knew where his work would lead. He was studying the laws which govern the emergence of the new—the dialectics of literature— that miracle of reflection which seems to reorient the reflected object.

" ... In order to analyse the relationship between the new and the old, Tynyanov began with the simplest analysis—that of the literary fact itself. The literary fact, as a communication of meaning, is perceived most acutely at the moment when a new element is introduced into a previously existing system, in other words, at the moment of change. What is important for genre is the conflict between systems: this conflict becomes part of the conceptual significance of the work and colours it. Genre is always on the move, which is why static definitions of genre need to be replaced by dynamic ones.

"Tynyanov remarked in general that genre is constantly being displaced; its evolution is a broken line, not a straight one. This displacement occurs at the expense of the fundamental characteristics of the genre ... It has always been known that there is such a thing as literary evolution, but no one has ever stressed the fact that this 'evolution' takes the form of leaps and transitions, the abruptness of which has always astonished and infuriated those who witness them. The classical writers gave way to the sentimentalists, they in their turn were replaced by the romantics, romanticism was replaced by realism. The transition between different systems has always been interpreted as a crisis.

"Tynyanov demonstrated that art had a definite purpose and he pointed out the presence of history in the very composition of the work, thus confirming the agelessness of the work of art. This eternal existence is not a tranquil one. The work needs to follow a course; it needs, as it were, to roll down the slope of time; it requires a new permutation of the meaning of events. Even now, people do not always realise that it was Tynyanov who in principle raised the question of the multi-faceted nature of the work of art. Now the first attempts are being made to create a mathematical theory of verse. Mathematical analysis encompasses the progress of verse and indicates the relationship between the language of a given poet and that of both literature and speech. But here we are faced with new difficulties. Language itself exists not as a single system, but as the interrelationship between several systems of linguistic constructions. The word has a history of its own, it evokes associations with other constructions of meaning and, by reinterpreting them, makes utterances more precise.

"Verse form consists as it were of several layers and exists simultaneously in several time periods. In his book *Archaists and Innovators* Tynyanov elucidated one distance of the interrelationship between different systems." (Shklovsky, *Ibid.*).

What was the chief idea underpinning Tynyanov's writings?:

> "In his work on the interrelationship between the poetics of the Karamzinists and the Archaists, and in his examination of the poetry of Kukhelbeker and Griboyedov, Tynyanov established above all that the verse of Griboyedov and Krylov was no chance phenomenon, but a regular development. At the same time he demonstrated or foresaw the law of displacement—the conflict of different systems within a living work."

And lastly:

> "The old lives on in the new but it is not only recognised it is reinterpreted as well, and the different function which it acquires gives it wings." (Shklovsky, *Ibid.*).

In their manifesto, *A slap in the face for public taste*, the futurists had thrown Pushkin, among others, overboard in the name of modern times ... It can hardly be said that this iconoclasm made much impact: no presence was more clearly felt, more vital, more poignant, than that of Pushkin in the Russian literature of the 1920s and 30s—in emigré as much as in Soviet writings. Mayakovsky himself admitted that he knew Pushkin by heart, and Livshits that he kept Pushkin "under his pillow", etc. Countless biographies, articles, and essays were devoted to the great romantic. This raises the problem of the relations between ancient and modern, between cultural tradition and cultural revolution. It is to the credit of the formalists that, behind their total, intransigent and indispensable rejection of the past, they demonstrated the deep bonds uniting the great futurist poets to the fundamental structures of the Russian language and its poetry.

While being the friends, defenders and interpreters of the futurists, Eykhenbaum devoted his life to Gogol and to Lermontov, and Tynyanov to Griboyedov and to Pushkin. Thanks to them, behind the apparent contradictions and the violent slogans, the futurists' revolt shines forth in its true colours: not as a superficial desire to shock the bourgeois mind, as it has sometimes been presented, but as a determination to bend a society bogged down in conservatism to a great force for change, to a great dream of freedom, of fulfillment, that had been foreshadowed and felt by the great Russian poets in the past, who had opposed and fallen victim to the ruling and ambient oppression.

Consequently, we should not take the futurists' revolt against churches, museums and libraries at its face value; as with intellectuals and poets, oppressed during their lifetime yet integrated after their death, it was aimed not so much at the things themselves, but at the signs of an embourgeoisement, of a conformist, conventional way of life which nauseated them. Their revolt was aimed at the cadaverous stench which emanated from the family, the altar and the fatherland. They were animated by a revolutionary conception which saw life and art as being indissolubly linked, a unitary, progressive conception for whose holders the October Revolution seemed a golden opportunity.

It is hard to resist the fascination of this great creative dream of an all-embracing revolution, a revolution on every front, which inspired the revolutionary artists and writers of those times, following Mayakovsky, Meyerhold, the Vesnin brothers[2] and Leonidov, Malevich and Tatlin, Ehrenburg and Lissitzky, etc.

They had grasped the vanity of a revolution that left the old aesthetic and the old way of life intact. This impulse, which drove them to reject a monotonous, clinging existence in favour of an open, alive one, was shared by other poets and artists abroad, for it ignored frontiers. The word internationalism, like the terms modernism, revolution and progress then meant something. The period that followed was marked by the massive comeback of conservatives of every stripe, who succeeded in stifling this liberating upsurge beneath the harsh yoke of a state once more deified.

The two dominant trends in the avant-garde, "left art", merged in the Lef constructivism. The end of Lef coincided with the official condemnation of formalism; and when Mayakovsky went over to the RAPP, against which he had always fought, this move could only be interpreted as an admission of failure. One cannot help thinking, though, that for a moment everything was, or had seemed, possible.

Yury Tynyanov's critical work leaves us with an echo of this freedom, of this creative energy which inspired Soviet letters and art in the 1920s. Without this freedom, without this élan, are not poetry, thought, and creation doomed, compromised, in their practice, in their very existence even?

1   Cf. Georges Poulet's communication to the "Colloque de Cerisy": "His entire work is impregnated with the spirit of the author. As he makes us read it, he awakens in us an analogy he has felt or thought. Understanding a literary work is, in a certain sense, allowing the person who wrote it to reveal himself to us in us. It is like Ulysses pouring blood into the ditch, allowing phantom states of the soul to spring to life again and take form within our own souls". ("Une critique d'identification", in *Les chemins actuels de la critique*, coll. 10/18, p. 277.)

2   Anatole Kopp, *Town and Revolution: Soviet Architecture and City Planning 1917-1935*, London 1970.

*Interval** —(To Boris Pasternak)

"Here dwelt poets…"
Blok

1

Writing about verse is now almost as difficult as writing the verse itself. And writing verse is almost as difficult as reading it. Such is the vicious circle of our times. As time goes by there is less and less verse, and in fact we are faced today not with poems, but with poets. And this is not such an insignificant difference as it might appear.

Three years ago prose firmly ordered poetry to clear out. The place of the poets, who were retreating in some panic, was completely taken over by prose writers. In the same process, poets became unusually scarce, while the numbers of prose writers grew. Many of the prose writers did not yet exist at that time, but nevertheless were considered to be fully existent, and so actually appeared. There was a great deal of hurrying, and premature, hasty births took place: the "Serapion Brothers",[2] for example, were translated into Spanish long before they had written anything at all in Russian. We could all see clearly that prose was winning and poetry was retreating, we even welcomed this for some reason (we had begun to get very bored with poets' soirées). But precisely what was involved, what would come out of this victory and where poetry's retreat would eventually end—this we failed to give any attention to. Now poetry has finally "retreated" and things do not look at all simple.

The fact remains a fact: prose has won. Formerly, when a reader got hold of a journal or an almanac, he used to rush first of all for the verses and only when he had then fallen into a rather dreamy state did he look through the prose. The reader who has evolved in recent times cautiously avoids the poems, as he would friends who have grown too old, and makes straight for the prose. Instead of poetesses we now have prosewomen. (Most recently, the reader has in a way taken to

*Article written in 1924, published in 1929 in *Archaists and Innovators*.

avoiding both verse and prose. He is as yet a timid reader, one who has not yet confessed to this; nevertheless, he may well be the most intriguing reader—he goes directly to the chronicles, the reviews and polemical articles—to those journalistic backyards from which a new type of journal is emerging.)

And so, we have a "flowering of prose". This position is, so to speak, an accepted one and I do not even intend to challenge it. According to the critics, there is no difficulty now in writing a story that is no worse than those of Lev Tolstoy. And, it is true, the production of prose is growing, while that of poetry is falling. Prose writers and poets have set their watches differently. The time of verse is not now established by the date of its appearance; the time of prose is established in advance. Meanwhile, however, the relations between the vanquished and the victors are, I repeat, not at all simple or straightforward.

Prose now lives by the immense power of inertia. It succeeds in overcoming this inertia only with great effort, one small step after another, and this effort itself is becoming more and more difficult, and apparently more and more pointless. It sometimes seems that it was the inertia itself, and not the writer, who wrote the story, ending it in the obligatory manner with the death of the central character or, at least, of Europe. For poetry, however, the period of inertia is at an end. Neither a poetic passport nor affiliation to a school will save the poet now. The schools have all vanished, movements have terminated their existence in an orderly fashion, as if by command. Having grown up in geometric progression, they then split up into different groups and finally disintegrated; when this happened, the self-determination of minor poetic nationalities had to be achieved within the space of someone's flat and, finally, each poet was left to himself.

All this is now a long-established situation, but just about two years ago even the emotionalists, who declared that love, together with certain other more or less joyful feelings, was the best thing in the world—even they seemed to be considered half a school and half a movement.

This replacement of schools by solitary individuals is characteristic of literature in general, but the extreme swiftness of the replacements, the ferocity of the struggle and the rapidity of the collapses reflect the tempo of our century. Things happened more slowly in the nineteenth century. Our poets always live to see the replacement of their movements—Blok's death was *too* ordered.

The poetic inertia has come to an end, the groupings have

intermingled, the scale of the whole affair has become immeasurably greater. Completely different poets are uniting with each other, names remote from each other are now standing side by side. The lone individuals have survived.

And the game of poetry is now being played at an elevated level. Verse is transformed speech; it is human speech which has outgrown itself. The word in verse has a thousand unexpected nuances of meaning, verse gives a new measure to the word. New verse is new vision. And the growth of these new phenomena occurs only in those intervals in which inertia ceases to operate; strictly speaking, we are only familiar with the action of inertia—the interval in which there is no inertia seems to us, by the optical laws of history, an impasse. (In the final calculation, every innovator works for inertia, every revolution is produced for a canon.) History, however, has no impasses. There are only intervals.

One solitary poet told me that "every hour changes the position". Verse itself has become the poets' favourite theme. The better half of Pasternak's poems are about verse, Mandelstam writes about "the native sound-scale", Mayakovsky about "poetic blinkers".

It is difficult to talk about the works, the completed poems, even more about the books produced in an interval. It is easier to talk about the poets who pass through it.

2

"Ill repute has rumbled out ... "

There is no need to observe any poetic order of precedence in an interval. Let us take Esenin[3] first. He is one of the most characteristic poets of the interval. When the lull sets in after a battle, one is struck by the terrain. When inertia comes to an end, the first requirement is to check one's own voice. Esenin checks his by resonance, by echo. This is the normal way.

When things get difficult for literature, people start to talk about the reader. When it is necessary to redesign one's voice, they talk about resonance. This method sometimes succeeds: the *reader*, when brought into literature, turns out to be the literary motor which was all that was needed to shift the word from its dead stop. This is a kind of "motivation" which makes it possible to get out of impasses. In poetry this is sometimes stated by a change in intonation—in the address to the "reader", the entire intonational structure changes. In prose, first-person narration is designed for the reader, forcing him to "act out" all the speech. And an "internal" design of this sort with the reader in mind can help in periods of crisis (Nekrasov).

But there is also another address to the reader: verse can be made a cliché, language a routine. Such a mode of address impoverishes.

Esenin retreats without stopping.

Esenin's previous lyrics were, of course, profoundly traditional; they derived from Fet,[4] from conventional poetic "populism" and from the primitive understanding of Blok which Esenin had gained from Klyuev.[5] In fact, Esenin had no strength in terms of novelty, leftishness or independence. His most unconvincing tie was with the imagists,[6] for all that they also were neither new nor independent— indeed, no-one knows whether they even existed. Esenin's strength lay in the emotional tone of his lyric writing. Emotion in verse that is naive, primordial and therefore unusual, alive—that is what Esenin rests upon. Esenin's entire poetic effort is a ceaseless search for decorations for this naked emotion. At first it was Church Slavonicisms, a diligently sustained rural touch and an equally traditional "peasant Christ"; then, swearwords taken from the poetic practice of the imagists, words which constituted the same kind of decoration for the Esenin emotion as the Church Slavonicisms had.

The art which rests on this powerful, primordial emotion is always closely linked with the personality. The reader sees the man behind the word, he guesses at the "individual" intonation behind that of the verse. This is why the literary personality of Blok was so exceptionally powerful in verse (not the living, "biographical" Blok, but a verse Blok, one of quite a different order and design). This is why we find a remarkable force in Esenin's *Pugachev*, where this emotion shone out with a new light on a remote theme, gave it an extraordinary new life and brought it closer to us:

"My dear ones, my good ones! ..."

The literary, poetic personality of Esenin has expanded to the limits of illusion. The reader treats his poems as documents, or a letter received in the post from Esenin. This is certainly a powerful and a necessary phenomenon. But it is also a dangerous one. A collapse, a disintegration may occur—the literary personality may escape from the poems and live without them, while the abandoned poems grow poor. The literary personality of Esenin—from the "radiant monk" in the Klyuevian skull-cap to the "foul-mouth and trouble maker" of

Tavern Moscow—is profoundly literary. His personality is almost a borrowing: at times it seems that he is a remarkably schematised, inferior Blok, a parodied Pushkin; even a mongrel dog at village gates barks at Esenin in Byronic manner. And nevertheless, this personality, linked with the emotion, was sufficiently convincing to push his verses into the background, to grow into a unique, extra-verbal, literary fact. In Esenin's last poems the "personality" played out its last act. No more "the monk in the skull-cap", nor the poet "knocking back the drink". The "trouble-maker" has repented of his "scandals", the dramatic tension has slackened. The personality no longer veils the poems. But at the same time, if the spectator is distracted from the actor, the drama, as Lese-Drama, becomes questionable; if the title is removed from a picture, the picture will become an oleograph. The poet who is so dear to worshippers of "inspiration", those who complain that literature has become "craftsmanship" (i.e. art—as if it had not always been so), discovers that the "inspiration" is much more literary than "craftsmanship". With his primitive emotional strength, the almost ruthless directness of his literary personality, Esenin used to conceal the literary quality of his poems. Now he resembles at times an anthology "from Pushkin to the present day":

...I have visited the places dear to me...
...Yes! Now the decision is made. Never to return
I have left my native fields.
...Ah, what an amusing loss...
...The golden, distant expanses...

But perhaps even this is not so bad? Perhaps these are necessary banalities? After all, the emotional poet has a right to banality. Trite words have a remarkably powerful effect precisely because they are trite, because they have come to be used almost every minute. Hence the magnetic power of the gypsy vogue. Hence the banalities of Polonsky,[7] Sluchevsky,[8] Annensky[9] and Blok's Apukhtinian[10] laments. But this is precisely the case, that in seeking to level out his lyric along the line of simple, primordial emotion, Esenin in fact translates it into disappointing traditions that are not at all simple. There are disappointing traditions: those that have been worn down. (Thus Blok, as a tradition, has also been worn down for us today.) There are commonplaces which cannot in any way assume the place of poems; there are poems which have become "poems in general" and have ceased to be poems in particular. Rosenheim[11] is (and was) disappointing (and to think that he was once compared to Lermontov);

the tradition of Rosenheim—the platitude in verse—is also disappointing. But Esenin heads directly for just such general poems:

> And the sad conversation flowed out
> In warm tears onto the dusty pages.

This banality is too epic, too detailed to be categorised along with
the above. Here the intonation lies, here there is no "address" to anyone, but there is a set verse intonation in general. This is a withdrawal to the platitude of "verse in general" (in fact—to the affected
verse of the end of the nineteenth century). Resonance deceived
Esenin. His poems are poems for light reading, but to a great extent
they cease to be poems.

3

"Au dessus de la mêlée"

Another withdrawal.
One can attempt to withdraw and stand to one side. This position is
reasonably grand and tempting.

As Esenin makes his withdrawal to the reader's level, so the role of
Khodasevich[12] is in withdrawal to the level of literary culture.

But, in the end result, this withdrawal as well unexpectedly takes
shape as a withdrawal to the reader's conception of verse culture.

We have a rich verse culture (immeasurably richer than the prose
culture).

We have a more profound memory of the nineteenth century than
people of the nineteenth century had of the eighteenth. In 1834
Belinsky[13] wrote a courageous piece of nonsense about the eighteenth century in *Literary Reflections*; he declared his ignorance with
pride, even with enthusiasm—all with the aim of reaching the
required proclamation (as completely untrue then as it is today): "We
have no literature". Our Thirties have not yet begun, but there will
certainly be no discovery of this negative America even in the Thirties.
We are denied this. We have one of the greatest verse cultures; it was a
movement, but in accordance with the optical laws of history it
addresses us above all through its own works. The Pushkinian era saw
just as fierce a battle raging around the poetic word as in our times;
and the verse of this era was a powerful lever for it. This verse comes
down to us as a solid body, a completed thing, and it needs a whole

archeology to discover in the solidified object the movement that was once there.

> Thus the raging current, having frozen,
> Hangs above the abyss,
> Losing its former threatening roar,
> Retaining its appearance of movement.

The simplest approach is the approach to the thing. It is enclosed within itself and may serve as an excellent frame (if the middle is cut out).

Today's meanings do not fit well into verse which has been "handed down by the centuries". Pushkin and Baratynsky,[14] were they alive in our era, would probably retain their principles of construction, but would probably also renounce their verse formulas, their solidified bodies. The Smolensk market in the two-foot iambics and the manner of Pushkin and Baratynsky is, of course, a thing of ours, a thing of our era, but, as a fact of verse, it does not belong to us.

This does not mean that Khodasevich has no "good" or even "fine" poems. They do exist and it is possible that in twenty years' time the critics will declare that we underestimated Khodasevich. The "underestimations" of our contemporaries are always a doubtful point. Their "blindness" is fully conscious. (This applies even to such underestimations as that of Tyutchev[15] in the nineteenth century.) We consciously underestimate Khodasevich because we wish to see our own verse, we have a right to this. (I am talking not about new metre in itself. The metre may be new, but the verse old. I am talking about that novelty of the interaction of all aspects of verse, which gives rise to a new poetic meaning.)

However, Khodasevich possesses some verse to which he himself apparently pays no attention. This is his *Ballad* ("I sit, lit from above"), with its sinister angularity and the deliberate awkwardness of its verse. It is a note in verse. "Step over, jump over"—a note almost Rozanovian in tone, with muttering domestic rhymes, unexpectedly short—like the sudden intrusion of a note-book into the classroom of the elevated lyric. Both fall outside his canon. But Khodasevich's normal voice, his full voice is not real to us. His verse is neutralised by the verse culture of the nineteenth century. The reader who sees only solidified bodies in this culture demands that the poet see better than he does.

4

"And her swift feet grew rooted to the ground".

There is another danger: to see one's own works as solidified bodies—to fall captive to one's own verse culture.

This is first and foremost a question of themes. Whole movements may fall captive to their own themes—history teaches us this. How surprised our schoolchildren would be, if they were to learn that the themes of "sentimentalism"—its "love", "friendship", "pathos"—do not characterise the movement itself at all (and consequently "sentimentalism" is not sentimentalism at all). Yes, love, friendship, sorrow for lost youth—all these themes emerged in the process of work, as the authentication of original principles of construction, as the justification of the chamber style of Karamzinism and as the "parlour" rebuttal to the lofty and grandiose themes of the elders. But then, then the theme itself was canonised and became the moving force—Karamzin[16] surrendered to Shalikov.[17]

But an example closer to us is that of symbolism, which only towards the end became aware of its own *themes* as the principal factor, as the moving force—and then went in pursuit of its themes, and departed from living poetry.

It is the same with individual poets. Our era, which talks frequently and enthusiastically about Pushkin, in fact learns little from him. But Pushkin is incidentally characteristic in his retreats from old themes and his espousing of new ones. The evolutionary line between *Ruslan and Lyudmila* and *Boris Godunov* is of vast length, but the interval here only lasted 5 years. This transition was always a revolutionary act for Pushkin. Thus in the end he withdrew to history, prose and the journals—and, together with them, new themes. We find it difficult to understand the boldness of his transitions. We prefer to hold onto our own themes. Our era prefers to study from Gogol—from the Gogol of the second part of *Dead Souls*, who was led along by his theme; our poets wander about, their heads lowered, captives of their own themes.

They do not even remember the heartening example of Heine, who escaped to freedom from the canon of his own themes, from the "Heine manner", as he himself wrote. And what themes! Love, which became a canon for the entire nineteenth century. He, like Pushkin, is not ashamed of betrayals. In poetry fidelity to one's themes is not rewarded.

At the moment, Akhmatova[18] is a captive of her own themes. The theme leads her along, the theme dictates images to her, the theme silently hides the entire verse from view. But it is curious that when Akhmatova began, she was considered new and valuable not for her themes, but *despite* her themes. Almost all her themes were "suppressed" by the acmeists. And her theme was interesting not in itself, but because it was alive with some kind of intonational perspective of its own, a kind of new verse perspective in which it was presented; it was necessary by virtue of its almost whispered syntax and the unexpectedness of its normal vocabulary. Her chamber style and the domestic tone of her awkward words was a new phenomenon; and the verse itself moved around the corners of the room. Not for nothing is Akhmatova's word organically linked to the particular culture of metrically foregrounded words (the phenomenon for which the inaccurate and ugly term of "pausality" [*pauznik*] has become established). This was connected quite naturally with the narrowed range of her themes, with the "small emotions" which were like a new perspective and led Akhmatova toward the genre of "stories" and "conversations", a genre which had not been established or canonised before her appearance. It was these "stories" which became linked together into miscellany-novels (B. Eykhenbaum).

The theme itself had no life beyond the verse; it was a verse theme, hence its unexpected nuances. Verse grows old, like people. The old age of verse consists in the disappearance of the nuances and the complexity, the smoothing over of all difficulties—instead of a problem, an answer is provided straight away. A characteristic poem in this sense was *When in the anguish of suicide*, a poem remarkable for other features as well. And it is characteristic also that Akhmatova's verse has gradually moved away from metre, which was organically related to her word in the beginning. Her poems have levelled out, the awkwardness has vanished; the verse has become more "beautiful", more detailed; the intonations are paler, the language more elevated; the Bible lying on her table, once simply an accessory in the room, has become the source of images:

> She looked, and, fettered by the pain of death,
> Her eyes could no longer watch;
> And her body became transparent salt,
> And her swift feet grew rooted to the ground.

This is the theme of Akhmatova: her principal theme attempts to vary and renew itself at the cost of Akhmatova herself.

5

"Without an epigraph"

But the theme itself has nothing to gain from holding the poet captive. In doing so, it remains simply a theme; it loses its necessity and in the end itself decomposes.

The restless Vyazemsky[19] attacked Zhukovsky[20] in the following manner: "Zhukovsky more than other poets ought to take care to avoid monotony: he has an awful tendency to fall into habit. There was a time when he lit upon the thought of death and every poem he produced ended with his funeral. The presentiment of death *is impressive when it suddenly bursts forth*; but if we see a man expecting death every day, while he continues to flourish, then his presentiment eventually makes us laugh … Evdokim Davydov tells of how the mutilated Evgraf Davydov used to tell him that he thought constantly about death: "Well, you think you're going to die in the evening; well, old chap, so you order them to give you some tea, well, old chap, you drink the tea and you think you're going to die, well, you don't die, old chap; you order some supper, old chap; well, you have supper and you think you're going to die; well, you finish your supper, old chap, and you're not dead, so you go to bed; well, old chap, you fall asleep and you think you're going to die, old chap; but you wake up again in the morning, old chap; so you're not dead yet; well, old chap, you order them to give you some more tea, old chap".

Even a theme such as death, which would seem to be so immune from the parodist, is obviously capable of giving rise to humorous parody, as well as a treatment diametrically opposite in tone. The measure of all themes is the same: whether they are domestic or universal, they are necessary, until they fall outside the scope of the work and provoke a change in treatment, when they thrust out beyond it.

6

"This theme will come,
And will command:"

The theme crushes Mayakovsky as well, it breaks out of him. Russian futurism was a breakaway from the middle verse culture of the nineteenth century. In its bitter struggle and conquests it is kin to the eighteenth century, extending a hand to it across the head of the nineteenth century. Khlebnikov[21] is akin to Lomonosov. Mayakovsky is akin to Derzhavin.[22] The geological shifts of the eighteenth century are closer to us than the peaceful evolution of the nineteenth. But nevertheless we are not the eighteenth century, and therefore we must talk first about our Derzhavin and only afterwards about Lomonosov.

Mayakovsky revived the mightiness of image which had been mislaid somewhere since the time of Derzhavin. Like Derzhavin, Mayakovsky knew that the secret of the mighty image lay not in its "loftiness", but simply in the extremity of its interlinked levels—the high and the low, in what the eighteenth century called "the closeness of unequally elevated words", and also "the harnessing together of quite remote ideas".

Mayakovsky's clamouring poetry of the mass-meeting, designed for the resonance of public squares (just as Derzhavin's verse was constructed for the resonance of palace salons), was no relative of the verse of the nineteenth century; this verse gave birth to a particular system of verse meaning. The word occupied a whole verse, it stood out; therefore, the sentence (which also occupied a whole verse) was equated with the word—it contracted. The semantic weight was redistributed, and in this Mayakovsky resembles comic poetry (the fable also involved the redistribution of semantic weight). Mayakovsky's verse is always poised on the narrow edge between the comic and the tragic. The genre of the public square, the "burlesque" was always both a supplement and a stylistic means of "elevated poetry", and both strands— the high and the low—were equally hostile to the basic material of "the middle style".

But if the whispered style of the chamber is threatened by the danger of the middle-range voice, the danger facing the poetry of the public square is that of the falsetto.

This danger is present in Mayakovsky's latest works. His accurate poetic aim is a combination of the two levels—the high and the low, but they are moving further and further apart: the lower level is moving into satire (*The Mayakovskyan gallery*); the high level into the ode (*To the Workers of Kursk*). The pure satire and the pure ode alike lead to the disappearance of Mayakovsky's keenness and his two-level system. Satire has opened up a path towards Demyan Bedny [Demyan the Poor][23]—poor for Mayakovsky in any case, while the pure ode has rapidly degenerated into "greatcoat verses". Only the Chamber Theatre [24] puts on plays which are acted in shouts from beginning to end.

It is the theme which incites Mayakovsky to take this divided path—
the theme which now surfaces above his poems and is no longer
contained within them—a persistent, pure theme which provokes self-
repetition.

> This theme will come,
>   will command:
>   —Truth!—

> This theme will come,
>   it commands:
>   —Beauty!—

This theme dominates the verse. And Mayakovsky's verse has
palpitations. From his former, line-based verse, with its foregrounded,
clamouring, weighty words, Mayakovsky has moved imperceptibly,
stepping here and there, towards traditional metre. Certainly, he
blatantly parodies this verse, but secretly he has moved closer to it:

> In this theme,
>   both private
>   and trivial,
> Resung many times
>   And more than five
> I whirl like a poetic squirrel
> And want to whirl again.

And already without parody:

> Running from the Germans,
>   Fearing the French,
> The eyes
>   Of those squinting
>   at a tasty morsel,
> While trudging along
>   panting from the burden,
> Hiding in the heart of Russia
>   near Kursk.

Line-based verse becomes for Mayakovsky in his latest works a means
of soldering together different metres. Mayakovsky is seeking an
escape from his verse in the *parodic consciousness of verse*.
(Mayakovsky took the first steps along this path with the success in
150,000,000 of his unexpected Koltsovian lines.)

In *About This* he re-tested and explored all the verse systems, all the set genres, as if seeking an escape from himself. In this work Mayakovsky echoes the *Backbone Flute*, which contains his early poems and sums up. Here Mayakovsky attempts to shift literarified everyday life, to take aim again with the word at the thing, but it is difficult to come down from falsetto, and the deeper the rut that has been dug into poetry, the more difficult it is to stop the wheel just spinning round on the spot. Mayakovsky introduced into verse in his early lyrics the *personality* of the unworn "poet", not a diffuse "self", and not the traditional "monk" and "trouble-maker", but a poet with an address. This address of Mayakovsky's is constantly broadening; biography, real life and memoirs all grow into verse (*About This*). Mayakovsky's most hyperbolical image, in which the high level, intensified to the point of hysterics, is linked with the street—is Mayakovsky himself.

If it goes just a little further, this hyperbolical image will thrust its head out of his poems, burst through them and take their place. In *About This* Mayakovsky emphasises once again that the elemental material of his words is hostile to the plot epic, and that the uniqueness of his large form consists precisely in the fact that it is not an "epic", but a "great ode".

Mayakovsky's position is a special one. He cannot rest tranquilly on his canon, which has already been picked over by eclectics and epigones. He is sensitive to the underground promptings of history, because he himself was once just such a prompter. And this is why he, as a poet who has not done much theorising, is so conscious in the period of the "interval". He deliberately returns to the theme "both private and *trivial*, resung many times and more than five" (and immediately makes it a mighty one in the old way); he consciously cripples his verse in order to free himself finally from the "poetic blinkers":

> At least without metres,
> At least without rhymes.

And, in the end, sensing his powerlessness, he comes out onto the old, well-tried street that is so inextricably linked with early futurism. His advertisements for Mosselprom, cunningly motivated as participation in production, are a withdrawal made in order to gain new strength. When the canon begins to repress the poet, the poet escapes with his craftsmanship into everyday life; thus, Pushkin wrote semi-epigrams and semi-madrigals in scrap-book albums. (From this point of view, complaints that poets are "wasting" their talent are apparently ill-founded; where it seems to us that they are "wasting" talent, they are in fact acquiring it.) Verse is faced with such tasks in everyday life that it has to come down from its usual haunts whether it wants to or not—that's what it's all about.

Compliments are not given lightly in our times; the madrigal has given way to the advertisement. Mayakovsky's madrigals to Mosselprom are the kind of "poetic debauchery" that is sometimes very necessary. But:

> Both the verse
> And the days are not the same.

And the street is not the same. Futurism has withdrawn from the street (strictly speaking, it has already ceased to exist); and the street is not concerned either with futurism or with poetry.

> Gathering the late fruit of their cruel experiences,
> They hurry to balance income with expenditure—
> They have no time for jokes...
> > or to argue about verses.

And if they do argue about verses, then it is done in a businesslike manner, with plans and estimates, in which everything is calculated in advance "as in a chemist's". Will cold-blooded Mosselprom[25] make Mayakovsky fertile in the way that the fervid poster of Rosta[26] did once?

7

> *"But I, if you understand,*
> *have a chance to live!"*

There is another reason why this exit onto the street is of interest. Every *new* phenomenon in poetry is revealed first of all *by a newness of intonation*. Akhmatova possessed new intonations, and so, although different ones, did Mayakovsky. When intonations grow old and cease to be noticed, the poems themselves are noticed less and less. In going out onto the street, Mayakovsky is attempting to change his intonation.

Recently there emerged a new poet, in whom a kind of new intonation was faintly perceptible—Selvinsky.[27] He brings to verse a roguish intonation, the intonation of gypsy romance. In his "rogues' lyrics" Selvinsky is a Babel[28] in verse:

> And I took myself past like some kind of fop,
> Threw off my cap and winked:
> "You didn't have any luck today, dear Madam Death,
> Adieu until the next time".

And here, in his *Robber*, it is not, of course, the introduction of thieves' slang into the verse that is really important: with the aid of Trakhtenberg's little dictionary the poem can be quite easily translated into Russian (just as, with the aid of the *Introduction to the Study of Language*, the works of the remaining authors of *General Change*[29] can be easily decoded). What is interesting here is the new intonation which has come in from the street.

Gypsy intonation has already succeeded in gaining its literary status—there exists an *elevated* gypsy lyric. Selvinsky provides a new gypsy intonation, one that has not yet degenerated:

> I look to see, are they hot or cold
> Under the knife your woman's caresses.
> You squabble and throw up the dust.
> You. The stallions. My ones. The Obolenskys.

Verse *almost* becomes an open stage. Selvinsky, by good fortune, has an unusually poor tradition; sometimes such poor traditions produce living phenomena. As long as this tradition does not turn out to be the usual poor *literary* tradition—his "poems in the crowns of sonnets"; this is precisely a poor, but usual literary tradition.

But the *Gypsy guitar waltz* is a gypsy waltz, it cannot be read but has to be sung—from the open stage. Poetry gains nothing from this, although it does not lose anything either. Whether Selvinsky will be able to avoid bad literature and the real open stage, and develop into a living phenomenon—that is a question for the future.

8

*"The vast, clumsy
Creaking turn of the wheel"*

In its "withdrawals" the twentieth century instinctively clutches at the verse culture of the nineteenth century; it instinctively tries to inherit its legacy. The poems expiate their guilt before their predecessors; we are still apologising to the nineteenth century. But meanwhile, the leap has already been made and we recall our grandfathers sooner than our fathers, who struggled against the grandfathers. We have a deep memory of the nineteenth century, but in fact we are already far removed from it:

> What would you have said, on seeing this temptation?
> Our age has insulted you in insulting your verse!

The silent conflict between Khlebnikov and Gumilev[30] recalls that between Lomonosov[31] and Sumarokov.[32] And there was probably an element of love in both battles.

Khlebnikov's activity came to rest on the boundary between two verse elements. Velimir Khlebnikov is dead, but he is still a living phenomenon. Just two years ago, when Khlebnikov died, he might have been called a semi-lunatic versifier. No-one would say this now; the name of Khlebnikov is on the lips of all poets. Khlebnikov is now threatened by something quite different—his own biography. It is a biography that is exceptionally canonic, the biography of a madman and a seeker, who died a hungry death. But biography—and most of all death—erases a man's work. People remember the name and respect it for some reason, but what the man did is forgotten with amazing rapidity. There is a whole series of "greats", who are only remembered by their portraits.

And if the study of Pushkin was for so long excluded by the study of his duel, then who knows what role in all this was played by all the speeches and verses which have already been delivered, are still delivered and will go on being delivered on his anniversaries?

Without naming Khlebnikov, and sometimes without knowing about him, poets make use of him; he continues to be present as a structure, an orientation. At the same time, as a theoretician, he is confused with *zaum* alone, and is thought to be a poet "not for reading". (There have indeed been such poets. Lomonosov from the very beginning "had no need of the trifling honours of a fashionable writer", in Pushkin's diplomatic phrase.)

His linguistic theory has been hastily christened *zaum* and people have contented themselves with the view that Khlebnikov created meaningless sound-speech.

But the real essence of Khlebnikov's theory lies elsewhere. He transferred the centre of gravity within poetry from questions of sound to the question of meaning. He revived in the meaning of the word its long-forgotten kinship with other words close to it, or he *introduced* the word into relationship with words which were strange to it. He achieved this by consciously recognising that verse was a *structure*. If different but like-sounding words are placed in a *series* or structure, they become relatives of each other. Hence Khlebnikov's "declension of words" (*bog* [god]—*beg* [flight]), hence his new "etymology", which has been ridiculed in our time just as much as Shishkov's[33] "etymology" was indicted in his. But nevertheless Khlebnikov did not claim that his theory possessed scientific truth (as Shishkov did); he considered it a principle of construction. Khlebnikov thought of himself not as a scholar, but as "a railway engineer of artistic language".

"There are no railway engineers of language", he once wrote. "Who would travel from Moscow to Kiev via New York? But what line of modern artistic language is free from such journeys?"

"This is because any single everyday meaning of a word excludes all its other meanings, just as by day all the stars of the night disappear. But to the astronomer the sun is exactly the same kind of speck of dust as all the other stars". Everyday language is to Khlebnikov "the feeble visions of the night"—"the night of everyday life". Khlebnikov therefore sees literary language, which follows everyday language, as a wheel spinning round on the same spot. He preaches "an explosion of linguistic silence, of the deaf-mute layers of language".

An explosion produced systematically, a revolution which at the same time constitutes a structure. (He made his own theory into a poem as well—hence his verbal series, the unusual juxtaposition of words with numbers and his number poems.)

Khlebnikov's last works, which were printed in *Lef—Ladomir* and *Razin's Boat*—are like a sum-total of his poetry. These pieces could have been written today.

An almost meaningless phrase sounds almost understandable in an Onegin stanza; almost understandable, it gains a new colouring in the variable verse system, where the iamb breaks into trochee, and the trochee into iamb. The normal thing is abnormal and amazingly complicated when presented in elevated language.

Here is an image, the novelty of which lies in the fact that it is familiar to everyone in everyday life: the private residence of Kshesinskaya:[34]

> The sea will remember and tell
> With its thunderous word—
> The castle of lace won by the girl
> By the dance of the girl before the throne.

The sea will remember and tell
With its thunderous pealing,
That the palace was won with a dance
Before the executioner of a hundred peoples.

Archaic language, hurled into the present, does not carry it backwards, but simply paints it in special colours by bringing ancient
times closer to us. The themes of our reality have an almost Lomonos-
ovian sound to them—but, strangely, they become newer as a
result:

Fly, human constellation
Ever further into space
And pour the dialects of earth
Into the single conversation of mortals.
... Wiping commerce from the face of the earth
And bringing down the castles of auctions,
From the ruins of stars you will build a roof—
The glass bell of capitals.

But it is not for the "revival" of themes that Khlebnikov is important. He is still first and foremost a poet-theoretician. The foreground
of his poems is occupied by bared construction. He is a poet of
principle.

There is no true theory of construction for poetry, nor any false one.
There are only those that are historically necessary or unnecessary,
those that are useful or useless, just as in literary conflict there are no
guilty parties, but there are defeated ones.

To the verse culture of the nineteenth century Khlebnikov opposes
principles of construction which in many ways resemble those of
Lomonosov. This is not a return to the old ways, but simply a struggle
against the fathers, in which the grandson turns out to resemble the
grandfather. Sumarokov struggled against Lomonosov as a rationalist:
he exposed the falsity of his construction and was defeated. It needed
Pushkin to declare that "the direction Lomonosov took was harmful".
He was victorious by the very fact of his existence. We are faced with a
protracted period of Khlebnikov's influence: the long-drawn process
of joining him to the nineteenth century and his infiltration into its
traditions. And we have still got a long way to go to the Pushkin of the
twentieth century. (One must not forget, in this connection, that
Pushkin was never a Pushkinist.)

9

... things tear off their masks.

The rebellion of Khlebnikov and Mayakovsky shifted literary language from its place, and revealed in it the possibility of a new colouring.

But at the same time this rebellion did succeed in moving the word quite far aside. Khlebnikov's things reveal themselves mainly through their principle. The rebellious word has broken away, it has shifted from the thing. (In this, the "self-valuable word" of Khlebnikov coincides with the "hyperbolical word" of Mayakovsky.) The word has become free, but it has become too free, it has ceased to adhere. Hence the pull of the former futurist nucleus towards the thing, the bare thing of everyday life; hence the "denial of verse" as a logical outlet. (Too logical: the more infallible logic is in its application to things in process, and literature is such a thing, the more straightforward and correct it is, the less right it turns out to be.)

Hence the other pull—to take aim with the word at the thing: somehow to turn both words and things, so that the word doesn't hang in the air and the thing is not bare; to reconcile them, to intermingle them in brotherly fashion. At the same time this is a natural pull away from hyperbole, a longing, while standing already on a new level of verse culture, to use the nineteenth century as material—not starting from it as a norm, but not being ashamed of kinship with the fathers.

Here lies Pasternak's mission.

Pasternak has been writing for a long time, but he did not immediately move into the front ranks—this happened only in the last two years. He was very necessary. Pasternak gives us a new literary thing.

Hence the unusual necessity of his themes. His theme does not protrude in any way, it is so firmly motivated that somehow it is not even discussed.

What themes bring verse and thing into confrontation?

First of all, the wandering and the birth of verse among things.

> The shoots of the downpour sink in clusters
> And long, long before the dawn
> They scribble their acrostic from the roofs,
> Setting the bubbles to rhyme.

The word has mingled with the downpour ("downpour" is a favourite image and landscape for Pasternak); the verse has intertwined with the surrounding landscape and with the images that have been blended together by sounds. Here we almost have "meaningless sound-speech", but nevertheless it is implacably logical; this is some kind of illusory imitation of syntax, but here, however, an infallible syntax.

And as a result of this alchemist's verse operation the downpour begins to be verse: "both the March night and the author" walk together, changing position to the right on the square "in dactylic hexameter". As a result, the thing begins to come to life:

The slanting pictures, flying in torrents
From the highway which blew out the candle,
From hooks and walls to escape to rhyme
And to fall into time, I shall not break them of this.
What of the fact that the universe wears a mask?
What of the fact that there are no such breadths,
Whose mouths they would not have volunteered
To close up with putty for the winter?
But things tear off their masks
They lose their power, they discard their honour,
When they have a reason to sing,
When there is a pretext for a downpour.

This thing has not only torn off its mask, it "discards its honour". Thus were created Pasternak's "Pushkin variations". The "swarthy adolescent" who had become oleographical has been replaced by the descendant of the "flat-lipped Hamite", wandering among sounds:

But interrupting the rustle of the fruit-clusters,
A thunderous roar died and tormented.

The Pasternakian Pushkin, like all the things in his verse, like the attic which "will begin to declaim", tears the mask from himself and begins to wander through sounds.

What themes make up the best trampoline from which to hurl one-self into the thing and awaken it?—Illness, childhood, in general those *chance* and therefore intimate angles of vision which usually get varnished over and forgotten.

Thus they begin. At about two
They tear away from the wet-nurse into a fog of melodies.
They chirp and whistle—but the words
Appear about the third year.

... Thus they are revealed, hovering
Above the wattle fences, where the houses should be
The seas, sudden as a sigh,
Thus will begin the iambs.
... Thus they begin to live by verse.

The strangest definition of poetry that has ever been made becomes intelligible:

Poetry, I shall swear
By you, and finish, with a wheeze:
You have not the bearing of one with a silver tongue,
You are summer with a seat in third-class
You are suburb, and not refrain.

Perhaps only Verlaine, the poet who felt a troubled attraction towards the thing, could have made this definition.

Childhood, not the "childhood" of the anthology, but childhood as a turning-point in vision, mixes the thing and verse, so that the thing comes to stand beside us, while verse can be explored with the hands. Childhood justifies and makes necessary images which weave together the most incommensurate, varied things:

Christmas will glance like a young jackdaw

The distinctive quality of Pasternak's language lies in the fact that his difficult language is more exact than exact—it is an intimate conversation, a conversation in the nursery. (Pasternak needed the nursery in his verse for exactly the same reason as Lev Tolstoy needed it in his prose.) Not for nothing is *My sister, life* essentially a diary with its conscientious indication of place (*Balashov*) and its indispensable notes at the end of the sections (indispensable firstly for the author, and then for the reader): "These amusements ceased when, on leaving, she handed over her mission to her successor" or "That summer we left for there from the Paveletsky station".

This is why Pasternak possesses prosaic elements, a domestic practicality of language—it comes from the nursery:

The sky is in an abyss of pretexts,
For playing jokes.

Pasternak's linguistic exaggerations also come from children's language:

The storm, instantaneous for ever.

(In Pasternak's early works this intimate prosaic quality was different, it reminded one of Igor Severyanin:[35]

> Beloved, without delay
> Without allowing the dawn to disperse from the road,
> Reply as soon as light with its bearer
> On the course of your trial).

Hence also the strange visual perspective, which is characteristic of the invalid—attention to things close at hand, beyond which there immediately extends an endless expanse:

> A yard away from the window,
> Penetrating the strands of the burnous,
> He swore by the ice of the heights:
> Sleep, my dear, I will return like an avalanche.

This is the same as illness which projects "love" through "the eyes of medicinal phials".
The same also as any chance angle of vision:

> The cup of cocoa evaporates in the pier-glass,
> The tulle sways, and—by a straight
> Path into the garden, into the wind-fallen trees and the chaos
> To the swing runs the pier-glass.

It is for this reason that Pasternak's stock of images is special, taken at random. The things in it are somehow not very closely linked, they are only neighbours, they are close only in contiguity (the second thing in the image is always very humdrum and abstract); and the chance element reveals itself as a far stronger connection than the densest logical one.

> The rain thumped at the doors
> And there was a smell of wine-bottle cork.
> So smelt the dust. So smelt the tall weeds.
> And if one looks into it,
> So smelt the maxims of the gentry
> On equality and brotherhood.

(These semi-abstract "maxims", as an element in a comparison, stand side by side with a whole vocabulary of such abstractions in Pasternak's work: "motive", "right", "extract". It is curious that in this he coincides with Fet,[36] in whose work also "motive", "right" and "honour" are found in most unexpected combination with the most concrete things.)

There is a phenomenon called "false memory". Someone is talking to you, and you have the feeling that all this has already happened, that you once sat in exactly the same spot, that your companion was saying exactly the same thing, and you know in advance what he is going to say. And your companion indeed says exactly what he ought to. (In fact, of course, the reverse is the case—your companion speaks and you think *at that same time* that he once said exactly the same.)

Something similar happens with Pasternak's images. You are not familiar with the link between things which he provides, it is a chance connection, but when he has produced it, it somehow seems as if you can recall it, as if it has already existed somewhere before—and the image becomes a necessary one.

In fact, both the image and the theme are necessary, in that they do not protrude, and they are a consequence of poetry, not a cause of poems. The theme will not come out, it lies in the cavernous bodies and the uneven surfaces of the verse. (Unevenness, cavernousness indicate a young fabric; old age is as smooth as a billiard ball.)

The theme does not hang in the air. The word has a key. The key exists in the "chance" vocabulary and the "monstrous" syntax:

> Of careful drops.
> Youth in happiness swam, as
> In the quiet snore of a child
> A sleep-creased pillow-case.

And the "free word" itself does not hang in the air, but stirs up the thing. To do this, it must come into collision with the thing; and it collides with the thing—on emotion. This is not the bare, everyday emotion of Esenin, set as a theme and thrust forward from the very beginning of the poem; this is a vague, musical emotion, akin to that of Fet, which seems in the end to resolve itself, dawning in every word and every thing.

This is why the traditions or, more exactly, the points of support which Pasternak indicates for himself are the emotional poets: *My sister, life* is dedicated to Lermontov,[37] the epigraphs in it are taken from Lenau and Verlaine; this is also why Pasternak's variations are permeated by the themes of the Demon, Ophelia, Marguerite and Desdemona. He even has a romance in the style of Apukhtin:[38]

> My mad age, when shall I bring to reason
> The darkened tempo of the unfathomable past?

But, above all, he echoes Fet:

The boat rocks in the sleepy breast,
The willows have bent over and kissed the clavicles,
The elbows, the rowlocks—oh, wait,
After all, this could happen to anyone!

One is disinclined to attach historical labels to living people.
Mayakovsky is compared with Nekrasov.[39] (I myself have sinned
even more by comparing him with Derzhavin, and Khlebnikov with
Lomonosov.)

That was my sin, but this bad habit is caused by the difficulty of
foretelling and the fact that one must be circumspect. For this, I shall
refer to Pasternak[40] himself (and, at the same time, to Hegel):

One day Hegel unintentionally
And probably by chance
Called the historian a prophet,
One who foretells backwards.

I shall restrain myself from predictions about Pasternak. We are
living in a crucial time and I do not know what his future course will
be. (This is a good thing. It's very bad for the critic to know what the
poet is destined for.) Pasternak ferments, and his fermentation affects
others—it is no accident that no poet finds himself so often in the
verse of others as Pasternak. He not only ferments, he is also an agent
of fermentation and leavening.

10

*"I have forgotten the word that
I wanted to say."*

A poet who is apparently close to Pasternak, but is in fact alien to him,
in that he has arrived from the other direction, is Mandelstam.[41]

Mandelstam—a surprisingly frugal poet—produces two little books,
a few poems per year. However, he is a weighty poet, and his books are
alive.

This feature—a frugality and sparseness of verse—has been known
in others as well; it has occurred at different times in history. As is well
known, the model of it is Tyutchev—"heavier than many volumes".
This is not a convincing argument, because Tyutchev is not a frugal
poet at all; his compactness is not the result of frugality but of his

fragmentary approach; this fragmentary nature stems from his literary dilettantism. There is, however, another kind of frugality—that of Batyushkov, who worked on verse language during the initial period of a new verse culture. This kind of frugality is more characteristic.

Mandelstam resolves one of the most difficult problems facing verse language. Even the old theoreticians were familiar with the difficult concept of "harmony"—"harmony demands the fullness of sounds, depending on the scope of the thought"; in this area, the old theoreticians seem to have a presentiment of our own time and request that "harmony" and "melody" not be merged into one.

Lev Tolstoy, who understood Pushkin well, wrote that Pushkin's harmony stems from a special *"hierarchy of objects"*. Every work of art places equal objects into a hierarchical series, while it includes different objects in an equal series; every construction regroups the world. This is particularly evident in verse. The weight of meaning in words is redistributed by verbal coercion itself, by the equality (or inequality) of verse to verse and by the foregrounding, or non-foregrounding within verse. It is here—in the special hierarchy of *objects*—that Pasternak's significance lies. He regroups objects, and dislocates our perspective on things.

But verse as structure does not just regroup; the structure has an ability to colour things, it possesses *its own* strength; it produces *its own*, *poetic* nuances of meaning.

We have lived through the time when metre or rhyme, "musicality" as ornament, could be a novelty. But on the other hand (and here lies the basis of the new verse culture, which also constitutes Khlebnikov's principal significance), we have become very sensitive to the music of meanings in verse, to the order and structure in which words are transformed in verse. Mandelstam's role lies here—in the particular *nuances* of words, in the special music of meaning. Mandelstam drew his musical verse from the nineteenth century—the melody of his verse is almost that of Batyushkov:[42]

> I to the round dance of the shadows trampling the gentle
> > meadow,
> With a singing name joined myself,
> But everything melted away, and only a faint sound
> Remained in my cloudy memory.

But Mandelstam needs this melody (in the same way, incidentally, as Batyushkov did) for particular purposes, it helps him to knit together and construct nuances of meaning in a special way.

The words which are equated with each other through a single, well-known melody are coloured by emotion; their strange order and their hierarchy become necessary.

Every reorganisation of melody by Mandelstam is above all a change in the structure of meaning:

> And I thought: why wake
> The swarm of lengthened ringings,
> In this eternal strife to try to catch
> The wondrous Aeolian structure?

The structure of meaning in Mandelstam is such that *one* image, one word series takes on a decisive role for a whole poem and imperceptibly colours all the others.

This is the key to the whole hierarchy of images:

> ... How I hate the *odorous*, ancient *fellings*,.
> ... With toothed *saws* they *cut* deep into the walls
> ... Even into *timber* the hot axe did not *cut* ...
> ... Like a transparent tear on the *walls* stood out the *resin*,
> And the town feels its *wooden ribs* ...
> ... And the arrows fall like dry *wooden rain*
> And other arrows grow on the earth like the *hazelnut-tree*.

This key even restructures the image of blood:

> ... *The dry noise of blood* will not subside
> ... But the *blood* gushed to the *stairs* and went over
> to the attack.

The key is still more noticeable where Mandelstam changes the "extended" melody to a short structure:

> I do not know since when
> This *song* has begun—
> Is it not by it that the *robber rustles*
> And the *mosquito prince rings*.
> ... To *rasp* a *match*, with one's shoulder
> To *shake* the night awake.
> To *raise like a stuffy rick*
> *The air*, that is tormented by the hat,
> To *shake up the bag*,
> ... So that the bond of pink blood,
> The *ring* of these *dry grasses*,

> *Purloined* may be found
> Through *age, hay-loft, sleep*.

Age, hay-loft and sleep have become very close in this rustling of
verse, they have become overgrown with special nuances. But we find
the key in the following poem:

> I up a step-ladder
> Climbed to the *dishevelled hay-loft*—
> I breathed the milky *dust* of the *stars*,
> I breathed *the matted clumps of space*.

But the key is not even necessary: there is always a "purloined
bond" in Mandelstam. It is created *from verse to verse*; the nuance,
the colouring of the word in each verse is not lost, it solidifies further
in the following verse. Thus we find in his last poem (*The First of
January 1924*), an almost lunatic association—"underwood" and
"pike's bone". This seems to be ready-made for those who like to talk
about "nonsense" (these people stand out for trying to use their key
to open someone else's house, even though it is not locked).

But nevertheless these strange meanings are justified by the progress
of the whole poem, a progress from nuance to nuance, leading finally
to the *new meaning*. This is the main point about Mandelstam's
work—the creation of special meanings. The significance which he
gives to words is deceptive and oblique; his are the kind of meanings
which can only emerge in verse, which can become necessary only
through verse. These are not words, but the shadows of words.

In Pasternak the word becomes an almost tangible poetic thing; in
Mandelstam the thing becomes a poetic abstraction.

This is why he is successful with the abstract philosophical ode, in
which, as with Schiller, "sober concepts perform a Bacchic dance"
(Heine).

This is also the reason why the theme of the "forgotten word" is
characteristic of Mandelstam:

> I have forgotten the word that I wanted to say.
> ... Oh, if the shame of sighted fingers could be returned,
> And the swollen joy of recognition.
> I fear so much the sobbing of the Aonides:
> The mist, the ringing and the abyss.
> ... Still not of this the transparent affirms.

It is for this reason as well that he knows, better than any other

contemporary poet, the power of word colouring—he loves proper
names, because they are not words, but the nuances of words. It is for
its nuances that language is important to him:

> Sweeter than the singing of Italian
> Is for me my native language
> For in it secretly babbles
> The spring of foreign harps.

Here is one "foreign harp", built up *almost* without foreign words:

> I have learnt the science of parting
> In the bare-headed laments of the night.
> The oxen chew and the waiting lengthens—
> The last hour of the city *vigils*.

Here is another:

> Let us go where there are various sciences,
> And the trade is *shashlik* and *chebureki*,
> Where a notice displaying trousers,
> Gives us an understanding of man.

It needs only a minor foreign inoculation of this receptive verse
culture for "parting", "bare-headed" and "expectation" to become
Latin in the form of "vigils", while "sciences" and "trousers"
become "chebureki" [meat pasties].

Mandelstam's confession about himself is characteristic:

> And with lime in the blood for a foreign tribe
> The night grasses to collect...

His work on the literary language is the work of one who is almost a
foreigner.

And this is why Mandelstam is a pure lyricist, a poet of the small
form. His chemical experiments are only possible in a small space. The
question of going beyond the lyric (his love for the ode) is quite alien
to him. His nuances are unthinkable in the space of an epic.

Mandelstam has no hard cash words. He has nuances, promissory
notes, which are transferred from line to line. For the time being, this
is his strength. I say for the time being, because in the period of an
interval hard cash most often turns out to be false. We have already
seen this in talking of Esenin.

11

"The ballad, naked speed…
…And a picket has been sent to the epic".

"The style of the ballad is not very young"; one might rather say it has
grown old twice. The ballad as a genre was exhausted in less than two
years. Why?

We still retain an attitude to genres which regards them as ready-
made things. A poet gets up from his seat, opens a cupboard and takes
out the genre he needs. Every poet can open that cupboard. And there
is no shortage of these genres, beginning with the ode and ending
with the long poem. There must be enough for everyone.

But the interval teaches us otherwise. It is an interval precisely
because there are no prepared genres, because they are created slowly
and in quite anarchic manner, and are not for general use.

Genre is created when the verse word possesses all the qualities
necessary, given their reinforcement and extrapolation, to produce the
appearance of enclosure. Genre is the realisation, the solidification of
all the fermenting, dawning powers of the word. Therefore, the convincing new genre emerges only sporadically. Only occasionally does
the poet fully realise the quality of his word, and it is this realisation
that leads him to a genre. (This was Pushkin's strength. *Evgeny
Onegin* shows how the distinctive quality of the poetic word is *pro-
jected* into genre, and *itself* seems to create it.) It does not need saying
that this quality of the poetic word which, once it is solidified and
recognised leads to genre, is to be found not in metre and not in
rhyme, but in the semantic uniqueness of the word by which it lives in
verse. It is for this reason that the eighteenth century could create only
a *humorous* verse tale, and the nineteenth century only a *parodic* epic.

Poets are now looking for a genre. This means that they are attempting to become fully conscious of their poetic word.

It was Tikhonov[43] who initiated the ballad of our times:

The ranks of the dead—the well-worn fact,
Packets with delivery to the house,
Horses and nails I took
To your aim, ballad.
Ballad, naked speed,
The slope of romance,
I have given you gait and growth

I have burnt out your name by memory.
Go to others, merry one
Serve them, as you have served me,
Live straight and red-haired.

This is an important farewell, and the definition that is given is a true one: the ballad is "naked speed",

Lake to lake, the meadows at a gallop.

The ballad was created on the basis of an exact word, a word almost prosaically honest—not for nothing is Tikhonov one of the circle of prose-writers.[44] In his ballad verse, the word lost almost all its poetic colours and became the fundamental basis of the plot, the point on which the plot rested. The plot drum beats out the tapping of words which are as exact as a calculation:

Bread, two pieces
Of sugared fruit-drop,
And in the evening over and above the ration
Six ounces of lead.

And the plot, without hesitating, without being transformed in verse, flies with "naked speed" across three, four or five stanzas down "the slope of romance".

Tikhonov's ballad made a great impression. No one before had put the question of genre so directly, or had consciously perceived the poetic word as a factor in the movement of the plot. Tikhonov in his ballad took to the extreme that tendency in the poetic word that could be called *Gumilevian*;[45] he revealed the genre towards which the poetic word was directed.

Do you remember what happened then? Conscientious, but naive imitators, who thought that you could take a genre ready-made out of the cupboard, began to copy Tikhonov's ballads in a great hurry, sometimes changing the proper names, the status of the heroes and the punctuation marks.

Tikhonov himself did not stop at the ballad, and in this perhaps lies his vitality. The ballad word strives for speed, but is incapable of coping with wide expanses. It is delivered with a blue packet to the house in the seventh stanza.

Tikhonov fell victim to the epic. He avoided Zhukovsky's temptation, that of joining several ballads together, which produced in its time the *Twelve sleeping maidens*, but all the same no poem emerged.

The verse tale is considered by us to be the self-evident form for the epic. We forget that *Ruslan and Lyudmila* was for a long time a *non-genre*: people brought up on the epic refused to consider it a *genre*; in the same way, *Evgeny Onegin*, with which it was difficult to come to terms after *Ruslan and Lyudmila*, was also considered a *non-genre*. The verse tale was a younger epic, in which all the originality lay in the fact that the poetic word was constructed on a pivot of prose, the plot.

Meanwhile, the descriptive poem, the elder of the two, did not possess this prosaic pivot at all, and in it the word was developed on the principle of the image.

The symbolists were under the hypnosis of the verse tale of the nineteenth century in their large-scale works. It was no accident that even Vyacheslav Ivanov used such a ready-made thing as the Onegin stanza when he had to write a long poem. (Nobody remembers that once even the Onegin stanza was not a prepared thing.) It was Khlebnikov who produced the turning point, Khlebnikov whose poetic word develops according to other laws, changing from stanza to stanza (more correctly, from paragraph to paragraph, sometimes from line to line—the concept of the stanza as a unit fades in Khlebnikov's work), from image to image. In *Chess* Tikhonov achieved a descriptive line poem. Just as the verse tale of the nineteenth century was a rebuff to the pure descriptive poem, so the pure descriptive poem becomes with Khlebnikov a rebuff to the verse tale.

But if the ballad is "naked speed" and therefore hostile to the epic, if it comes to an end too quickly, the descriptive poem, on the other hand, is static and has absolutely no end.

In Tikhonov's long poem *Face to Face*, there is already a hero journeying across the configurations of the descriptive poem, and the configurations themselves are even stirring. The poem marks a new stage for the poet; here description is established on plot, linked with it. The descriptive configurations which are divorced from the ballad by the basic principle of construction are built on *ballad material*. This tendency in Tikhonov's large form is certainly going to become more marked.

The case of another poet presents an interesting revolution in genre, a revolution in the reverse direction. A. Aseyev[46] is a poet who approached the weight of the foregrounded word gradually. Already in his *Rusty Lyre*, the impression is of a single verbal solidification disintegrating into stanzas and sentences:

And here
The factory [*Zavod*]
Of the supplest steel songs,
And here—
Of yawnings [*Zevot*]
Autumnal the world so fresh,
And here—
Roars [*Revyot*]
Of the strongest winds the roar ...
And here
The gavotte [*Gavot*]
On the strings of all the trees.

(Apparently, this device of his arose from the single-word refrain of songs, which Aseyev loved.)

From here it is but one step to *The Northern Lights* and *The Future Ones*:

Twist the strings'
Screws.
Through the night of moons
The blue flow,
Through the day blow
For the smoke
Across the ice.
Scalds!

Here every word is a step in a rhythmical progression. (The piece itself has the sub-title, *Flight*.)

And, at the same time, Aseyev is always striving towards distinct genres, even if they are his own: his *Choice* begins with "songs" and it contains a "folk-tune"; it is characteristic of Aseyev to construct his poems in chapters, which reveals an attraction towards plot, a weariness of amorphousness. Aseyev goes over to the ballad. His ballad, as distinct from that of Tikhonov, is constructed not on the exact word, not on a prosaically swift plot, but on the *foregrounded* word (indeed, almost foregrounded out of the verse itself). This word of his has retained its kinship with the song, from which it was drawn out (at first as a refrain); this is why Aseyev's ballad is strongly marked by the *stanza*, with its melodic movement. (In Tikhonov, this would be a *line*.) Aseyev's ballad is one of song:

White tusks
beat
The quarter-deck.
Into the noisy foam
The bowsprit
is buried.
Who says,
storm—
nonsense,
if a cliff—point-blank!

(Polezhayev[47] once operated with the same melodic and, at the same time, foregrounded word.)

The sections of the ballads are distinguished from one another by their melodic development—the melody illustrates the plot, as music does a cinema film. This melody gives one the opportunity of mastering anew unexpectedly strange patterns. Such is the assimilation of Koltsov's[48] verse.

That country will stand
That land will bloom
Where lies the tomb
Of the twenty six.

And therefore Aseyev's ballad is longer than Tikhonov's: for the same reason, it does not contain any straightforward development of plot (cf. *The Black Prince*). The Tikhonov ballad and the Aseyev ballad are different genres, because various different verse elements have condensed into these genres.

But this difference also proves to us that genre only ceases to be a "ready-made thing" and becomes a necessary link when it is a result, i.e. when it is not prescribed, but recognised, as the direction of the word.

Meanwhile, Pasternak has sent a picket into the epic.

His *Lofty Illness* presents the epic, outside plot, as a slow rocking to and fro, a slow growth in theme—and the realisation of it by the end. And one can understand that here Pasternak coincides with the poetic word of Pushkin and attempts to renew *the principles of the Pushkinian image* (which was a fulcrum for the Pushkinian epic):

In those days on all fell the passion
For stories, and winter at night

Did not tire of moving the lice,
As horses move their ears
So stirred of quiet darkness
The ears showered with snow,
And with fairy tales we tossed
On the mint spice-cakes of our pillows.

It is also characteristic that this revival is not sustained in the poem: towards the end it is replaced by the "bare word", somewhere it gets deluged in associative waste, while the four-foot iamb breaks, time and again.

The epic has still not come off; that does not mean to say that it *must* come off. Its appearance in our time is too logically necessary, and history has often been deceitful, giving us, instead of one expected straightforward event, not another unexpected but also straightforward one, but a third one, quite sudden and complex into the bargain, if not a fourth and even a fifth one as well.

The experiences of Tikhonov and Pasternak teach us differently. What we value in the period of an interval are not "successes" and "ready-made things". We do not know what to do with good things, in the same way as children do not know what to do with toys that are too good. We need a way out. "Things" may well be "unsuccessful", what is important is that they bring closer the possibility of "successes".

1   Yury Tynyanov (1895-1943).
2   "The Serapion Brothers": see note 29, p.97.
3   Sergei Esenin (1895-1925). One of the greatest modern Russian poets. Born of peasant parents, he remained faithful all his life to the old rural and patriarchal Russia. He had an instantly successful literary début in Saint Petersburg in 1915. At first influenced by Klyuev, another peasant poet, he later joined the imaginist movement. Joined the left wing of the Socialist-Revolutionary Party and adopted the ideas of the philosopher and historian Ivanov-Razumnik, the creator of Scythism. He welcomed the revolution with Messianic fervour for the same reasons as Blok, Bely and Klyuev. Married Isadora Duncan in 1922 and travelled in Europe and America. Returned to Russia disenchanted, began drinking uncontrollably and committed suicide in 1925. He admirably expressed the torments and contradictions of the Russian peasant soul in the face of the necessities of the new era. He also sang *Moscow Slums*.
4   Afanasy Fet (1820-1892). Lyric poet. Despite a relatively small output, he was one of the most important lyric poets of his time. Together with Tyutchev he was the leading representative of "art for art's sake" and heavily influenced the decadent and symbolist poets, who regarded him as a forerunner.
5   Nicolas Klyuev (1887-1937). Together with Esenin, he was the principal representative of the "peasant" current in modern Russian poetry. Brought up among a

sect of old believers, he arrived in Petersburg in 1912 and published his first volume of poetry (*The Carillon of Pines*). His personality and his poetry, with its naive mysticism, charmed the literary salons at a time when the fashion for "primitivism" was at its height. People were rediscovering primitive and savage art, and Klyuev naturally slipped into this trend. He enjoyed a period of glory under Blok's protection. But he soon came into conflict with the achievements of the new Russia. He created a poetic language of his own of great verbal wealth.

6 The Imaginists. A group of poets founded in 1919 under the leadership of Vadim Shershenyevich (born in 1893). Like the futurists, the imaginists set themselves up as the Revolution's exclusive poets. Their poetry was inspired by the English imagists and by Ezra Pound and was founded solely on the importance they accorded to metaphor. In addition to Shershenyevich (*The Horse as Horse*, *2 + 2 = 5*), the group included Marienhof, Kusikov, Rurik Ivanyev and Esenin.

7 Jakov Petrovich Polonsky (1819-1898). Belonged to the "art for art's sake" group of poets. He was close to Fet. His poetry drew its inspiration above all from his love of nature, and his output includes some very fine poems.

8 Constantine Sluchevsky (1837-1904). Advocated art for art's sake; his pessimistic poetry heralded the decadentism of the end of the century.

9 Innokenty Annensky (1856-1909). Taught Greek at the Tsarkoye Selo High School while pursuing a highly fertile literary career at the same time. Brilliant translator of European poets, literary critic, author of tragedies; owes his posthumous glory to his poetry (*Calm Songs*, *The Cypress Casket*). He frequented symbolist circles but stayed independent of them. He chiefly influenced the acmeists, whose merit it was that they were the first to recognise his true worth.

10 See note 38, below.

11 Rosenheim: revolutionary poet, second half of 19th century.

12 Vladislav Khodasevich (1886-1939). Poet and critic. Emigrated in 1922 and lived in Germany until his death. Occupies a very special place in contemporary Russian poetry. Originally a symbolist and belonging to the avant-garde he claimed to have been influenced by Pushkin, to whom he devoted a highly pertinent essay. He published a remarkable volume of memoirs (*Necropolis*).

13 Vyasaryon Belinsky (1810-1848). Was the greatest nineteenth-century Russian literary critic.

14 Evgeny Baratynsky (1800-1844). Intimate friend and rival of Pushkin. Elegiac poet in his youth, developed in the direction of a pessimism which inspired poems of sombre grandeur (*The Last Death*, *The Last Poet*).

15 Fyodor Tyutchev (1803-1873). Highly important poet despite the slimness of his output. Admired by his contemporaries and especially by Tolstoy. Underwent a period of neglect before being rediscovered by the symbolists, whom he influenced greatly. His essentially metaphysical poetry owes much to German romanticism.

16 Nicolas Karamzin (1766-1826). Celebrated historian, author of a monumental *History of the Russian State*. Theoretician of language and literature; under the influence of western ideas (Rousseau, Herder) he introduced "sentimentalism" into Russia, a new literary sensibility that paved the way for romanticism.

17 Pyotr Shalikov (1768-1852). Imitated (poorly) Karamzin; with him, "sentimentalism" degenerated into milk-and-water sentimentality.

18 Anna Akhmatova (1889-1966). Poetess. Together with Gumilev and Mandelstam she formed the core of the acmeist group. Her poetry represents a return to familiar, everyday reality in reaction against symbolist evanescence. Banned under Zhdanov, her work is now universally admired as among the finest of our age.

19 Prince Pyotr Vyazemsky (1792-1868). Poet, critic and statesman. Friend of Pushkin. Although inferior to Baratynsky, he was one of the best poets in Pushkin's circle. Greatly influenced the literary life of his time.

20 Wasily Zhukovsky (1783-1852). Was the most important Russian pre-romantic

poet. Influenced by Karamzin, retained a constant attachment to "sentimentalism", but gradually evolved in the direction of romanticism following his contact with the English and German pre-romantics, whose themes he adopted.

21 Velimir Khlebnikov (1885-1922). One of twentieth-century Russia's greatest poets. Belonged to the cubo-futurist group ("Hileya") founded by David Burlyuk, but his attitude remained independent and reserved in spite of the glory that his name attracted very early on in avant-garde circles. He led a peripatetic life and his love of the East took him as far as Persia. Living a life of constant poverty he finally died of exhaustion in Siberia. His complete works were published after his death by Tynyanov and Stepanov (5 vols. Leningrad, 1928).

22 Gavril Derzhavin (1743-1816). With Krylov and Karamzin he was one of Russia's greatest eighteenth-century poets. He is especially noted for his great odes on philosophical subjects, and his energetic style and the sincerity of his inspiration— at once realist and grandiose—served to breath new life into the classical form.

23 Demyan Bedny (1883-1945). Proletarian poet, author of satires and fables. This poorly-talented writer owes his popularity to his skill as a versifier and to his choice of revolutionary and anti-religious themes.

24 The Tayrov Chamber Theatre was one of the bastions of avant-garde art and theatre in the 1920s. Its renown, together with that of Meyerhold and Vakhtangov, contributed greatly to the prestige of Soviet culture abroad. Costumes and scenery were mostly the work of Yakulov and Exter.

25 Mosselprom: state shops for which Mayakovsky wrote advertising copy.

26 Rosta: Russian Telegraph Agency, for which Mayakovsky wrote propaganda posters during the civil war (1919).

27 Ilya Selvinsky (1899-1968). The leading theoretician of Russian constructivism (1922-1926). Died leaving an abundant poetic and dramatic output of uneven quality.

28 Isaac Babel (1894-1941). Master storyteller (*Odessa Tales*, *Red Cavalry*). Babel counted himself among the "fellow travellers" and died in a camp, victim, like so many others, of Stalin's repression.

29 *Myena Vsyekh* (General Change): title of the first Manifesto of the Russian constructivist poets (Ilya Selvinsky, K. Zyelinsky, A. Chicherin), Moscow, 1924.

30 Nicolas Gumilev (1886-1921). Initially influenced by Bryusov and by Vyacheslav Ivanov, pupil and friend of Annensky, he broke away from symbolism fairly early on and founded acmeism which marked poetry's return to reality, to the concrete world and to plastic beauty. Gumilev claimed to be influenced by Théophile Gautier, whose *Emaux et Camées* he translated. His taste for exoticism and adventure is reflected in his poetry, which exalts heroic and virile values. Gumilev's poetry is the expression of a flashing, myth-creating imagination (*Pearls*, *The Woodcutter*, *The Pall of Fire*). This great poet was shot by the Cheka for his part in an anti-Soviet plot. His work nevertheless continued to be published for some time afterwards.

31 Mikhail Lomonosov (1711-1765). Illustrious mathematician, chemist, physicist and poet. The greatest thinker of his time. He has been called the "Peter the Great of Russian culture". He was the true founder of Russian literature. In addition to his theoretical writings, in which he was the first person to lay down the principles of grammar, prosody and style, he also left a large body of inspired poetry in every genre (odes, tragedies, epic and lyric poems, epistles, etc.).

32 Alexander Sumarokov (1717-1777). This contemporary of Lomonosov was a fine poet, but it was in the theatre that he achieved his greatest successes. He was the embodiment of fidelity to the classical rules and for this reason was known as the "Racine of the North".

33 Admiral Alexander Shishkov (1754-1843). President of the Academy and leading traditionalist. He accused Karamzin of seeking to destroy the purety of the Russian

language. He sided with ecclesiastical language as opposed to popular language. He is often referred to as the archetypal cold-blooded, narrow-minded pedant.

34 Celebrated ballerina.

35 Igor Severyanin (1887-1941). The first Russian poet to openly claim to be a futurist; founded the ego-futurist group. Was much in vogue for a few years, and his poetry soirées were all the rage (1909-1913). Despite his ridiculous posing and his affected snobbery, he played a part in the revival of poetry at the beginning of the century. His poetry bears witness in particular to a remarkable degree of melodic and verbal inventiveness.

36 See note 4, above.

37 Mikhail Lermontov (1814-1841). The greatest Russian poet after Pushkin. Killed in a duel at the age of 27, in the Caucasus, to which he had been confined. He expressed the bitterness and the revolt of his generation with quite exceptional lucidity and profundity.

38 Alexis Apukhtin (1840-1893). Early beginnings as a poet in the footsteps of Nekrasov and right from the outset formed part of the democratic, radical trend in literature. But he soon changed direction and sources of inspiration, specialising in the melancholy complaint, a genre that was to earn him success. He became a fashionable author. However, the musicality of his verse had a marked influence on the symbolist and decadent poets, and on Alexander Blok in particular.

39 Nicolas Nekrasov (1821-1877). A poet whose merits have often given rise to controversy. A victim, in his own time, and even long after his death, of the rigours of the censorship, his work, which until then had been available only in fragmentary and mutilated form, was only published completely after the Revolution and thanks to the untiring efforts of Korney Chukovsky. He created a poetry that was democratic and popular in inspiration, and his journal, *The Contemporary*, served as a focal point for protesting youth whose thirst for change and whose social aspirations were to prepare the ground for the coming revolutionary struggles.

40 Boris Pasternak (1890-1960). One of the greatest Russian poets of the 20th century. Achieved fame in 1922 with the publication of a collection of poems entitled *My Sister, Life*. He started off close to futurism, although he never went as far as that movement did, and he held himself apart from the great debates and controversies that raged in literary circles during his lifetime. Even so, Bukharin described him in 1935 as the "greatest living Russian poet". The last years of his life were darkened by the scandal which his novel *Doctor Zhivago* provoked in the USSR, and they were poisoned by his winning the Nobel Prize. His poetry, which dealt with Nature and things, succeeded in according a cosmic dimension to the most fleeting and most intimate moments and details of life.

41 Osip Mandelstam (1892-1943). One of the three great acmeist poets, along with Akhmatova and Gumilev. He was never recognised by a regime which he, on the other hand, had hailed from the outset. What he could never renounce were his love, his idea—as courageous and as irreducible as they were exemplary—of a poetry, the grandeur and wretchedness of which embodied better than anyone else in those troubled times. Arrested and deported, he perished in a camp. His sparkling, difficult work has never been republished in his own country, but it has been published in full abroad in Russian, and has been translated into German and English.

42 Constantin Batyushkov (1787-1855). Anacreontic and elegiac poet, heavily influenced by Greek and Roman antiquity, which set him apart from the poetry of his time.

43 Nicolas Tikhonov (born in 1896). Of proletarian origins, he took part in the civil war as a cavalryman in the Red Army. It was from this experience that he drew his material for his early poems. In the heyday of formalism he lectured at the Institute for the History of the Arts. At the same time, he belonged to the "Serapion

Brothers'' Group. His work has been praised for its healthy and positive determination to attune poetry with manly action and down-to-earth reality. He revived the ballad form.

44 Namely the "Serapion Brothers", mentioned earlier (see note 29, p.97).

45 Gumilev (see above, note 30).

46 Nicolas Aseyev (1889-1963). Poet. Together with Pasternak he belonged to a futurist group called "Centrifuge". He then proposed to "merge pure classical lyricism with the conquests of cubo-futurism". In 1922, he joined the LEF under the influence of Mayakovsky and henceforward devoted himself to singing the praises of the construction of socialism.

47 Alexander Polezhayev (1805-1838). Elegiac poet, influenced by Lamartine and called the "Russian Lamartine".

48 Alexis Koltsov (1809-1842). Poet who drew his inspiration directly from the wellsprings of folklore and who sought to combine poetry with popular lyric song.

YURY TYNYANOV

About Khlebnikov*

It is possible to talk about Khlebnikov without discussing symbolism
or futurism, and it is not necessary to talk about *zaum*[1] either. I say
this because the approach along these lines has so far meant that
people have talked not about Khlebnikov, but about "and Khlebnikov": "Futurism and Khlebnikov", "Khlebnikov and *zaum*". Rarely
do people talk about -"Khlebnikov and Mayakovsky"[2] (although
they have done), but they quite often refer to "Khlebnikov and
Kruchenykh".[3]

This all seems to me quite wrong-headed. First of all, neither futurism
nor *zaum* are in any way simple entities, but rather conventional names
used to cover different phenomena, a lexical bond which unites different words,—something like a surname, which is possessed by different
members of a family and even by people who simply happen to share
the same name.

It is surely no accident that Khlebnikov called himself a *budetlyanin*
[a personal noun based on *budet*, the third person singular of the
future tense of the verb "to be" in Russian] and not a futurist; neither
is it an accident that this word did not gain currency.

Secondly, and this is the main thing, generalisations made at different times are based on different criteria. There is no such thing as a
general individual, a general human being: people are matched by age
at school, by height in the army. In military, medical and class
statistics, one and the same man will be recorded on different graphs.
Time passes—and it alters generalisations. Finally there comes a time
which demands *an individual*. Pushkin used to be written about as a
poet of romanticism, Tyutchev as a poet "of the German school".
Reviewers found such approaches easier to understand, and it was
more convenient for textbooks.

Movements disintegrate into schools, schools contract to circles.

*Introduction to the Complete Works of Khlebnikov (Leningrad, 11/1928).

In 1928 Russian poetry and literature wants to see *Khlebnikov*.

Why? Because suddenly one of the "ands" has begun to stand out as being of much greater importance than the others: namely, "contemporary poetry and Khlebnikov". And another "and" is growing all the time: "contemporary literature and Khlebnikov".

2

When Khlebnikov died, one extremely cautious critic, perhaps acting precisely from caution, called all his work "senseless attempts to renew speech and verse" and in the name of "literary conservatives, as well as others" declared his "unpoetic poetry" to be unnecessary. It all depends, of course, on what the critic understood by literature. If literature is understood as the periphery of production of literature and journalism, the facility of cautious thoughts, then he is right. But there is a literature which exists in depth, which is a fierce battle for a new vision, with successes which bring no reward and necessary, conscious "mistakes", with decisive uprisings, with negotiations, conflicts and deaths. And the deaths suffered in this cause are real ones, not metaphorical ones. They are the deaths of people and generations.

3

It is usually imagined that the teacher prepares the way for the acceptance of his pupils. In fact, however, the contrary occurs: the appreciation and acceptance of Tyutchev was prepared for by Fet and the symbolists. Features of Tyutchev's work which seemed bold, but unnecessary in the time of Pushkin, seemed illiterate to Turgenev— Turgenev corrected Tyutchev, the poetic periphery smoothed out the centre. Only the symbolists resurrected the true significance of Tyutchev's metrical "illiteracies". Similarly, Rimsky-Korsakov— according to musicians—used to correct the "illiteracies" and "absurdities" of Moussorgsky, only half of whose work has been published even now. All these illiteracies are illiterate in the same way as phonetic transcription is by comparison with Grot's orthography. Many years of secret, underground work by the fermenting agent have to pass before it can emerge on the surface not as an "agent" any longer, but as a "phenomenon".

The voice of Khlebnikov has already revealed itself in contemporary poetry: it has already fermented the poetry of some and has given individual devices to others. The pupils have prepared the way for the appearance of the teacher. The influence of his poetry is an accomplished fact. The influence of his lucid prose lies in the future.

4

Verlaine distinguished between "poetry" and "literature" in poetry. Perhaps there is both "poetic poetry" and "literary poetry".

In this sense, Khlebnikov's poetry, despite the fact that present-day poetry secretly feeds on it, is perhaps closer to, for example, present-day painting than poetry. (Here I am talking, of course, not about the whole of present-day poetry, but about the powerful current of middle-of-the-road journal poetry that has suddenly emerged.) Whatever the situation may be, present-day poetry has paved the way for the appearance of Khlebnikov in literature.

How does poetic poetry take on literary form and penetrate literary poetry?

Baratynsky wrote:

> At first thought it embodied
> In the concise poem of the poet,
> As a young girl is *mysterious*
> To the inattentive world;
> Then, growing bolder, it
> Is already evasive and voluble,
> Visible from all its sides
> Like an experienced wife,
> In the free prose of the novelist;
> An old gossip, then
> She, raising a brazen shriek,
> Produces in journal polemics
> What has long been known to all.

If one discards the reproachful, sarcastic tone of the poet-aristocrat, what remains is an exact formula, one of the laws of literature.

The "young girl" retains her youth, despite the novelist's prose and the journal's polemics. It is just that she is no longer a mystery to an inattentive world.

5

We are living in a great time; surely no-one could possibly doubt that fact. But the standard of measurement by which things are judged is for many rooted in the past, while for others it is purely parochial. Greatness is attained only with difficulty. The same is the case in literature. Dostoevsky wrote to Strakhov[4] about his book on Lev Tolstoy, saying that he agreed with everything in the book, except for one point: that Tolstoy had said a new word in literature.

War and Peace had already appeared by then. In Dostoevsky's opinion, neither Lev Tolstoy, nor himself, Dostoevsky, nor Turgenev, nor Pisemsky[5] had said the new word. Pushkin and Gogol had said a new word. Dostoevsky did not say this out of modesty. He demanded high standards, but in addition—and this is the main thing—it is difficult for a contemporary to perceive greatness in what is contemporary to him, and it is even more difficult to perceive any new word in what is contemporary. The question of greatness is decided by the centuries. Contemporaries always have a feeling of failure, a feeling that literature is not succeeding, and the new word in literature is always felt to be a particular failure. Sumarokov, a talented man of letters, gave the following opinion about Lomonosov, the writer of genius: "mediocrity of rhymes, difficulty arising from the non-distribution of letters, pronunciation, the impurity of verse composition, the obscurity of logical connection, the violation of grammar and orthography, and everything that is harsh to the delicate ear and abhorrent to the unspoilt taste".

He chose as his device the verses:

> Excess in poetry is always decay:
> Have abilities, art and diligence.

Lomonosov's verses were and remained unintelligible and "meaningless" in their "excess".

This was failure.

The essence of Lomonosov, however, gave life to the literature of the eighteenth century, in Derzhavin. Russian poetry, including Pushkin, was brought up on his struggle against Sumarokov. In the eighteen-twenties Pushkin diplomatically excused him also from "the honours of the fashionable writer", but studied him closely. And Lermontov as well made use of the stanzas of Lomonosov. The sparks of Lomonosov flash here and there in the verse material of the nineteenth century.

Behind Lomonosov stood chemistry, a great science. Without it, he would probably have been out of favour as a poet. One should not be afraid of one's own vision: Khlebnikov's great failure was a new word in poetry. It is as yet impossible to foretell the scale of his fermenting influence.

6

Khlebnikov himself knew his fate. Laughter held no terrors for him. In *Zangezi*, a romantic drama (in the sense in which Novalis used this word), where mathematical computations become a new poetic material, where numbers and letters are linked with the downfall of cities and kingdoms, the life of a new poet with the singing of birds, and laughter and grief are necessary for serious irony, Khlebnikov presents the voices of his critics in the voices of the passers-by:

"Fool. The prophesy of a fool from the woods ..."
"He looks nice. Feminine. But he won't last long."
"He wanted to be a butterfly, that's what the cunning
                                    fellow took a fancy to."
"Raw material, real raw material his prophesy. A raw
                                                    block."
"He lies divinely. He lies like a nightingale at night."
Something earthly! Enough of the sky! Strike up the
                                            Kamarinskaya!
"Thinker, say something jolly. The crowd wants some-
                                            thing jolly."
"What can you do—it's the after-dinner hour."

And the thinker replies:

"I am such a one."

7

In the same work, Khlebnikov says:

It is for me, the butterfly, who has flown .
Into the room of human life,
To leave the writing of my dust
Along the severe windows with the signature of a prisoner.

Khlebnikov's handwriting did in fact resemble the dust with which the butterfly is showered. The childlike prism, the infantilism of the poetic word, stood revealed in his poetry not by "psychology", but in the elements themselves, in the smallest fragments of phrase and word. The child and the savage were a new poetic personality which suddenly blended the rigid "norms" of metre and word. The childlike syntax, the infantile "look!", the consolidation of the transient and voluntary changing of verbal categories—all these elements struggled with naked honesty against the dishonest literary phrase, which had grown remote from people and the reality of every passing minute. It is pointless to apply to Khlebnikov the word which seems significant to so many people: "searchings". He was not "searching", he was "finding".

This is why his individual verses are like simple finds, as simple and irreplaceable as the separate lines of *Evgeny Onegin* were in their time:

> How often we later regret
> What we have earlier thrown away.

8

Khlebnikov was new vision. New vision alights simultaneously on different objects. Thus they not only "begin to live by verse", in Pasternak's remarkable formula, but also to live by the epic.

And Khlebnikov is our only epic poet of the twentieth century. His lyrical small pieces are that same writing of the butterfly, sudden, "endless" notes, extended into the distance, observations which, either in themselves or in their related forms, will become part of the epic.

At the most crucial points in the epic, the epic emerges on the basis of the fairytale. This was how *Ruslan and Lyudmila* emerged, defining as it did the course of the Pushkin epic and the verse tale of the nineteenth century; thus also emerged the democratic *Ruslan*—Nekrasov's *Who is Happy in Russia*.

The pagan fairytale is Khlebnikov's first epic. The new "light poem" in the pre-Pushkinian sense of that term, almost anacreontic (*The Tale of the Stone Age*), the new rural idyll (*The Shaman and Venus, Three Sisters, Forest Yearning*) are presented to us by Khlebnikov. Of course, those who read *Ladomir, Razin's Boat, Night before the Soviets* and *Zangezi* approach these poems as juvenile works by the poet. But this does not diminish their significance. Such a pagan world, close to us, stirring nearby, merging imperceptibly with our countryside and our city, could only have been constructed by an artist whose verbal vision was new, childlike and pagan:

Blue flowers
Threaded into your buttonhole by your Beloved.

9

Khlebnikov is not a collector of themes set for him from outside. It is questionable whether this term—a set theme, a task—exists for him. An artist's method, his individuality, his vision themselves grow into themes. Infantilism, a primitive, pagan attitude towards the word, ignorance of the new man naturally leads to paganism as a theme. Khlebnikov himself "foretells" his own themes. One must take into account the strength and the wholeness of this relationship, in order to understand how Khlebnikov, a revolutionary of the word, "foretold" the revolution in his numerical article.

10

The fierce verbal battles of futurism, which overthrew the conception of the well-being of the word, its slow and regular evolution, were, of course, accidental. Khlebnikov's new vision, which blended the small with the large in pagan and childlike fashion, was not reconciled with the fact that the most important and intimate thing does not fall to the solid and dense language of literature, that this principal thing, with its minute-by-minute significance, is pushed aside by the "packaging" of literary language and declared a "chance feature". And it is this *chance feature* that has become for Khlebnikov the principal element of his art.

It is the same in science. Minor mistakes, "chance features", explained by the old academics as a deviation caused by incomplete experimentation, serve as a catalyst for new discoveries: what was explained by "incomplete experimentation" turns out to be the action of unknown laws.

Khlebnikov the theoretician becomes the Lobachevsky of the word: he does not reveal the small defects in the old system, but opens up a new structure which derives from their chance displacements.

The new vision, very intimate, almost infantile ("the butterfly"), turned out to be a new order of words and things.

People hurried to simplify his linguistic theory, since it was called *zaum* and contented themselves with the belief that Khlebnikov created "meaningless sound-speech". This is not true. The entire essence of his theory consists in the fact that he has transferred the centre of gravity in poetry from questions about sound to the question of meaning. For him, there is no sound that is not coloured by meaning, there is no independently existing question of "metre" and of "theme". The "instrumentation", which was applied like sound-imitation, became in his hands a weapon for changing meaning, reviving the long-forgotten kinship of the word with other familiar words and bringing out a new kinship with strange words.

11

"The dreamer" did not divide being and dreaming, life and poetry. His vision became a new structure, he himself "a railway engineer of artistic language". "There are no railway engineers of language", he wrote. "Who would go from Moscow to Kiev via New York? But what line of contemporary artistic language is free from such journeys?" He preaches "the explosion of linguistic silence, of the deaf-mute layers of language". Those who think that his speech is "meaningless" do not see how revolution can be at the same time a new structure. Those who talk about Khlebnikov's "nonsense" ought to re-examine this question. This is not nonsense, but a new semantic system. Not only was Lomonosov "meaningless" (this "nonsense" or "meaninglessness" provoked Sumarokov's parodies), but there are parodies (many of them) of Zhukovsky, in which this poet, who serves now as a primer for children, is ridiculed for being meaningless. Fet was complete nonsense to Dobrolyubov.[6] All poets who even partially altered semantic systems were declared meaningless, but then became intelligible, not by themselves, but because the readers raised themselves to their semantic system. The verses of the early Blok did not become more intelligible by themselves; but who now does not "understand" them? And those who nevertheless want to place the centre of gravity in the question of Khlebnikov right on the problem of poetic nonsense should read his prose: *Nikolai*, *The Hunter Usa-Gali*, *Ka* and other works. This prose, semantically as lucid as that of Pushkin, will convince them that the question is in no way one of "nonsense", but of a new semantic structure and that this structure gives different results on different material—from Khlebnikovian *zaum* (one of meaning, not of nonsense) to the "logic" of his prose.

If one wrote a phrase that was absolutely bereft of meaning in an irreproachable iamb, it would be almost intelligible. And how many of Pushkin's terrible "nonsenses", blatant in his time, have faded for us because of the accustomed nature of his metre. For example:

> Two sweet shadows, two given by fate
> To me angels in former days ...
> *But both with wings* and with flaming sword,
> They guard and both take vengeance on me.

How many have stopped to think about the fact that the wings here appear quite illicitly as a threatening attribute of the angels, contrasted to their pleasant meaning, wings which in themselves are not threatening at all and are so customary in poetry for angels? And how much has this "nonsense" deepened and broadened the course of associations?

But a subtle, genuine record of human conversation, without authorial comments, will appear meaningless; while the variable system of verse (now an iamb, now a trochee, now a masculine, now a feminine ending) gives to even the traditional verse speech a variable semantics, a meaning.

Khlebnikov's verse speech is not a constructive glue. It is the intimate speech of modern man, seeming as if overheard on the side, in all its suddenness, in its combination of an elevated level and domestic details, in its abrupt exactness, given to our language by the science of the nineteenth and twentieth centuries, and in the infantilism of the city dweller. There are commentaries to his poem *Gul'-Mulla*, written by a man who knew Khlebnikov during his wanderings through Persia—and every fleeting image turns out to be exact, only not "retold" in a literary form, but created anew.

12

Before the judgement of Khlebnikov's new structure, literary traditions are thrown wide open. The result is a sweeping dislocation of traditions. *The Tale of Prince Igor's Campaign* suddenly appears more modern than Bryusov.[7] Pushkin enters the new structure not in the fossilised, undigested chunks flaunted by stylizers, but in a transfigured form:

Obviously, thus the sky wished
To serve secret fate,
In order the cry of love and food
To instill in all existing.

Lomonosov's and Pushkin's odes, *The Tale of Prince Igor's Campaign* and the *Sobakevna* from *Night before the Soviets*, which echoes Nekrasov—all these are indistinguishable from each other as "traditions": they are all included in the new system.

The new structure possesses coercive strength, it strives to broaden itself. Opinions may be divided about Khlebnikov's numerical researches. Perhaps they seem to the specialist to lack foundation, while to the reader they are merely interesting. But if new phenomena are to emerge in literature, what is needed is relentless intellectual activity, and belief in it, together with the scientific processing of material—even if such work is unacceptable to science. The gap between the methods of science and art is by no means so large. Only that which in science possesses self-sufficient value can be a reservoir of energy for art.

Khlebnikov was able to produce a revolution in literature because his structure was not exclusively literary, because he comprehended by it both the language of verse, and the language of numbers, both chance conversations on the street and the events of world history, and because for him there was very little distance between the methods of the literary revolution and those of historical revolutions. Even if we concede that his numerical historical poem may not be scientific, and that his angle of vision is purely poetic, nevertheless *Ladomir*, *Razin's Boat*, *Night before the Soviets*, the sixteenth fragment from *Zangezi* and *Night Search* are perhaps the most significant statements about the revolution that have been made in verse.

If a knife was concealed in the fingers,
While vengeance opened wide her eyes,
It was time that howled: give,
While obedient fate replied: so.

13

Poetry is close to science in its methods—this is what Khlebnikov teaches.

Poetry must be as open as science is in facing phenomena. And this means that when it comes across a "chance feature", it must reorganise itself so that the chance feature ceases to be chance.

The poet who approaches the word and verse as an object the function and use of which he has long been familiar with (and perhaps has become slightly bored by) will approach the thing in everyday life like a hopelessly old acquaintance, however new the thing may be. The stance of a poet usually demands looking at things from above (satire) or from below (the ode) or with the eyes closed (the song). As for the poets whose verse appears in journals, they can look sideways, seeing things "in general".

Khlebnikov looks at things in the same way as a scientist who is penetrating a process and its development regards phenomena—with a level gaze.

For him there are no *things* soiled in poetry (beginning with "the rouble" and ending with "nature"), he does not believe in things "in general"—but in the individual thing. It moves and develops, is correlated with the entire world and therefore is valuable.

Therefore, to Khlebnikov there are no "inferior" things.

His village poets do not picture villages as a condescending dacha-owner from the towns would see them. (How much smugness there is in our rural lyrics—in all those village songs about the rye and blue-eyed peasants. They remind one not so much of Karamzin as of Wolf's children's books, in which children are represented in pictures as little grown-ups with big heads but no whiskers.) It is the same with the Orient: in *The Pipe of Gul'—Mulla* there is no European Orient, none of the patronising interest or the excessive admiration. It is in a level, balanced way that the standards of themes change and re-evaluation of them takes place.

This is possible only when the word is viewed like the atom, with all its processes and its construction.

Khlebnikov is not a collector of words, not a private landowner, not a rogue out to shock. He treats words like a scholar re-evaluating his standards of measurements.

His word "*raklo*" from Kharkov, which is normally only good for humorous verse, enters an ode as an equal guest: "*Rakly*, madmen and jokers".

Ancient European things are entwined into modern speech, broadening it both geographically and historically:

And to the ounces rush the Valparaisos,
To the Honduras roubles hurled themselves.

Khlebnikov has no "poetic economy", he has a "poetic observatory".

14

So Khlebnikov's poetic personality changed: the wise man of Zangezi, the pagan from the forest, the child-poet, Gul'-Mulla (the priest of flowers), the Russian dervish, as they called him in Persia, were all at the same time a railway engineer of the word.

Khlebnikov's biography—the biography of a poet who stands outside bookish and journal literature, fortunate and unfortunate in his own way, complex, ironical, "reclusive" and sociable—has a terrible ending. It is connected with his poetic personality.

However strange and impressive the life of this wanderer and poet may have been, however awful his death, the biography must not crush his poetry. One need not be distanced from a man by his biography. Such cases are not rare in Russian literature, however. Venevitinov,[8] a complex and interesting poet, died at the age of twenty-two, and since then people have really remembered only one thing about him—that he died at the age of twenty-two.

15

This man need not be included in any school or any movement. His poetry is as unique as the poetry of any poet. And one can learn from him simply by following the paths of his development, his points of departure and by studying his methods. Because it is these methods that contain the moral of the new poet. It is a moral composed of *attentiveness and fearlessness*: attentiveness to the "chance" (which in fact is characteristic and real), crushed as it is by rhetoric and blind habit; a fearlessness of the honest poetic word, which goes onto the paper without literary "packaging"—a fearlessness of the necessary word, which cannot be replaced by any other, "not begged from the neighbours", as Vyazemsky put it.

And what if this word is that of a child, what if the most banal word is sometimes the most honest? This is precisely where Khlebnikov's boldness lies—in his freedom. All literary *schools* of our time, without exception, operate on prohibitions: you can't do this, you can't do that, this is banal, that is silly. But Khlebnikov existed by virtue of poetic freedom, which was a necessity in every given instance.

1928

1   *Zaum*: transrational language in which words, completely stripped of their meaning, are employed solely for their phonic and emotional value. It was Alexis Kruchenykh who invented this new form of poetic expression and who devoted himself exclusively to illustrating this new definition of poetry, one that corresponded to a new definition of the word "as such". Other poets that wrote poems in *zaum* did so only partially or episodically. In particular, they included: Zdanevich, Petnikov, Elena Guro, and Khlebnikov, but none of them wrote exclusively in *zaum* as did Kruchenykh.

2   Vladimir Mayakovsky (1893-1930). At first drawn to painting, he studied at the Moscow School of Fine Art, but it was advice and encouragement from David Burlyuk which made him decide to become a poet. This led him to "Hileya" and to the cubo-futurist adventure, when, still alongside the impetuous David, he wrote his manifesto (*A slap in the face for public taste*) and his first volumes of poetry (*The Cloud in Trousers*). He hailed the Revolution enthusiastically and decided to devote his art and his strength to it. During the civil war, he played an active part in the revolutionary propaganda effort, writing poems and posters for Rosta (Russian Telegraph Agency). In 1922, he formed the LEF (Left Front), a constructivist movement to which most avant-garde artists and writers flocked. But gradually his dream of attuning poetry to revolution and of creating a new culture and a new man came to nought. In 1928, he was obliged to abandon the hopes that he had placed in the LEF. Together with Meyerhold, he wrote and staged satirical plays in which he poked fun at bureaucratic manners and at the bourgeois life style that had crept back following the introduction of the NEP.

    Beset by almost general incomprehension, if not hostility; cut off from youth; entangled in a heartbreaking and impossible dilemma, he finally joined the RAPP (Association of Proletarian Writers) which he had always denounced. He committed suicide in 1930, for reasons that have never fully been made clear.

3   Alexis Kruchenykh (1886-1968). Cubo-futurist poet, friend of Khlebnikov and Mayakovsky, he was one of the noisiest and most intransigent members of the avant-garde. He wrote the libretto for the Matyushin's opera, *Victory over the Sun*, which was a landmark in the history of art and the modern theatre on account of the superb sets by Malevich (1913). He is chiefly known for having invented *zaum*, a transrational, phonic form of poetry which inspired poets more gifted and more discerning than himself (Khlebnikov).

4   N.N. Strakhov. Critic with slavophile leanings, friend and associate of the Dostoyevsky brothers with whom he founded the journal *The Times*.

5   Alexis Pisemsky (1820-1881). An important writer who admirably depicted his age in his novels and plays. His talent for satire and his passion for truth earned him many enemies, but Turgenev and Leskov greatly appreciated him.

6   Nicolas Dobrolyubov (1836-1865). Together with Chernyshevsky and Pisarev he was one of the leading theoreticians of democratic radicalism, seeking to focus the attention of art and literature solely upon social and moral problems. Wrote for Nekrasov's journal *Contemporary*. His "utilitarist" views had tremendous influence in his time.

7   Valery Bryusov (1873-1924). His *Masterpieces*, inspired by the French symbolist

poets, provided the starting signal for Russian symbolism in 1895, and he was to take the lead in the movement. He enjoyed a considerable reputation and influence. His tireless curiosity, the variety of his themes and his skill did not always make up for a certain academic coldness. Beneath his poses as "seer" lay a mind that was, at bottom, cynical and positivist. He encouraged the acmeists in their early days and was one of the first leading representatives of the old "intelligentsia" to go over to the Revolution and to join the Communist Party.

8 Dimitry Venevitinov (1805-1827). A remarkable poet, friend of Pushkin. Belonged to the "Philosophers" Group. Wrote poems of very great formal beauty. Aspired to create a philosophical poetry in which lyricism would be combined with profundity of thought. A disciple of Schelling and Goethe, he also wrote essays in which he emerges as the theorist of "romantic idealism".

SECTION III

Socialist Revolution and Cultural Revolution

Preface

Nicolas Gorlov has been absent from Soviet literature since the time of Stalin, and we know practically nothing about him except that, according to his own account and to that of Trotsky, he belonged to the generation of the old Bolsheviks and was an ardent partisan of the LEF and Mayakovsky. Above all, he wrote a book called *Futurism and Revolution* in which he frankly and vigorously questions the politics of Russian futurism and its relations with Italian futurism.

In *Literature and Revolution*,[1] Trotsky previews Gorlov's book in the following terms:

"In Gorlov's unpublished work, which, in my opinion, traces incorrectly the international origin of Futurism, and which violates a historic perspective and identifies Futurism with proletarian poetry, the achievements of Futurism in art and form are very thoughtfully and weightily summarised. Gorlov points out correctly that the Futurist revolution in form, which grew out of the revolt against the old aesthetics, reflects in the plane of theory the revolt against the stagnant and smelly life which produced that aesthetics. And that this caused in Mayakovsky, who is the greatest poet of the school, and in his most intimate friends, a revolt against the social order which produced that discarded life with its discarded aesthetics. That is why these poets are organically connected with October. Gorlov's outline is correct, but it must be made more precise and definite. It is true that new words and new word combinations, new rhythms and new rhymes were necessary, because Futurism, in its feeling for the world, rearranged events and facts, and established, that is, discovered, for itself new relationships between them."

In fact, we should see Gorlov's pamphlet as a reply to Trotsky, who had rounded on formalism in *Literature and Revolution*, had expressed serious reservations concerning futurism, and regarded proletarian literature with complete scepticism. In this, he was expressing a view very close to that of Lenin whose traditional tastes in art and literature and whose hostility to modernism were well known. Nevertheless Trotsky was, together with Bukharin, the most sensitive and the most open-minded among the Soviet leaders where aesthetic questions were concerned, and his book is remarkable for its cogency, the breadth of its reflection, and its tolerance with regard to intellectuals and artists. But even he mistook the significance of the struggle being waged by ''left'' thought and art, just as he underestimated what was at stake; Gorlov was one of the few people to have understood this.

His book belongs to the LEF tradition, for it summarises the fundamental ideas of this movement on the cultural revolution to be carried out simultaneously with the socialist revolution. It represents an exemplary attempt (albeit, alas! an isolated one on the part of a politician) at harmonising aesthetics and lifestyle with the new economic and social structures born of the revolution. At that time, more than at any other, people believed in the possibility of casting down the tyranny of academicism and tradition which were the expression and auxiliaries of a suffocating form of life, and of building a new culture to meet the needs of the new world. These were the ambitions, this was the meaning of the constructivist movement that sprang up all over the place in the name of a new urban environment and technology, a movement that was represented by LEF in Russia, by the ''Esprit-Nouveau'' in France, and of which Ehrenburg's and Lissitzky's *Objet* was to be the most short-lived, and most accomplished achievement.[2]

The constructivists were concerned not merely to substitute a new kind of beauty (from the dynamic beauty of the futurists to the surrealists' convulsive beauty) for the old clichés of stereotyped beauty; they sought also to create a new man, freed from the bourgeois shackles which they assimilated to the platitudes of everyday life.

No one had made this combat, which dominated his entire life and work, his own more than Mayakovsky. And it would be utterly to misconstrue his death to refuse to see it as a confession of failure, of bankruptcy, whose ramifications spread well beyond his personal case to embrace the entire European avant-garde of the 1920s, marking an end to its hopes and struggles for the liberation of man. What Mayakovsky had sought in poetry was what Leonidov had sought in architecture,[3] Tatlin in painting, Meyerhold in the theatre, Eisenstein and Vertov in the cinema, and the formalists in the science of literature.

It was Gorlov's chief merit that he found the link between aesthetic problems and those of the *byt*,[4] and that he perceived a single front on which revolutionaries should do battle against the bourgeois mind. This was one of the leitmotivs of the LEF, whose leading theoretician, Chuzhak, drew his inspiration from Marxism in claiming that art was a form of production and that futurism was the only possible road to proletarian culture.[5]

LEF fought both against the structures of bourgeois society and against psychologism: all literature, all art, all criticism, any aesthetic arising out of it, was regarded as reactionary and passéist. This explains why the contribution of the formalists, and particularly of Osip Brik, was so important to LEF.

We are familiar with the deep bonds that united the two movements[6]: they converged in constructivism, with which what was known as left art, that is, the avant-garde, became identified[7] in 1922. The fundamental idea of the formalists was the autonomy of literature (Jakobson suggested replacing literature with literality). This theory is directly derived from the futurist slogans relating to the autonomy of the word and of language. The work of literature is a thing in itself, with its own specific laws, and which cannot be explained in terms of factors that are foreign to it: biography, sociology, etc.

This was a liberating principle. It was the fruit of reflection on futurist poetics, on the *zaum*, on the attempt to create a purely phonic poetry, and it in turn came to be an instrument for the emancipation of poetry itself, by shedding light on its own meaning.

People were thus called upon to weigh anchor and to come to terms with reality by means of a new system of signs. While the October Revolution had given meaning to futurist experiments, without them the Revolution itself would have lost all meaning: forms and ideas are indissociable, the social revolution must be accompanied by a revolution in everyday life itself, and in the aesthetic that expresses it.

The break with the past could never be anything but total. There was no point in overthrowing bourgeois power and eliminating the bourgeois class, unless one destroyed that class's thought, customs, morality and culture as well. Hence the constant parallel which Gorlov strives to maintain between the role of Marxism in politics and that of futurism in aesthetics. This need for cultural revolution has always impressed itself upon Marxist intellectuals concerned with coherence and truth (cf. Nizan).[8] But we have to admit that a cleavage very soon developed between the transformation of the economic structures and the backwardness of mentalities, which irresistibly produced a backlash: this split gradually widened to the point of total rupture (cf. The Congress of Kharkov).[9] This contradiction between politics and aesthetics was to pave the way for Stalinist intrigues. The reversion to academicism, the rejection of anything smacking of creative experiment went hand in hand with the deviations condemned by the 20th Party Congress. Still, we should never forget that there was a time when people really did believe that the cultural revolution would imbue the socialist revolution with its full meaning. Then, avantgarde poets strove to create a new vision of man and of the world in harmony with the new conditions of life which were seeking to drive out the old man and the old world with it. They identified poetry with revolution, the liberation of language with the liberation of humanity. When, later, words began to betray ideas, the subjection of language had no other purpose than the subjection of man. It was in the name of this totality, of this unity, of this merger between the essence of modernism and that of revolution, that LEF denounced a counter-revolution in form in the work of the communist poet Bryusov,[10] and that Mayakovsky heaped scorn on the academicism of the so-called proletarian poets. Among the many different movements, groups and circles that squabbled over and shared the Russian literary scene at that time, LEF, the last avatar of Russian futurism, stood out by the radicality of its ideas and the cogency of its positions as much as by the scope of its aims. We may ponder the totalitarian character of the ideology that it expressed, in respect of which, in spite of its internationalism and its links with European constructivism, it does indeed appear to have been a typically Russian phenomenon. Berdyaev wrote on this question in *The Russian Idea*: ''It is most important to bear in mind that Russia has a penchant for totalitarian doctrines, for a totalitarian conception of the world. Only doctrines of this kind stand any chance of success in our country. This is a manifestation of the Russian's religious caste of mind. The intelligentsia has always sought to forge for itself a coherent and totalitarian Weltanschaung in which 'pravda-justice' joins hands with 'pravda-truth'. Via a totalitarian form of thought, it was seeking a form of perfect life, and not just perfect embodiments of philosophy, science or art. This kind of total thought can even be regarded as the sole passport to membership of the intelligentsia'' (p. 38). These words may very well be applied to the Lef formalists and futurists and their thirst for totality. Their aim was that ''form of perfect life'' which Berdyaev spoke of; they wanted to transform man, to put a generous, open, and, above all, free ''new spirit'' in the place of the bourgeois mentality and its mean-minded egoism. They knew how illusory would be the economic and social liberation sought by Marxism in the absence of an interior, spiritual liberation. It was for this reason that they did their utmost to spread the revolution to the *byt*, to the lifestyle, to every aspect of everyday life. For them the political revolution was supposed to trigger, make possible, a poetic revolution: poetry would burst in upon life, all our lives, everyday life. The reign of Caliban would yield to that of Ariel. Some people have claimed that the futurists wanted to destroy poetry. It seems to me, however, that what interested them was not so much poetry itself as poetry as a genre, imprisoned within precisely defined limits and subject to rules; their concern was to free it from this constricting framework, to emancipate it from this secular millstone, to liberate it from this bed of Procrustes. We should see their fight against poetry as a fight against a certain conception, a certain use of poetry, the legacy of a past which they hunted down in all its forms, whose every trace they sought to extirpate. For this, they had to cast down the old idols, to eradicate definitions which had served the Tsarist system as so many ploys for conditioning and neutralising a formidable potential revolt. The futurists let go the reins, threw open the cages and gave free expression to that power against which those in authority had hitherto so carefully protected themselves; so carefully that they had placed it in the hands of an élite of submissive eunuchs, priests or agents, depending on the circumstances, obtaining their services and the servility of their muse by bribery.

LEF grasped this power in order to scatter it throughout the streets, among the crowd, among men. Mayakovsky and Brik wanted to make everyday life a marvellous thing. The reign of the bourgeois was to be succeeded by that of the poet; that of gravity by lightness; in a word, liberty. The bourgeois is someone who grows his roots in things; he is a reified, petrified, congealed thing: an oyster in its shell, surrounded by all the instruments of his well-being, by all the futile objects of his comfort. He protects himself with a kind of carapace against all that threatens to disturb him, to trouble his selfish, sated tranquility, against all that is liable to expose him to the rhythms and blasts of the world. The poet, on the contrary, is defined by his lack of worldly goods. St. Francis taking the vow of poverty was thereby taking a vow of poetry. By renouncing the world he gained the world. He renounced ownership, vanity, the mean and peaceful security of the slave, and his freedom opened up to infinite perspectives. Poetry begins with the irrepressible need to drop everything. Poetry is the down-at-heel vagabond with holes in his pockets; Khlebnikov, the nomad without hearth or home, dying of hunger at the end of his long wandering in the desert, is the incarnation of the poet's renouncement and poverty. This spirit of wandering and escape, this refusal to appropriate things and beings (refusal to become attached and to settle down) is the diametrical opposite of European embourgeoisement. This is the asiatic "way": a quest for cosmic harmony, for complete harmony between man and the universe. Poetry, for Khlebnikov, was identified with a metaphysic of language which expressed this oriental disposition of the Russian soul. He turned implacably towards the East in order to escape the fundamental alienation which the West represented for him. In order to live in poetry, he had to break down all barriers. Through their hatred of the West, the supporters of *zaum* perpetuated the most extreme tendencies within the ancient slavophile current.

Leontiev and Dostoyevsky despised and loathed catholic and bourgeois Europe for the same metaphysical and moral reasons as Khlebnikov. They shared the same cosmic sense of liberty; they felt the same loyalty to a deep-seated anarchy which they opposed to the hierarchy, the order, the pigeon-holing, the spirit of rivalry and conquest that had been imposed upon them by European capitalism. Reactionaries they may have been, but they were nonetheless anti-capitalist and anti-bourgeois.

For the futurists, it was neither accidental nor without significance that the revolution had arisen in the east of this Europe whose values they detested. They saw it not so much in terms of the impact of borrowed ideas foreign to the Russian soul (cf. Dostoyevsky in the *Devils*), as the East's revenge over the West. They based their internationalism upon this asiatic messianism, and their openness, their attempt to create a common world-front of all who wished to couple poetic revolution with social revolution, was based upon these premises. After all, was not the revolution the child of two messianic creeds: Marxist messianism, and the more specifically Russian messianism (oriented eastward). That, at least, is what Berdyaev thought:

"The messianic idea of Marxism founded upon the notion of the proletariat's mission became identified and confused with the Russian messianic idea. What predominated in the Russian communist revolution was not the empirical proletariat, but the idea of the proletariat, its myth. But this communist revolution, which became the true revolution, represented a universal messianism; it sought to bring happiness into the world and to free it from all restraints". Through their quest for a totality in which man could at last fulfil himself, through their hunger for fullness and their vision, which was turned towards ends rather than means, the Russian futurists belonged to that Russian Idea which Berdyaev spoke of. Their myth, too, was eschatological and their aspirations messianic.

1   Trotsky, *Literature and Revolution*, The University of Michigan Press, 1966, p. 145.

2   Published in three languages (Russian, German, and French) in Berlin, and fired with the purest internationalism, this journal sought to act as a rallying point for Europe's progressive élite. The only three issues to see the light of day stand as a moving testimony to the spirit of the 1920s, to the great abortive dream of the Russian constructivists. *Object* was intended above all to effect a junction between the Russian and European avant-gardes.

3   See Anatole Kopp's very fine book: *Town and Revolution ... op. cit.*

4   The word *byt* is too rich in meaning to be translated with precision. Usually it refers to everyday life, routine life, in a pejorative sense, with its conventions and rituals; it is associated with the most hateful form of alienation, the force of routine, "getting into a rut", the slavery of material comfort. It corresponds, finally, to the notion of "embourgeoisement". One of the essential, constant themes of the Russian intelligentsia since the nineteenth century had been precisely this revolt against the *byt*. Happiness and the fulfillment that comes from authentic creativity were to be wrested from the *byt*. Freedom, true life, were possible only after victory over the *byt*. Love and poetry, too, were its opposites; cf. Mayakovsky's parting shot: "The barge of love has shattered against everyday life". At the time of the NEP, Zabolotsky and his friends vituperated against the new *byt* (*novy byt*).

5   Chuzhak: "The proletarian Socialist revolution is the social base of futurism". Tretyakov: "The task of futurism is identical and parallel to that of communism", (*LEF*, no. 1). "LEF shapes a communist vision of the world" (*Ibid.*).

6   Futurism and formalism: the friendship between Mayakovsky and Osip Brik is well known, too. The leading Russian futurist and the most prominent figure of *Opoyaz* together founded the Left Art Front (LEF).

7   The word "left" referred to the avant-garde in literature and art as opposed to academicism and passeism.

8   Paul Nizan citing Emmanuel Berl: "As between culture as heritage, as the sign of heritage, and the proletariat, the mass of non-inheritors, there is no possible reconciliation, because culture is a system of values arrayed against the proletariat and shall necessarily remain so". And Nizan adds: "We must not be afraid to say so: bourgeois culture is a barrier. A luxury. A corruption of man. A product of idleness. A counterfeit of man. A weapon. The very justification of the economic and political power of one class over another." (*Pour une nouvelle culture*, p.27).

9   The International Congress of Revolutionary Writers was held in Kharkov in 1930. It led to the condemnation and disappearance of avant-garde tendencies and paved the way for the 1934 Congress of Soviet Writers, where the principle of Soviet realism was definitively established as dogma, and where the progressive aesthetic of the 1920s was catalogued as petit-bourgeois decadentism. This was the first serious blow to freedom of creation and expression, the first attempt to subordinate art and literature to a single line. The theses of the French surrealists, among others, which upheld the rights of poetry, were rejected, provoking a serious crisis in their group (the break with Aragon).

10 See Arvatov's article in *LEF* no. 1, 1923: "A counter-revolution in form"

(Bryusov). "This reactionary socialo-artistic movement, of which Bryusov appears to be the spokesman, has now spread widely throughout the Republic. Bryusov's work is not an isolated phenomenon, an individual or unique fact. Read the proletarian poets, open an issue of *Krasnoy Nivy*, *Izvestia* or *Pravda* and you shall find a continual *Bryusovshchina*. Communist youth is learning from Bryusov; it is practically as if the whole province was working for Bryusov and the Bryusovians; the St. Petersburg acmeists turn out to be the natural brothers of Bryusov, as are the Moscow neo-romantics and the other groups or circles. *Bryusovshchina* is a grave, dangerous social phenomena which is now, unfortunately, being cultivated in the Soviet State".

NICHOLAS GORLOV

On Futurisms and Futurism*

(*Concerning Comrade Trotsky's article*)

Art is one of the most complex superstructures and yet it is still the one that is studied less than any other by us Marxists. Our party has still not managed to gain control of art in theoretical terms. And this is understandable: until now the party has had to expend its energy with the greatest urgency on one front after another. However, the further we go, the more often our attention is drawn to this new front.

Our revolution has slowed its pace, but has not stopped.

In deepening, the revolution has come closer to everyday life.

Everyday life is our new front. Art is our weapon on this front.

It used to be that art existed outside the party and the party existed outside art. Comrade Trotsky, by his articles on everyday life, culture and art, has upturned soil of almost maidenly virginity: these articles give rise to the most vital and urgent questions of our cultural present; party thought has been given a good hundred thorough jolts. More than that, Comrade Trotsky has not just upturned the virgin soil, he has also had partial success in working it. Partial, but not complete success. Some of it, it seems to me, needs to be worked over again.

I shall attempt to show this in an article about futurism, dealing with it not as a whole, but only with those aspects in which the social nature of futurism and its attitude to the revolution is established and illustrated.

Futurism or futurisms

While on the one hand Comrade Trotsky admits the kinship between Russian and Italian futurism, on the other hand, he distinguishes sharply between the former and the latter. By his way of thinking, Italian futurism is the ideology of the imperialist bourgeoisie, while Russian futurism is the rebellion of persecuted intellectual

*Published in *Lef* (1924, n.4).

bohemianism. (Persecuted by whom? by the bourgeoisie, naturally?) The distance between these two is surely enormous. Aesthetics is a part of ideology. Can one ideology be shared by persecutors and persecuted; by the bourgeois and the rebels against the bourgeois? Marxist consciousness cannot accept this stretching of interpretations.

True, in the manifesto of the Italian futurists war is glorified as the hygiene of the world, while Russian futurism from the beginning has been against war. But the key to the solution of this contradiction is given us by Comrade Trotsky himself.

He writes:

For its war the bourgeoisie exploited with the greatest scope *feelings and attitudes, predestined by their nature to foment revolution.*

Futurism (revolutionary art), just like Marxism (revolutionary science), is predestined by its nature to foment revolution. But the bourgeoisie exploits to counter-revolutionary ends both Marxism and futurism.

The parallel between Italian futurism and Menshevism suggests itself, all the more so because they both came to grief on their attitude towards war.

Menshevism unwittingly serves the cause of imperialism. But none of us would call it an ideology of imperialism. Nor is it necessary to give futurism such a name.

The key to the way out from this contradiction is in Comrade Trotsky's hands, but he does not open the door.

The rebellion of the romantics and the rebellion of the futurists

It is, of course, correct that the social nature of futurism is not defined simply by the fact of its noisy protest against contemporary life and art. The romantics also rebelled, castigated philistinism and one of them even wore a red jacket. But nothing terrible came of this.

However, if the social nature of an artistic school cannot be deduced simply from the fact of its rebellion, no more is it possible to deduce the fact of rebellion from a game of marbles, if one ignores the social nature of that rebellion.

Plekhanov, from whom Comrade Trotsky borrows the information adduced above about the romantics, provides us in the same article with a good criterion for the weighing of artistic rebellion on social scales.

Aesthetic rebellion within the boundaries of class he characterises as hopeless and pessimistic. Why hopeless? Because the rebellion relies on the same economic relations as those which created the living conditions contemporary to it—the object of its rebellion. Why pessimistic? Because there is no way out of this bewitched circle.

This is what Plekhanov himself says of the romantics: "To the romantic circles belonged young members of the bourgeoisie, who had nothing against the named (bourgeois) relations, but who were aroused at the same time by the dirt, boredom and philistinism of bourgeois existence".

We are confronted by a discord between a social group and the milieu which was its origin. But where is this group aiming for ideologically? From society towards the individual personality, from socially useful art towards art for art's sake, from the ideology of bourgeois civic consciousness towards the ideology of the parasitic aristocracy, i.e. not forwards, but backwards.

"At that time the romantic school was dominated by the fashion of having a complexion as pale as possible, even to the point of being green and almost corpse-like. This gave a man a fateful Byronic appearance, bore witness to the fact that he was tormented by passions and tortured by pangs of conscience, made him interesting to women". Alfred de Musset, quoted by Plekhanov, calls the romantics "expansive souls, striving towards the infinite".

If we recall the old memory of the years 1907-1910, when our intelligentsia strove towards the individual and the infinite, and take into account the fact that the flowering of romanticism in France coincided with the period of the restoration, together with the fact that here in Russia, romanticism also flowered "under the sceptre and the orb" (Zhukovsky), then the social nature of the romantic "rebellion" will become clear to us.

Many are misled by the revolutionary background of some of Victor Hugo's works. But in their most vital feature these works are profoundly reactionary, for, surely, no works oppose individuality to the collective more blatantly than those of Hugo.

Remember Gauvain and Cimourdain, Jean Valjean and Javert. Hugo attempts to instil into us revulsion and horror towards Cimourdain, the iron man of revolution.

All his sympathies go to Gauvain, the betrayer of the revolution.

It is the same with Jean Valjean and Javert. The former is the personification of heavenly justice, while the latter personifies the cruel, unrelenting community, ignorant of mercy.

The romantic movement in its social essence was nothing more than a re-examination of the principles of 1793. This re-examination did not go beyond the limits of class (it even moved backwards), as it was advantageous to a certain section of the bourgeoisie—that which had already come to birth and had especially strengthened itself during the period of the restoration—the parasitic bourgeois aristocracy. This re-examination stood, therefore, without hope and tinted with pessimism, opposed as it was to the elemental power of the developing bourgeois economy and the rebellion which had grown up against it.

Is this similar to the futurist rebellion? Similar, inasmuch as reaction is similar to revolution.

About the futurists and the classics

Here we need consistency.

Comrade Trotsky says: "It cannot seriously be thought that history will simply preserve futurist works and present them to the masses many years later, when they [the masses] have matured. This surely would be the purest ... passéism".

This is, of course, correct. But the conclusion which seems to follow logically from the above is that to present the masses now with the preserved classics means just as much that one is struggling against history, acting like the purest passéist.

However, Comrade Trotsky finds that the classics are very necessary to the masses at the moment. In his opinion, the call to break with the classics makes sense only in so far as it is addressed to the intelligentsia, which is a captive of the old literature.

"The working class need not and cannot break with literary tradition, because it is not in its clutches. It is not familiar with the old literature, and so needs only to enter its world, only to assimilate and absorb Pushkin, in order to triumph and overcome it".

It is true that the working class has some advantages, compared with the intelligentsia.

The first point in favour of the working class is the fact that "it is not familiar with the old literature". But when it does discover the old literature, it will lose this advantage.

The second plus for the working class is the fact that the economic polarity between its interests and the interests of the bourgeoisie is a precondition of ideological polarity (for the elaboration of its own class culture).

It is clear that only by standing on the basis of his class culture can the worker not only assimilate Pushkin, but also overcome him. Otherwise ... Pushkin will throw him to the ground.

This gives rise to the question: is the worker sufficiently well armed by his culture to withstand this competition?

There can only be one reply: from the political point of view (after six years of mass struggle with the old order) he is armed, but from the aesthetic point of view (in relation to the old way of life) he is almost unarmed; politically he will overcome Pushkin, but aesthetically he will be crushed by him, as from this angle he has nothing with which to resist Pushkin.

Parodying a little (but just a little) the thought expressed by Comrade Trotsky, I could say thus: to the intellectual Marx it was necessary and important to escape from the clutches of bourgeois economics, but the worker, leaving to one side Marx's experience, needs to adhere to it.

It may indeed be said in objection to this that we have no Marx in art.

That's true, there is no Marx, but we do have his dialectic.

The law of development of art and of science is one and the same: in both spheres the preserved classics are of use only for the historical archive.

In both spheres every one of us must avoid constructing his psyche on his own, setting aside the experience of others.

In art, as in science, the worker must avail himself of the experience of *that part of the intelligentsia which has escaped from captivity*; otherwise, he inevitably falls temporarily into a void.

Comrade Trotsky does not make clear what a worker should assimilate in Pushkin and the other classics. Ideology? But surely it is a class-based, aristocratic, bourgeois, at best petty-bourgeois ideology. Objective truth? But art is not objective cognition, it is subjective attitude. It is nothing other than public (always class-based) emotion. Art is inseparable from the image, as the image is from life. And therefore art cannot go beyond the boundaries of class, without denying what in the revolutionary order is the image of class—its way of life. Even Comrade Trotsky himself comes close to this thought. "In the sphere of poetry"—he says—"we are dealing with a perception of the world in terms of images, and not with a scientific cognition of the world. Life, personal circumstances, the circle of the personal experience of life therefore exercise a determining influence on artistic creation".

But unfortunately Comrade Trotsky turns this true thought like a spear not against the old literature which sits up to its ears in the old way of life, but against futurism, which, although conceived in the womb of the intelligentsia, has torn itself away from the old bourgeois way of life and strives for a new definition in the revolution.

Contrasting art to science, Comrade Trotsky denies the possibility of the intelligentsia's anticipation of proletarian ideology in art.

This denial has no justification in theory or in practice.

Science operates on the structure of life, art on its mode. Changes and contradictions in the structure of life correspond to changes and contradictions in the mode of life. If contradictions in the structure can be apprehended and synthesised by thought, then contradictions in the mode of life can be apprehended and synthesised by emotion.

The synthesis of the contradictions of a given structure leads to the denial of that structure—revolutionary politics. The synthesis of the contradictions of a given mode of life leads to the denial of that mode of life—revolutionary aesthetics. As far as practice is concerned, it is sufficient to point to the poem *Cloud in Trousers*, which, three years before the proletarian revolution, anticipated the ideology of the militant proletarian.

From the point of view of content, Pushkin is only a negative value for the working class.

There remains form: language, style, rhythm, rhyme etc.

But there are two sides to form.

One side is form as the image of content, as the concrete shell in which the content is revealed, the two in complete fusion.

As we deny content, so we at the same time deny this side of form.

The other side of form is technique, mastery, the ability to handle the material, the devices of old art.

In this aspect it is possible for the proletarian to approach the classics as well, but such an approach will be necessary only when his psyche is able to form art, and not at the present moment, when art must form his psyche.

Art and Everyday Life

To the question as to how our party should relate to art, Comrade Trotsky replies thus: the party accepts that art which the revolution accepts.

This reply seems too vague to me. Our revolution has approached everyday life through politics and economics. It is clear that we now have little in the way of a political criterion. We must re-examine and deepen our criterion.

At the present moment the only effective kind of art for us is art which has *completely broken away from the old way of life*, which has burnt the old ideological bridges and its aesthetic boats.

What sort of art should this be, can it be everyday art?

Everyday art—predominantly representative—corresponds to the statics, and not the dynamics of social life. In dynamic eras, such as ours, representation is the same thing as photographing the bricks of a building under construction.

Bricks can only be photographed by someone who stands apart from the building work—even more so, by someone who likes the bricks as bricks, or, to put it more clearly, by someone who would like to give life an order, as Joshua, son of Nun did to the sun: "stand fast and do not move". This kind of everyday art is always an admiration of life and it is extremely characteristic that everyday life in literature is now being earnestly promulgated by writers of petty bourgeois persuasion (Pil'nyak, Fedin, Zamyatin and others).

To build in art means presenting not the maximum of resemblance, but the maximum of expressiveness and class evaluation. The art of today is not analysis, but synthesis, not a portrait of a brick, but the plan of a building.

About Tradition

Comrade Trotsky, reproaching the futurists for their break with tradition in bohemian nihilism, offers them as an example to us, the Bolsheviks, who use revolutionary tradition for revolutionary aims.

This reproach is unjust, being based on a confusion of the functions of art and politics. The politician organises the masses for direct action. It is important for him always to have a stout rope to hand, so that he can haul those who have fallen behind up to those who are in the lead. Tradition serves as just such a strong rope for him. The politician must be *understandable* to the masses in *elementary terms*. In order to make the present more understandable, he naturally compares it with the past. But the organisational task of the artist is quite different: it is not the use of the existent psyche of the masses, but the formation of a new psyche, not hauling on an old rope, but the replacement of the old rope by a new one, not the grasping of tradition, but the rejection of it. For the artist the traditional image is already a worn-out and dead image.

About Evaluation

Now, to Comrade Trotsky's evaluation of Mayakovsky. Above all, about Mayakomorphism. Witty, but unjust.

"Mayakovsky populates the squares, the streets and the fields of revolution with himself ... In order to raise up man, he elevates him to a Mayakovsky ...".

And he does so correctly. Art is the self, always and only the self, i.e. a subjective organising principle, the emotional effect of an artist on the masses, however objective it may pretend to be.

Mayakovsky rejects pretence, lays bare the device and, by doing so, places a definite boundary between the old art and the art of revolution.

"Mayakovsky stands with one foot on Mont Blanc, and with the other on Elbrus" ... But, after all, even Comrade Trotsky himself affirms that the proletariat will rebuild mountains. Here as well, therefore, the present-day *self* of Mayakovsky is nothing other than tomorrow's proletarian *we*.

"In referring to the greatest events of history he adopts a familiar tone ..."

But here even our own revolutionary tradition must take Mayakovsky's part: let us not forget how in 1871 the proletarians of Paris flung a certain historical event into the dirt.

"Mayakovsky's works lack movement most of all" ... Why? Because there is too much of it, "an excess of urgency in images leads to tranquillity" ... The confession of one who is accustomed to proceeding in art according to Chekhovian pauses, not the pauses of revolution—I would add.

In Comrade Trotsky's words, "a work of art should present a maximum crescendo of image, idea, atmosphere, story opening and plot, not hurl the reader from one end to the other, even if the punches are the most refined in boxing imagery". But that is equivalent to saying that one cannot give expression in art to revolution, as it always hurls us about in zig-zags like that, not from bottom to top, but from top to bottom, not from the minimum of atmosphere to the maximum, but the reverse.

This we see in Mayakovsky as well: his poem *150 million* begins on the highest note—with the hungry howl of men and beasts, but finishes with a calm and satisfied "solemn requiem of peace". Mayakovsky gives our psyche a revolutionary shakeup. We who have been brought up in petty-bourgeois tastes, who have become accustomed to art as a buffer, to whips and scorpions, interwoven well in advance with roses, to the gradual crescendo of image and atmosphere, to story openings, plots and denouements, are suddenly unsettled by Trotsky with the thunder of his revolutionary drum.

The same must be said about the abundance of individual images, which seem to annihilate the unity of the whole. Here the matter is one of subjective perception, in that one is simply unaccustomed to perceiving a new thing which is quite unlike anything old. Our consciousness in the first instance stumbles on new images, new rhythms, rhymes and stylistic forms, and the defect in our consciousness seems to us to be a defect in the thing itself.

So far as objective, not subjective unity is concerned, then *Cloud in Trousers*, *150 million* and *Mystery-bouffe* are rare in their unity and wholeness. They are genuinely synthetic pieces. Despite their wide thematic range and the wealth of content invested in them, they are all compact and succinct to an extreme. They are not simply well written, but masterfully organised.

The synthetic quality of the whole is achieved in these works precisely as a result of the abundance (or synthetic quality) of the individual images.

Cloud in Trousers is a synthesis of a whole era, the sum-total of the old culture, all chipped and cracked on the eve of the revolution. Its social meaning is the preparation of the militant.

Mystery-bouffe encompasses the revolution in its initial period of radical class stratification and the conflict between class ideologies. Its social meaning is the struggle for the establishment of a class (the Civil War).

150 Million brings us to the moment when class ideology is established on the scale of the State (i.e. to the end of the Civil War and the beginning of the class war in international dimensions).

This is already a poem of world revolution.

Mayakovsky, like a sound drum, is always in the advance guard of the revolution. He always keeps time in the call to assembly.

Comrade Trotsky, while admitting the individual merits of the poem *150 Million*, does not recognise the poem itself, as a whole. He says:

"The author wanted to present an epic of mass sufferings, mass heroism, the faceless revolution of 150 million Ivans. But what resulted was a profoundly personal, individualistic poem". Why:

Because it contains a great deal of "unmotivated artistic arbitrariness". For example, "Wilson swollen in lard", "no inhabitant of

Chicago is of less than general's rank'', ''Wilson guzzles, the fat bulges, stomachs swell, storey after storey'' and so on.

In actual fact, Wilson is lean and not fat, Chicago is inhabited by workers as well as generals, and so on.

It seems to me that what we are faced with here is the same old naturalistic approach to the art of the new era, an era which has not the slightest need of naturalistic representation. Photographing the revolution (or the counter-revolution) means not presenting even one per cent of it and, in the other 99 per cent, presenting what does not characterise it at all.

Wilson is lean; perhaps he even has a sympathetic look, a pleasant smile, perhaps he is a good family man, loves Beethoven, strokes his cat etc. One might ask, does the worker who is struggling against Wilson need all these touching details of Wilson's profile?

Not in the least. Moreover: the everyday Wilson is for the worker not only an unnecessary truth, but a harmful lie. He knows Wilson as someone quite different: not Wilson the personality, but Wilson the representative of the collective of world suffocators, not the Wilson who smiles pleasantly at him from a portrait, but the Wilson who with one stroke of his hand sends ships to Archangel, in order to suppress his country with an iron blockade. Wilson for him is not a photographic but a synthetic individual. Such he is with Mayakovsky as well.

The worker, of course, is well aware that ''in Chicago there are, as well as generals, the workers of the slaughter-houses''. But the fact that he knows this well does not prevent him at any one moment from forgetting about it.

In 1871 the Parisian worker knew very well that Versailles was inhabited not only by members of the bourgeois class, but also by poor workers, while Paris was inhabited not only by poor workers, but also by bourgeois. Nevertheless, the Parisian worker directly contrasted a bourgeois Versailles to a workers' Paris. His ideas about one or the other were integral conceptions, because they were constructed not by rational but by emotional means. They were *the slogans of his struggle*. Such is our conception of Red Moscow, contrasted to the bourgeois capitals. Such also is Mayakovsky's artistic image.

Comrade Trotsky doesn't like the fact that Ivan has ''his hand stuck behind his belt''—''What'', he asks, ''is the justification for this careless attitude towards technology?'' But here Comrade Trotsky deserts not only his own naturalistic, but even the realistic position.

For this is indeed the most genuine Ivan and, moreover, not just our Russian one but, as is now clear, the world Ivan. This is what he is like and we must take serious account of it. The same story happens to him every time: before he can stir himself he has been cut with a wound four versts long, reaching even as far as Tula itself, and only after this do men crawl in plenty from his wound. The revolution is more an element than an organisation. It is a fact you cannot escape. Where is the contempt for technology, where is the bravado and the athletics? The very word "championship" sounds like irony and maliciously deceives those who trust it and await an engrossing struggle, with miracles of agility and athletics. Alas, as in any mass struggle, the matter is simply decided: "a wound four versts long and men crawling out of it".

Nor do I see anything criminal in the use of the word "to pocket". The harmful effect of the image "to pocket" is eliminated by the image "the wealth of all worlds", just as the harmful effect of the image "steal" is annulled by the image "loot".

Are Ivan and Wilson like the primitive characters of folklore and fairy tale?

Mayakovsky's epic shares with the folk epic its collectivism and the monumentality of its images. But the images of the folktale are analytical and allegorical. Mayakovsky's images are synthetic and realistic.

Nevertheless, there is much more similarity than with, for example, Pushkin's *Poltava*. But before reproaching Mayakovsky for archaism, should we not seriously consider whether this approach by the poet of revolution to the sources of collective popular creativity is accidental or not.

I think it is not accidental, in the same way that it is no coincidence that our single revolutionary of the theatre so far, Meyerhold, bases himself on old popular spectacles—the mystery, farce and carnival play, while the master of the revolutionary poster, Moor, draws his inspiration from the icon (whose stylistic, artistic, constructive and other merits, by the ways, came to be valued by our artists only after they had passed through ... Shchukin's[1] private residence).

Are we not dealing here with the law of Marx's dialectics—thesis—antithesis—synthesis?

Comrade Trotsky's prejudiced attitude towards Mayakovsky's poetry has prevented him from noting clearly enough the real shift, or rather the crisis of the poet. This is the poem *About This*. It is of dual nature: in it Mayakovsky gives everyday life a good pasting, but it gives him one as well. In Mayakovsky's poem he himself is divided into two—Mayakovsky the revolutionary is running errands for the

Mayakovsky who has arrived "from beyond seven years".[2]

Love, which once raised Mayakovsky to the revolution, has now tumbled him down among the bears.[3]

The old love is that *everyday life* which Mayakovsky did not manage to overcome. But, after all, that is the most difficult thing to do.

1   Famous Moscow dealer and collector.
2   Allusions to the poem *About This*.
3   Allusions to the poem *About This*.

NICHOLAS GORLOV

Futurism and Revolution

(*The Poetry of the Futurists*)*

What is Futurism?

Futurism has arisen on the border of two epochs. It is the art of a revolutionary watershed.

How should we characterise futurism? What clearly marks it off, in its first phase, from other artistic tendencies? It is the rebellion against old content and old forms, the destruction of an old aesthetic.

The basis of art is emotion. Futurism is the rebellion of emotion against the old pattern of life, against those old everyday forms of life in which life was set, under the sign of "private property".

I emphasise: it is not a direct rebellion against private property, it is a rebellion against the pattern of life created by it, against its everyday life. It is clear, however, that a direct strike against everyday life is at the same time an indirect strike against the social order which created this life.

That is why the bourgeoisie in all countries shuns futurism like the plague.

Futurism is an uprising against the everyday life of the old world, it is a revolution in art, a red flag, raised above one of the citadels of the bourgeoisie. Futurism is the same everywhere and everywhere it is under the red flag. It is shortsightedness that makes many of us mistake the red for the white (just as many mistake the white for the red). Thus, for example, comrade Lers (whom comrade Lunacharsky praises for his serious Marxist approach to contemporary art), in his book on "Russian futurism",[1] relates to futurism literally as he would to a weathercock: he heads in the direction it points. "Russian futurism", in his words "is a populist, intellectual, revolutionary movement in conditions of social reaction. It is ideologically hostile both to Western European futurism, the aesthetic ideology of

*Moscow, GIZ, 1924.

imperialism, and to the Russian decadent movement, the ideology of the industrial bourgeoisie, which stands on the threshold of imperialism, but it is also hostile to the coming proletarian ideology''.

And further on:

''The upsurge of the October Revolution made the most talented of the Russian futurists (Mayakovsky) hostile to the basic tendency (i.e. populist) of this movement''.

Russian futurism is a populist movement, Western European futurism is the ideology of imperialism and, in addition, we see the futurist Mayakovsky going close to the ideology of the proletariat in his works! In a word—it's not futurism but a chameleon.

How is it that comrade Lers created this chameleon?

In order to prove that Russian futurism is a populist movement, hostile to the proletariat, he recruits to the ranks of the futurists Esenin, Klyuev, Shershenevich and Mariengof, while quoting a couple of lines from genuine futurists which at a stretch (and mainly on a superficial reading and not on an understanding of their inner meaning) can be made to seem like populist sentiments. To these are added from the poetry of the ''recruited'' futurists a healthy dose of Kulak-philistine ideology. All this makes sense when the reader is offered such lines, under the imprint of futurism:

> ''O, homeland, happy
> And perpetual hour.
> There is no better, nothing more fair
> Than your bovine eyes...
> —Bless yourself on Mid-Whitsun
> And bless yourself at Christmas,
> So that those who thirst for an awakening
> Can assuage their thirst with the stigmata...'' (Esenin)

Or,

> ''And I am faithful to the weeping cradle,
> To the kindred grave of my mother, to the face of the
> granary...'' (Klyuev)

or Klyuev again:

> ''The sands of mighty Asia
> Will present a shroud to the factory chimneys.
> And the raven will sit down on the skull of steel—
> The nursling of dust, the lighthouse of fate''.

Or when Esenin compares the "idol" of the communists, Karl Marx, to a cow, then the reader can do nothing but agree with comrade Lers that the populist futurists are people who are harmful to the proletariat.

Now, about the second discovery of comrade Lers.

As proof of the fact that Western European futurism is the ideology of imperialism, comrade Lers quotes a series of statements from Marinetti's manifesto, and, giving them a narrowly political, and therefore extremely superficial evaluation, attempts to extract from them this perfidious ideology.

But how is one to reconcile imperialism with this sentence, for example:

"We glorify the huge crowds, motivated by work, pleasure or rebellion, the multicoloured, polyphonic waves of revolutions in contemporary capitals".

Comrade Lers answers us: the imperialist does not fear revolution, he is protected by mechanical mitrailleuses.

Let us suppose that he is as brave as all that, but even so, it's still a long way from "glorifying". To glorify means you must also sympathise. It's impossible both to sympathise and to train mitrailleuses at one and the same time. Bravery isn't the same as stupidity, and a class ideology cannot be an ideology which incites another class to conflict with it.

It's not an easy task to adapt futurism to imperialism and comrade Lers takes on an easier one: to adapt imperialism to futurism.

He creates the ideology of imperialism on the basis of Marinetti's manifesto—and an ideology results for which no imperialist would thank him.

And, in fact, what is the ideology of imperialism? Isn't it the same as the ideology of capitalism? Can imperialism be so ideologically detached from capitalism as to become a contradiction to it? This can in no way be justified—not economically, nor politically, nor historically (at present we are living through the phase of the collapse of imperialism and so we already have the right to talk of its history).

Imperialism is the last stage in the evolution of capitalism. In essence it is the beginning of a world economic crisis. On the economic side it is characterised by the flooding of the world market with goods. The moment is coming when all the wealth created by the ruling class threatens to crash down on its head. The capitalist begins to feel cramped among the machines and goods created by him: they begin to crush him. And so, imagine, just when technology, the machine and mechanised living are crushing a man, the same man begins to sing the praises of this technology, the machine, mechanised living. But, according to comrade Lers, this is precisely what imperialism is doing. It's clear why—because he has Marinetti's crib-sheet in his hands.

In fact neither imperialism, nor capitalism could have created the aesthetic of the machine, could have glorified the machine and mechanised life because their mission was not at all to mechanise life as a whole, or to create harmony in production. Indeed, partial mechanisation only emphasised the general anarchy in production and worsened the jolting over the economic ruts and bumps, frequently leading to crises of catastrophic proportions. The machine, which the capitalist has exploited as he has the worker, and not at all in the same way as the worker has used it, has created for the capitalist strikes and has hit his pocket very hard indeed. So what sort of aesthetic could come from this!

In order to transform the whole world into the kingdom of the machine, one must not only possess the machines, but become oneself part of a single machine—the world-wide human collective. Only the working class is destined to mechanise life in the true sense of the words. This is its ideology and it is extremely characteristic that it was acclaimed by the very first Utopian Socialists, such as Fourier and others. The bourgeois individualist, the master of the machine, didn't even wish to think that he could become part of it and always spat on mechanisation with contempt and disgust.

One cannot draw a sharp line between imperialism and capitalism, either in the political realm or in everyday life. This is so clear that there is hardly any necessity to prove it.

Imperialism cannot rebel against capitalism but Marinetti's manifesto is rebelling against something. Against what, then?

Against the everyday life which the old order has created.

If we put to one side the political yardstick and look at Marinetti's aesthetic manifesto from the angle of everyday life then the revolutionary significance of even this very first declaration of futurism becomes indubitable:

"We have listened", Marinetti writes—"to the exhausted prayer of the old canal and the grinding of bones of the old palaces, with their nature fashioned from greenery, and suddenly voracious automobiles have begun to bellow beneath our window. My friends, I said, let us go. Let us move. At long last mythology and a mystical ideal have been overcome. We will be present at the birth of the centaur and will see the flight of the first angels. We must shake loose the doors of life and test out the catches and bolts. Forward! Here is the first sun that has arisen over the earth. Nothing can be compared to the splendour of its red rapier which has flashed for the first time in our murky millenia''.

Marinetti contrasts the automobile to the mythical centaur, the aeroplane to the mythical angel, the machine to nature and matter to spirit. Materialism which shakes loose the doors of life, matter which breaks open the catches and bolts of the spirit—whose ideology is this?

Comrade Lers, we must assume, thinks as follows:

Capitalism created the machine, imperialism transformed half the world into the kingdom of the machine. Can, then, the imperialist not be a materialist? But in exactly the same way as the imperialist cannot glorify the machine, that is, use it as the basis for his aesthetic, so he cannot make the machine the starting point for his philosophy: he cannot attain the synthesis of the world under the sign of the machine, since under this sign his world (the capitalist order) is not only not synthesised, but collapses on its feet.

Of course, imperialism, viewed as a particular stage, is closer to socialism than capitalism is, but closer only materially, economically and technologically, and not ideologically.

The economics of imperialism, which lay bare a whole series of contradictions in the capitalist order, also contain a whole series of pre-conditions for the material reconstruction of the world on another economic basis (not private but collective property), but the ideology which is being born out of these pre-conditions will not, of course, be the ideology of imperialism, but the ideology of the rising class.

Marinetti's words are bright flashes of this new ideology.

Comrade Lers makes exactly the same mistake (the identification of a material pre-condition with ideology) when he interprets the following lines from the manifesto: ''The train gives every provincial the chance to leave his small town with its empty squares where the dust, the sun and the wind languidly amuse themselves, and to stroll of an evening through the capital, strewn with gestures, light and shouting. The alpine dweller can every day, with the help of a newspaper which costs one sou, tremble from anxiety along with the Chinese insurgents, the suffragettes of London and New York, with Doctor Carrel and the heroic sledges of the polar explorers''.

Comrade Lers elucidates: ''Imperialism is international, the imperialist can only very half-heartedly pretend that wars are the result of the dictates of the patriotic conscience and not the seizure of new markets, simply the competitiveness of trade ...''.

Imperialism is international and so ... it wishes to tremble as one with the Chinese insurgents?

It wants nothing of the kind!

Imperialism is international only economically and technologically: ideologically, it is shot through with nationalism. Nationalism is the very soul of imperialism. But economic and technological imperialism, that is, to put it at its simplest, continuous relations with the most distant countries, which were formed under imperialism and which have developed as it developed, create the pre-condition for a new ideology, which is not only not in harmony with imperialism, but is clearly hostile to it.

Marinetti, not politically, of course, but aesthetically, has reached internationalism, starting from everyday life. Comrade Lers has perceived this, but what has imperialism got to do with it?

Comrade Lers also perceived that Marinetti does not spare religion, the family, nor the state. But, surely, all these are pillars of private property! Marinetti takes arms against all the obsolete prototypes of The Beautiful, The Great, The Solemn, The Religious, The Light, The Seductive. In a few lines he gives the whole programme for a revolution in aesthetics. How alive the old prototypes of The Beautiful are we can see very well in our contemporary poetry, painting, theatre, in all the art of the USSR which even now for a good nine-tenths of the time is still chewing the cud of bourgeois aesthetics. Even our, as yet weak, proletarian poetry went astray at first in these bourgeois aesthetics by going to bourgeois "specialists" to learn about literature. And only Russian futurism, which raised the revolutionary banner, hoisted originally by the Italian futurists, has knocked, and continues to knock, well sharpened aspen stakes into the stinking, rotten beauties of the old world.

"We wish", says Marinetti, "to glorify the love of danger, customary energy, customary valour. The principal components of our poetry will be as follows: bravery, daring, rebellion. We wish to praise the incipient movement, delirious insomnia, the gymnastic step, the dangerous leap, the slap and the punch".

This is the aesthetic of rebellion. Who needs it: tottering capitalism which is doomed by history to perish in the great world-wide workers' rebellion, or the new, young, powerful class of the universal rebel?

And it is here that we see the aesthetic glimpse into the future.

Of course, acts like the slap and the punch, as in the work of Mayakovsky, for example, and the bloody carcasses of corn-dealers, are not part of the programme of the RCP (Russian Communist Party) but they are fully part of the everyday life of revolution, as its inevitable, elemental setting. On the road to revolution, we accept it not only as a programme, but as an elemental force.

It is clear from the quotations we have given that Marinetti does not express the ideology of imperialism. But what ideology does he express?

One cannot attach any political label to this ideology. It is the ideology of rebellion against the deadened forms of life of contemporary society, it is a revolutionary aesthetic. Marinetti is the revolutionary of everyday life. He approaches revolution not from below but from above, not from politics, but from aesthetics, not with the cold weapon of abstract thought, but with a fiery heart which cannot tear itself away from the concrete phenomena of life.

With his sensitive instinct he catches the contradictions of the bourgeois order, but he fails to discover through his consciousness their origin. His political consciousness lags far behind his aesthetic instinct. This is natural, just as it is natural that we encounter, at almost every step, good political revolutionaries whose aesthetic instinct is a good fifty years behind their political consciousness (for example, communists who publish Zhukovsky for the worker).

The revolution in everyday life which Marinetti proclaimed was unthinkable within the framework of the bourgeois order, but Marinetti thought of it in precisely this framework, since, I repeat, he was not a politician but an aesthetician. It is understandable that when he tried to fit his essentially revolutionary tendencies to old political forms, he came up with, at times, wildly absurd combinations.

Marinetti is the foe of stagnant, deadened everyday life, the enemy of every stasis.

"We declare", he says, "that the splendour of the world has been enriched by a new beauty: the beauty of speed. The racing car which seems to run on buck-shot is much more beautiful than the victory of Samothrace [a good imperialist!]. A static creation cannot be a masterpiece. There is no poetry but dynamic poetry".

Marinetti wants life to be transformed into dynamism, into creative movement. This is a revolutionary tendency.

But how are we to purge life of its age-old mustiness? With what are we to shake loose its tightly bolted doors and break open the catches and bolts? Through what storm are we to burst forth over the deadened patterns of everyday existence?

Marinetti gives his answer:

"We wish to glorify war—the unique purgative of the world—and militarism, patriotism, the destructive gesture of the anarchists, beautiful ideas, which bring only death, and contempt for women''.

And further:

''We will glorify the multicoloured and polyphonic waves of revolution in contemporary capitals''.

This combination—if we take it on its political level—is the most absurd: revolution and war which are two separate quantities, one a plus sign the other a minus, are added together and their sum comes out with a plus sign.

But it is clear that for Marinetti both war and revolution are not political but aesthetic categories. Both these categories are subordinated to a third which reconciles them. This third is the purgative of the world, the purifying storm, creative struggle, the dynamic of life.

If we approached this section of the manifesto and gave it a political evaluation, as comrade Lers does, then we would get something like the following dialogue:

''He glorifies war—this means he's an imperialist'', comrade Lers would say.

''He glorifies revolution and the destructive gesture of the anarchists—this means he's the enemy of imperialism'', I would say. And we will never come to terms with each other.

Marinetti perceives war aesthetically, from the outside, as an awakening from a lifelong hibernation, as an elemental force which churns up the stagnant patterns of everyday life, as a gust of energy, as movement. But he fails to see, fails to understand that it is, for all that, an ant-hill which has been kicked over and the whole meaning of the commotion which has arisen in the ant-hill (militarism, patriotism) is to protect, to preserve, to re-establish, to place everything on its old footing. What escapes from Marinetti is the notion that war is not an active, but a reactive dynamic, that it is an elemental force which asserts, reinforces and preserves the old forms of life against the elemental force which negates and destroys them—that is, revolution. And this is the reason why Marinetti's essentially revolutionary aesthetic is transformed into reactionary politics.

Marinetti's anti-feminism has the same origins. However strange it may seem, the starting point for this is again a revolutionary tendency:

''We wish to destroy museums, libraries'', says Marinetti, ''to fight against moralism, feminism and all opportunistic and utilitarian baseness''.

For Marinetti the feminine principle is an inert one. For him woman is an intermediary link between the graveyards of the old—the museums—and everyday life which adapts itself to the old (opportunism and utilitarianism). And one must admit that in those organisational forms of life which private property has created, that is indeed the case. Woman, estranged from the life of society, locked in the cramped box of the family, woman with the horizon of one who sits in a snail's shell, has become the bulwark of that very inert and dead existence which is inimical to every revolutionary.

Marinetti hates this existence and attacks woman as a guardian who preserves it, without understanding that she is a captive guard, placed at the doors of life by her all-powerful master—private property. Once this master has been toppled, all the guardians will abandon all the doors. Man is as wax in the hands of life and life can make of woman not only a candle of the Lord God, but something else which is much more useful.

There was a time when workers, who were good revolutionaries but poor politicians in their struggle against unemployment, smashed machines, because they failed to understand that the true culprit in their disasters was not the machine, but the owner of it. Exactly the same mistake has been made by Marinetti—a revolutionary in aesthetics—thanks to the narrowness of his political horizon.

Marinetti, as a member of the intelligentsia, is a man with a divided ideology: in politics he is old hat, and clings to old, habitual, inert forms, whereas in aesthetics he is an innovator and seeker of new forms. It is here that he lays down the first stones for the foundations of a new art.

I have lingered in such detail over Italian futurism because it is precisely this, thanks to all these awful words, militarism, patriotism, anti-feminism, which has been the cause of the confusion in the minds of the theorists of the new art. And it is this confusion which has led to the breaking-up of the understanding of futurism into such "component parts", from which absolutely nothing can then be formed.

Imperialist futurism (Marinetti), populist futurism (Esenin, Klyuev), quasi-proletarian futurism (Mayakovsky), futurism which encompasses the unencompassable, weathercock futurism—this is where one may end up, even using Marxist methods and taking authentic Marxism as a starting point.

And in actual fact, if futurism, as a form, can be applied to any content, then one must admit that form in art develops immanently, without any connection with the content. But we Marxists have never accepted and will not accept these metaphysics. For us, form is a complex of signs by which the content *becomes known*, that is by which it can be differentiated from any other content. And so we come to the following conclusion: the signs by which one may differentiate, one from another, imperialism, populism and a proletarian or (I will be precise) a quasi-proletarian ideology, are one and the same.

And so, there is futurism, but there are no futurisms. Those who, having invented a variety of futurisms, then place them on both sides of the barricades, are deeply mistaken, but no less glaring an error is made by those who, while recognising the ideological kinship and, consequently, the historical continuity between Russian and Italian futurism, then point at a few Italian futurists who have sullied themselves with fascism (including, it seems, Marinetti), and as a result, nod ambiguously at Russian futurism, saying, as it were, birds of a feather ...

But ... did Marxism cease to be a revolutionary ideology because our Mensheviks tried to adapt it to the dictatorship of the white generals?

In the same way, futurism will not cease to be a revolutionary aesthetic, even though a certain section of the Italian "futurists" have made attempts to adjust futurism to fascism. One may say in advance that apart from empty space, nothing will come of fascistic futurism, just as nothing came of Menshevik Marxism.

I will now move on to Russian futurism.

Russian Futurism

Russian futurism was born in the circles of the petty-bourgeois intelligentsia at the moment when a new revolutionary wave was already rising to replace outdated reaction. The workers' movement was spreading, professional and party work had come to life. The Lena shootings[2] of 1912 had stirred up the working masses throughout Russia. And in 1914, just before the war, barricades were erected in the streets of St. Petersburg.

We never forget all this when we write or talk about the history of our party, but, when the discussion concerns the origins of Russian futurism, I have many times been obliged to observe that memory fails many of my comrades and they reduce the whole period of 1907-1914 to one of utterly black, hopeless reaction.

The reaction which followed 1905 produced a crisis in the consciousness of our intelligentsia, but when a new revolutionary storm began to be felt in the air, it could not help but touch the intelligentsia. And if a significant (even the greater) part was still wallowing in an ideological bog (God—the Cosmos—Sex) then another, healthy section, close to the working class, could not but be stirred by this revolutionary ferment.

Such was the social terrain on which Russian futurism grew up. There can be no doubt that Russian futurism received its first jolt from Western futurism, in the sense of its ideological formation (and consequently, in the adoption of a new form). But Western futurism, despite having taken up the initial revolutionary positions (rejection of the old way of life) was not able to overcome ideologically the second, principal line of hostile positions (the old order) and froze motionless on the spot. Western futurism is like a plant which came to bud too early. It remains frozen and withered, caught out by a political frost.

The fate of Russian futurism turned out to be immensely more felicitous. It only slightly anticipated a warm, incipient spring—the Russian revolution. It grew in its sunshine ... And now we have before us not a withered crop but the young, strong, healthy tree of a new art.

The revolutionary spirit of Russian futurism was apparent from its very first steps. Scarcely yet able to talk, it delivered a "slap in the face of public taste" and cast from the ship of modernity the classics of Russian literature, declaring that for it "Pushkin has become Derzhavin". It offered a daring challenge to bourgeois, philistine everyday life, by crossing over the boundary of "the permitted", not only in art but in everyday life as well (Mayakovsky's yellow jacket etc.).

What is this?—charlatanism, adventurism, literary hooliganism!—such were the howls of the good bourgeois as they spat with disgust on futurism. They, of course, could not have behaved otherwise. But, however strange it may seem, even today there are still people, and moreover, revolutionaries, even communists who, in order to have done with futurism ("it must be harmful because intellectuals thought of it"), repeat the same things, word for word.

Charlatanism, adventurism, hooliganism—after all, these are precisely the attributes which the bourgeois accorded us, the Bolsheviks.

The futurists struck against the taste (and therefore, the life-style) of the bourgeoisie, while we Bolsheviks struck against their order. The futurists cast from the ship of modernity the old writers and poets, who were the former masters of our thoughts, while we Bolsheviks chucked in the same direction "the powers that be"—the Tsar, the landowner and capitalist. And at the same time as the futurists were turning Pushkin into Derzhavin, we Bolsheviks were already preparing to climb aboard the engine to project Russia a whole century ahead in the course of a few years. (How could Pushkin not become Derzhavin after all this?)

In 1913 the futurists were already creating a revolution, parallel to our own. A small group of futurists, like the small group of Bolsheviks operating at the same time, boldly set themselves up in opposition to all of bourgeois, philistine society and, untouched by the spittle and taunts, moved decisively ''against the current'', thereby revealing truly Bolshevik tenacity and stubbornness.

This alone demonstrates the immense store of revolutionary energy possessed by Russian futurism, and also shows that, although we are still dealing with the same old Russian intelligentsia, this intelligentsia is special, not flabby but flint-hard. It is the best part of the intelligentsia which has given us Marat, Babeuf, Marx, Lenin, Trotsky and other less notable but genuine, revolutionary intellectuals.

This is no accident, but almost a rule, a law that it is not members of the proletariat, but the revolutionary intelligentsia which forges the ideological weapons of the working class as it goes to storm terrestial and celestial power. After all, while the working class is materially oppressed, it is ideologically impotent. How is it to become conscious of itself and its position in the world when almost all doors which lead to knowledge are closed for it? The intelligentsia, though, has all the books in their hands—in the literal sense. Perhaps people will tell me that these books were bourgeois. What sense could come of a bourgeois intellectual reading a heap of bourgeois books? However, I will say that sense, all the same, did come of it, in the case of Marx and Lenin, for example, and this is why:

The bourgeois order bears within itself the seeds of its own death. And, long before its actual death, disease is sapping its strength. Economically, this is expressed in industrial crises and ideologically in the collapse of bourgeois ideology, that is, in the ideological contradictions which arise and grow greater, the nearer the bourgeoisie approaches its economic end. Bourgeois scholars, writers, poets, artists all the time, without realising it themselves, push the bourgeoisie into the grave. Specialisation in one field makes them ignoramuses in another. They chop through the branch on which they sit and do this with a light heart because they cannot see the whole tree. And it is hard for them to see the whole tree because bourgeois ideology, just like bourgeois economics, is anarchic: unlike Marxism and the feudal ideology of absolutism (everything being in the hands of God and the Tsar) all its parts are not clearly linked by any visible precise connection. Often, the right hand of the bourgeoisie does not know what the left is doing and in the end its poor head suffers from all this. Thus, for example, the "perniciousness" of Darwin's theory of the struggle for survival was perceived by the bourgeoisie only when this theory was implemented and transformed by Marx in his teaching on the class struggle. Similarly, when Galileo discovered that the earth revolves around the sun, the monks (the ideologues of absolutism) immediately got to the heart of the matter and straight away imprisoned him.

One can point to quite a few contradictions arising within bourgeois ideology.

Thus, Utopian Socialism, where it rejects the contemporary economic order, based on the exploitation of man by man, is, without any doubt, grist to the mill of the proletariat, whereas another section of its theory, which contains the recipe for the correction of human society, is based entirely on bourgeois ideology.

Russian Tolstoyanism can be viewed as part of the same category of social phenomena. And so can Nietzscheanism—the rebellion of the individual against the social chains which bind him (a contradiction within the framework of the bourgeois order which is insoluble, and which leads consciousness to a dead-end).

As regards bourgeois art, one finds even more ideological contradictions.

Elements of the decline of the bourgeoisie have long been blowing in the wind. They permeate even its science and its art, against the will of the bourgeoisie. But in order to catch them in such a dispersed state and give an accurate diagnosis of the patient's condition (that is, the bourgeois order in science and the everyday life of the bourgeoisie in art), one needs a universal intelligence, an emotion which is all-embracing.

The ideology of the new class which is marching to power is constructed by means of a synthesis of all the contradictions which stem from the ideology of the class which precedes it. This task (the synthesis) can, of course, only be tackled by people of great erudition, with a wide horizon, that is, the finest members of the intelligentsia, and not the first arrivals from the working class. In order to arrive at a negation of bourgeois ideology, to overcome it, one must first pass through it. This is so in science, as it is in art.

We see this happening in reality.

Marx and Lenin, the ideologists of the proletariat in the field of scientific thought, were intellectuals.

And the first pioneers in the field of artistic creativity were also intellectuals.

The Revolution in Language

The futurists, as I've already said, made the same revolution as we Bolsheviks, but made it from the other end.

The futurists became alienated from the old world through an emotional non-acceptance of its everyday life. And they began their revolution with a rebellion against this everyday life, with a total rejection of it, with merciless destruction. (They began by demolishing aesthetics. But everyday life and aesthetics are the same as a hut and its roof. When you demolish the roof, then you've already demolished the hut.) Everyday life in life as a whole is the same as language in art. Once the futurists had come to hate the old way of life, they also hated the old language. And it could not have been otherwise: the word is the image of everyday life: it often clings to it so strongly that you cannot tear it away. The word is formed by everyday life and everyday life is discovered through words. There are words and combinations of words which literally reek of everyday life, there are those which smell of it and those which have a faint odour of it, but the smell of everyday life is in almost every word we use (bearing in mind, of course, its usual, accepted application). Take such words as dreams—sadness—innocence—mysterious—dear—wedding— fiancé—fiancée—to court—noble—decent—enchanted—in love.

Don't they hit you with the powerful bouquet of the most authentic philistinism?

The futurists engaged in a war against the old, bedraggled word which stank of everyday life. They conducted a formal cleansing of "the great, free, mighty and beautiful Russian language", chucking onto the rubbish dump quite a bit of various verbal junk. But they did not restrict themselves to a simple sorting-out of words, the bricks of human speech. They got through to the clay as well—i.e., sound. And what the futurists did in this field can, without exaggeration, be called a phonetic revolution. This revolution places a distinct boundary between the old and new poetry, which can no longer be thought of without those rights and freedoms which have been gained by sound.

The futurists introduced the phonetic image into poetry.

What does this mean?

Until now, the phonetic image of the word was hidden from us by its semantic content. I repeat that the blame for this lies with the old poetry which never, or almost never, made any attempt to reveal the phonetic image. Of course, it is true that rhyme has long since existed in poetry but rhyme is only a part of the phonetic image, and it was used not at all to show up the phonetic heart of the word, it was a simple accent which ended the rhythmic wave. Its phonetic aspect counted for nothing. And so, before, such rhymes as the following were considered quite legitimate:

—vzoidyot/poyot
—kholmam/nebesam
—bodrit/lezhit
—voskhod/rastyot
—zemlyoy/tolpoy
—mestakh/rukakh, etc.

It is true that the symbolists, who preceded the futurists, also valued rhyme from its phonetic aspect and to a certain extent enriched it, but enriched it only quantitatively and not qualitatively. They were not able to break its numbed form, a form which was defined not by pronunciation, as we see in the futurists (e.g. golodnen'kimi/kolodnikami; raz by yeshchyo/pastbishcham), but by graphic form (e.g. per'yami/preddver'yami; mramore/za more), and they were unable to do this because they failed to notice the phonetic heart beyond the semantic heart of the word. (Certain symbolists did get quite close to the phonetic image. They even anticipated it in some of their poetry (Balmont's *Reeds* and others) but these anticipations seem accidental. The phonetic image for the symbolists was only a windfall. In the futurists, however, this windfall is transformed into a discovery: it demands the restructuring of the poetic line itself). The symbolists, like all their predecessors, saw in rhyme merely a phonetic accent. And all their work on rhyme only led to the strengthening of this accent.

We see the same thing in alliteration, which the symbolists also introduced into poetry.

But alliteration, like rhyme, was used by the symbolists, not to reveal the phonetic image, but as a phonetic accent.

"Chuzhdy chistym charam schast'ya" (Balmont).

Here the repeated use of "ch" at regular intervals is nothing but the tick of a metronome which marks off the sections of the rhythmic beat.

In this lifeless form, without the slightest reworking, alliteration was taken from the symbolists by some of our proletarian poets:

"Suchki sukhikh serdets ...
Sverkay, siyay, svetilo ..." (Gerasimov).

Gerasimov attaches the sound "s" just as easily to "dry twigs" (suchki sukhikh) as to "shining celestial body" (svetilo). As a result, as a sound it expresses nothing but a rhythmic accent.

But after all, what is a phonetic image?

It is the combination of the phonetic elements of the word, which act on our psyche quite separately from the semantic content of the word.

To convince ourselves that the phonetic image is not a mere invention, it is sufficient to remember how each new word acts on us the first time we hear it. In such cases, we usually, without thinking, define the word by its phonetic image: we say "what a beautiful word" or "how ugly" or "how funny" or "how vulgar" etc.

Wherein lies the secret of the impact of the phonetic image on our psyche?

Let us give the floor to the futurists themselves.

"The sound of a word, the phoneme, the specific phonetic construction illuminates a series of other words, phonemes, organically linked together by completely objective phonetic conditions. I term such a series a series of phonetic associations." (V. Kataev, from A. Kruchenykh: *A Displacement Theory for the Russian Language*.)

To put it more simply: one word, by phonetic combination, reminds us of a series of other words... And consequently, I would add, inevitably conjures up their corresponding semantic images.

The phonetic image is a reflection of the semantic image. We see exactly the same in music—the basic tone (the semantic meaning of a given word) and a series of overtones (the semantic images of words which arise in our minds by phonetic association). But good music results only when the overtones do not drown the basic tone. It is the same in poetry.

Examples of bad music:

"Pomnish"; tebe *osoblivo*
Nravilis' zuby moi."

"Osoblivo" (particularly) resembles "sonlivo" (sleepily). And so, in this instance, the phonetic image literally grates on our ears.

"O, krug truda, tvoyo kruzhen'ye
I tvoy vostorg i tvoy exstaz" (S. Malashkin).

Ex-stasy is a bit like ex-minister.

"My zvonkiye pesni zheleza i stali
Na plitakh skrizhaley naveki *vpisali*" (I. Ionov).

Here the phonetic image "pis" sharply contrasts with the semantic images, "sonorous songs, iron, steel, flagstones and law tables", and in such loud company sounds like a peep, if not worse.

An example of good music:

"I v tretiy, plesnuv, uplyvayet *zvonochek*
Sploshnym izvinen'yem: zhaleyu ne zdes". (Pasternak).

Here the semantic image (three bells) is reinforced and underpinned by three phonetic images—zvonochek—izvinen'yem—zdes'. You not only imagine, but actually hear the ringing as it dies down (zvono-chek—izvineniyem) and breaks off on the third stroke (zdes').

Another example:

"Mimo barov i ban'
Bey, baraban!
Baraban, baraban'.
Byli raby
Net raba
Baarbey
Baarban'
Baaraban ... " (Mayakovsky).

This is, again, alliteration, but alliteration which has reached the phonetic heart of the words. Here the phonetic image merges with the semantic: the repeated sound "b" is not a mechanical line beat but a really authentic drum roll. Moreover, we hear not only the beating of a drum but its echo, as it is reflected by the surrounding objects (barami (bars), banyami (bath-houses)). The bars and bath-houses are drawn into the picture by the phonetic image—and the drum is caught up in the frenzied, headlong gallop of sounds, and so strengthens the expressiveness of the basic semantic image to its ultimate.

Even from these few quotations it is clear that futurism enriched poetry by its discovery of the phonetic image. And poetic creativity is unthinkable without these new discoveries. Now we demand from it not only semantic expressiveness, but phonetic expressiveness as well. The soundless words of our classics and the nasal twang of the symbol-ists can no longer satisfy us. Moreover, this old poetry will soon seem to us the same amusing, childish prattle as the poetry of Tredyakovsky, Kantemir and Lomonosov. And, surely, this poetry appears amusing to us now mainly because of its wild, indigestible phonetic imagery:

"Elefanty, eleonty i lesnye sraki" (Tredyakovsky).

At this point one should mention a further peculiarity of the phonetic image: as the phonetic image does not depend on the meaning of the given word, so it frequently does not coincide with its graphic boundaries, and often is carried over beyond them. To put it more simply, the sounds of one word freely combine with those of neighbouring words and form with them independent phonetic images. These images live in the line quite separately, and sometimes leap out of it so strikingly that they completely eclipse the semantic significance.

Comrade Kruchenykh who first noticed this phenomenon termed it ''displacement''.

I will borrow a few examples from his book. ''Who can guess'', he asks, ''what the following mysterious line means?''

''Spletyakhu lu sosannoyu''.

This, in fact, is the dedication of the poet S. Rafalovich to Akhmatova and it is printed as follows:

''spletya khulu s osannoyu'', but reads as above. Do we have here some Church Slavonic verb or 'spletyaka' (a gossip): 'lu' (an abbreviation of 'lu-lu'?); 'sosanna' (is this a name or a derivative of 'sosat' (to suck)?).

Another example:

''*Uzruli* russkoy Terpsikhory
Nezrumy khranitel' *mogu chemodan* (moguchemy dan)
Vse te zhe *l'vy* inye devy?
Ot kaspiya *Danila* (do Nila)
Osla vo vsem otravu p'yushchim.
Ik mudromu startsu pod'yekhal Oleg.
Ishak tvoy zemlyu tyagotil''.

Such displacements were commonplace in the old, slightly deaf poetry. But can the new poetry survive with all these l'vami (lions), ishakami (donkeys) and chemodanami (suitcases)?

The futurists liberated the phonetic heart of the word which had been kept in chains by the old art. Why were neither the realists nor the symbolists able to do this? Well, because they themselves were slaves of the everyday life of the old world and, through it, slaves of the old word (that is, its semantic image). Take any symbolist, even the most ''revolutionary'', such as Bryusov, and you will without fail find in his work Eros, Hecate, altar, mystery, spells, beatitude, illumination, astrality, the calls of fate, and the blissful langour of humilitation etc.

Having begun a revolutionary purging of words by shaking out of them all this trash, the futurists could not help noticing that something remained from the completely cleansed word.

And this was the phonetic image which at this very moment, when the semantic image no longer stifled it, declared its right to live. And the futurists gave life to the phonetic image in poetry. They destroyed the old rhyme, constructed on the principle of graphic identity of word endings and constructed a new one—rhyme as a phonetic image. And by combining the phonetic and semantic images they achieved a kind of expressiveness and power of psychic impact in the line which you just don't find in all the poetry of the past.

People may reply that all these subtleties are no concern of the worker. Give him the content he needs, even if it is in an old form. But isn't this the same as saying: the worker doesn't need to know all the subtleties of Marxism, what need does he have of Marx and Lenin? Give him Bukharin instead. But aren't there workers who have already mastered *The A.B.C. of Communism*? And those who are given it today will master it tomorrow. They will say to you: give us something new which we don't know yet. Then you'll send them off to Marx and Lenin.

It's the same in poetry. Today the worker is satisfied by Dem'yan Bedny, the poetic equivalent of *The A.B.C. of Communism*. But tomorrow he will say: give me something new. But where will you send him—backwards or forwards: to Ostrovsky or Mayakovsky?

Comrade Lunacharsky has unwittingly created the slogan: "Back to Ostrovsky".

That means—back to the old word, and through it a road leads straight to the everyday life of old. Briefly, that is, back to capitalism.

It is time to understand that form and content are one, that the new content will inevitably be cramped in the old form, and that this old form has become for us a barrel organ on which you can play nothing but "Farewell".

Won't we ever give the worker the best music?

"No subtleties": a good slogan when you're talking of the struggle. But when culture is at issue, then we must say: long live subtlety of knowledge and of feeling!

One must know how to differentiate subtlety from ornateness, perversion and an individualistic psychic tendency. What I have said about the phonetic image is based on the objective laws of the construction of human speech and its perception. An art which is based on objective laws can be subtle, but cannot be perceived.

Word-formation on the Model of the Phonetic Image.

I will now pass on to the most extreme aspect of futurism which its struggle with the old word has taken so far, that is, the attempt by a few futurists to create a new language.

What has prompted this striving for a new language?

In his book *The Apocalypse in Russian Literature*, Kruchenykh says:

"Thought and speech do not succeed because they follow the experience of inspiration, and so the artist is free to express himself not only in the common language (concepts) but in his personal language (the creator is individual) and in a language which does not have a specific meaning (which is not frozen), in transrational language".

What is this personal language?

Kruchenykh elucidates:

"Words die, the world is eternally young. The artist has seen the world anew and, like Adam, gives it his names. The lily is beautiful but the word 'lily' is ugly, soiled and 'raped'. So I name the lily 'yeuy', and the primal purity is restored".

"Lily/yeuy"—at first glance this is merely amusing. But does this striving by the Futurists strike no chord in the psyche of the political communist?

Surely we communists are looking at the world anew and don't we have the desire to rechristen, give new names to everything that was despoiled by the odious political past? But, in fact, we have long been doing this: all civilian and military establishments and posts, certain towns, many streets, factories and villages have been rechristened. We have even rechristened ourselves (communists instead of Bolsheviks). We say, Red Army Member instead of soldier, artillery detachment instead of artillery crew, "spetz" instead of specialist, social-traitor instead of social-democrat, and many others. And in our everyday life we frequently come across simple renamings and neologisms: Maxim (an engine), limon, kerenka, kosay, bourgeouika (an iron stove), zakommisarilsa, general'stvovat', liberdanit', nepman, nepach and so on. The striving to rename and form new words is inevitable in a revolutionary age. It is inevitable, firstly because the revolutionary consciousness, in rejecting the old, obsolete and odious order, cannot come to terms with the old labels which remind it of this order; and, secondly, because the new order of life, the new relations between people and things cannot be accommodated in the old lexicon. The creation of life demands creation of the word. Here we see once more the close link between content and form.

Creation of the word is now taking place in actual life. How, then, could it not take place in poetry? And on principle, no communist should nor could object to the desire of the poet to liberate the eternally young world from words which have been despoiled at the hands of decrepit everyday life.

The revolutionary artist, like every other artist, is individual (that is, in creation he always expresses his own personal emotion), but he is not individualistic, that is, he always creates what the masses demand, what they need.

To create what the revolution demands is good, but to replace "lily" by "yeuy" is worse. Why is this? Is the principle at fault? No, the artist is to blame. Kruchenykh is a one-sided artist and a one-sided revolutionary. He is a wrecker in artistic terms. And this means he is no longer a futurist: he is a former futurist.

Futurism is dynamic. Anarchistic rebellion is only the first stage, which it passed through long ago. Kruchenykh is static: he has not shifted an iota since 1913.

In the course of these ten years a huge gulf has appeared between Kruchenykh, who has all the time rebelled from exactly the same position, and Mayakovsky, who has gone forward by gigantic strides, together with the revolution. I think that they'll soon lose complete sight of each other, unless we see a displacement on the part of the theorist of displacements, from "the phonetic image of the revolution" towards the meaning of this image. (In the first two numbers of *LEF*, some of Kruchenykh's verse has been published: *Rur* and *On the first of May*. It looks as if this "displacement" has already begun). Kruchenykh is a wrecker in the field of art. He also wishes to build but only by first leaving not a single stone standing from the old world. But a revolution is not made in such a bear-like fashion. It destroys only those forms of the old order which cannot be adapted to the new order. This is true in economics, so too in politics, and the same in science and art. Revolution does not kill the old language, but restructures, purges and renews it.

By calling "lily" "yeuy" Kruchenykh shatters the organic wholeness of language, he kills language itself as a factor of the social order. In the name of social rebellion he performs an anti-social act: he is a poor revolutionary.

It is exactly the same with transrational language. Transrational language is one which has no specific meaning, a language based on the phonetic image rather than on semantic content. But the phonetic image, as I've already said, is nothing other than a reflection of the semantic image. A striking, fully realised image is replaced by one that is unspecified, vague and half-realised. As a general rule, the emotional effect of such an image is much weaker than that of a direct semantic image. And although Kruchenykh tries to assure us that, in terms of expressiveness, normal language is one thousand times weaker than transrational language, his transrational poetry convinces us of precisely the opposite. It is true that there are instances when a pure phonetic image (some unfamiliar word or name heard for the first time) evokes in us a powerful and profound emotion. But this only happens when we ourselves conceive of a sharp, precise semantic content beyond the phonetic image which is not clearly understood by us. In such moments we become creative artists. How does this come about? In most cases, the semantic image is attached to the given phonetic combination by way of association: the unfamiliar words phonetically remind us of a series of other, familiar words. At the same time, the collision of these words in our minds offers an accidental, sometimes highly complex and subtle harmony, which merges into a living, striking and new image, which is consequently highly charged with emotion. Thus, I remember, I was once deeply stirred by the name of a town in Palestine which I had come across for the first time—Kyriafiarim. I had a clear picture of sand bathed in sunlight, of a woman's name which someone had spoken, the image of a woman, even the glint of the sun and the rustle of yellow, definitely yellow, silk.

Reducing the word "kyriafiarim" to phonetic images we get a whole harmonic series: Kyria (Kyrie Eleison—Syria) Kyr-ria (reminiscent of the name Mariam or Maria) fia-rim (again a feminine image—fia, combining with one of sunlight—Rim (Rome)).

But the substitution of the semantic image for the phonetic can have another origin: not through external, but internal association, not as a result of memories of other words, but as the last link in a chain of harmonious emotions.

In his story *The Peasants* Chekhov tells of the magical effect which the reading of the Gospel word "dondezhe" (until) had on the simple peasant heart. It's possible that some phonetic association was involved here too, but that is not the main point. It is well known that from the very first words of the gospel reading the simple believing soul is raised to a higher level, unusual images awake in his consciousness, which come not from this world and which, when linked to one another, and to the images which are dimly perceived during the reading, gain in intensity, like waves during a flood. One may term what results a gradual accumulation of creative energy. This energy seeks an outlet and, at last, encountering the first transrational word which occurs, such as "dondezhe", is released within the believer and fills him with its content. The word "dondezhe" takes on a specific semantic colouring and when the passage is read again, its impact is no longer arbitrary but returns to the listener as though part of the emotional charge which has been expended.

And so we see that transrational language, viewed as a pure language of sounds, as speech liberated from any semantic meaning, has in poetry zero significance, or at least, an infinitesimally small importance. In fact, transrational language is the same as semantic language. The only thing is that transrational language approaches the image not in a direct way, but indirectly. Transrational language is a semantic echo, a reflection of other words. But the echo is only audible when it is distinct. And transrational language affects us more powerfully when the semantic image is more vividly reflected. Transrational language does not destroy semantic language, it only extends its boundaries. The phonetic image does not oust the semantic image from poetry, but, by uniting with the latter and assisting it, gives together with it the maximum emotional expression. So any attempt to eliminate meaning from poetry for the sake of sound's hegemony is doomed to failure. To replace the poetry of words by a verbal echo not only weakens its impact, but also disorganises it. The poet who undertakes this task ceases to be a poet (if one does not take into account infinitesimally small units). But Kruchenykh undertook precisely this task. He wished to kill meaning in poetry, but only killed himself as a poet.

As one element, transrational language is of great value in poetry: as a phonetic image, acting in conjunction with the semantic, it has already been introduced into poetry and has gained a strong place. Transrational language will find (and is already finding) application not only in the choice of words for their phonetic image but in the restructuring of the words themselves. But ... there's no need to break open your own head, even with such a revolutionary weapon as a universal world language; there's no need to arm sound against sense. Otherwise poetry will become an empty sound.

The old language is no longer suitable for us. It is like a large house in which there are very few rooms. We need a lot more rooms and the purpose of many of them will be different; we do not need drawing-rooms, billiard-rooms, servants' quarters etc.: we need work rooms, libraries. Yes, we will reconstruct the house, but not in a bear-like fashion. The foundations and the external walls will do us, and even inside there will be a lot we won't need to break up. Let us break things up sensibly.

Word Formation on the Model of Sense and Sound.

The reconstruction of language is a task which Russian futurism has opportunely suggested. This is its revolutionary merit.

In poetry, the revolution, as content, also determines the revolution in form, that is, the words. The revolution as word, just like the revolution as deed, proceeds along two basic lines: the destruction of old, obsolete forms and the creation of new ones which correspond to the new content which is flooding into life. Every revolution is at one and the same time both destruction and creation, but creation more than destruction. The new life created by the revolution will, without doubt, be more organised, and therefore more complex, more multifaceted in its concrete (economic) forms than the old life. It is clear that it will also develop into a more complex and multifaceted organisation in its ideological forms. The language created by revolution should be wider, fuller, richer, more subtle than the old language. And so, by no means the last place should be accorded to new word formations and new words in the creation of the new language. But we do not conceive of this creation except on the organic base of the old language: words should be born of other words—only then will they be living words. A word that is invented is a still-born word.

The revolution has posed the following tasks for the poet, the creator of the word:

1 To remove from poetry the old verbal rubbish and consign it to the museum of history (i.e. all those Eros's, Hecates, Alcmenes, charms, scales, enchantments, prayers, mysteries etc.)—briefly, to smash utterly the verbal bourgeoisie and, at the same time, to do so without any New Economic Policies,[3] of which there can be none in ideology.

2 All words which have been stained by a more or less prolonged complicity with the bourgeoisie and which have the odour of its life should be rinsed and ventilated in the air of revolution: in other words, they should be given a new, revolutionary application.

3 To create new words parallel to the new life that is being created.

And we see all these three tasks being fulfilled in the work of Mayakovsky, who began to create a poetic revolution even before the political one.

Compare his lexicon with that of any of his predecessors and, even at the most superficial glance, you cannot miss the fact that what he has done could not have been achieved without a thorough-going revolutionary purging.

To say nothing of such rubbish as vials, charms and Alcmenes, but even such generally used words as *charmed, mysterious, delightful, blessed, captivating* etc., which came up literally every ten lines in the old poetry—hardly any of this will be found on a single page of "The Complete Works of Mayakovsky". Words which are rooted in everyday philistine life, words which are themselves hereditary and respectable philistines, are in even more disgrace than the bourgeois and landowning words. He uses the last words quite frequently in his poetry, but how he uses them! He places them in the sort of setting which is literally a concentration camp. He uses a word so as to pour scorn on its meaning. He resurrects the old form to make more certain of killing the old content. So, for example:

> "*Let us pray to the Lord God*".

And further

> "*God made of meat*"
> "*God made Man*"
> "*God* runs with my poetry under his oxter ... *Jesus*, raising his crown of thorns, bows amiably. *Guardian Angel* is the tenant in riding-breeches. I ask for your body, as Christians ask '*give us this day our daily bread*' ... Bullying *Tsars* stroll, watched by nannies ... *It is easier for a camel to pass through the eye of a needle* than for such an element to come to me. *In your name* we fight so as to stand on our hind-legs in thunder and smoke ... Let us turn the wheel of *inspiration* ... The town there stands on one electro-dynamo-mechanical screw.
>
> "You then, begin to make *miracles* ... Is not the weathervane purified by *God*? Wilson's drawers are not drawers, but a *sonnet*. The favourites of the *muses* and fame, burdened by baskets, go to the market ..."

Here we constantly see one and the same thing: the divine, the regal, the magnificent are brought down to earth and are presented in such a pointed, usually comic contrast with their usual representations that absolutely nothing remains of the divine, the regal and the magnificent.

But Mayakovsky is not just tossing out words. Holding the verbal bourgeoisie under a red guard and not admitting the hereditary philistines with their scent of geraniums, eau-de-cologne and cats, he makes full use of the remaining verbal fraternity. Mayakovsky frequently finds an excellent application even for empty, average words, words which have been trivialised and soiled by too frequent usage. He does so by presenting them in new, unexpected combinations, and reveals in them a new emotional richness which, as it were, has remained hidden from us until now.

For example:

> "Your son is *wonderfully* ill ... I was spinning like a *poetic* squirrel ... The ocean is offensively *big* ... Work flowers in the hand like a *rose* ... The *roses* of the capitals with the petals of the squares ... *The day arises* ... Suddenly the storm clouds and the other clouds raised in the sky an *unbelievable* rolling ... And in the sky a *sunset*, as *red* as the Marseillaise, trembled as it died ... "

Let us now go on to word formation. Mayakovsky never makes up words. His words multiply by a process of germination. They grow like branches on the tree of language. Because of this, Mayakovsky's language, for all its novelty and external esotericism, is social from first to last. There is no trace in him of individualism. This is the authentic language of the revolution.

Mayakovsky's devices for word formation can be reduced to the following general principles:

1 Abbreviations.
2 A change in their endings.
3 The use of new prefixes.
4 Transformation of a verb into a noun, a noun into a verb, and adverb or adjective into a noun etc.
5 The merging of two words into one.
6 The use of a word in the plural instead of the singular, and vice versa.

Here is a series of new verbs, formed with the prefix 'vy-' (out of):

Vyshchetinilis', vymolodi, vyznakom', vygromil, vykosilas',

vymechtal, vytomlen, vymozhzhu, vymchi, vyzaryu, vyzhuyut, vyshchemil, vylaskat', vyzhiret', vydivit', vyvertelsya, vyfrantil, vyzlit', vyvostriv, vykaymil, vylyubil, etc.

If you compare these new forms with those in common use: oshchetinilis', omolodi, oznakom', razgromil, pokosilas', mechtal, istomlen, razmozhzhu, pomchi, ozaryu, razzhuyut, prishchemil, oblaskat', razzhiret', or ozhiret', udivit', razozlit', navostriv, okaymil etc., then the latter forms seem cachectic and enfeebled. But, quite apart from the shift in energy occasioned by the new formations, in most cases, they also change the meaning of the words. The prefix 'vy' indicates a process that has reached its limits, has been completed and exhausted. The words formed with this prefix by Mayakovsky clearly indicate: the end has been realised, nothing remains.

Moreover, because of the prefix, several of the words take on a specific social coloration. Thus, for example, "vyzhuyut, vyshchemil, vyzhiret', vyvertelsya, vyfrantil, vylyubil"—these are none other than clear labels affixed by the poet to things and phenomena from a social order to which he feels hostile.

> "But I have no time for pink flesh which has been *chewed out* (*vyzhuyut*) for centuries". ("Backbone—Flute").
>
> "I go, in the dawn of shining eyes, towards all those who have *ground out* (*vyshchemil*) their teeth with malice". ("War and Universe").
>
> "Your thought, dreaming on a softened brain, like a *fattened-out* (*vyzhirevshy*) lackey on a soiled couch". ("A Cloud in Trousers").
>
> "And now a stomach has *spread out* (*vyvalilsa*) onto the stage, shaken by the fire of the orchestra".
>
> "Suddenly the flashing navel stopped, and was *spinning out* (*vyvertelsa*) like a top". ("War and Universe").
>
> "The fattened earth, like a mistress which Rothschild has *loved out* (*vylyubil*)".

Here are some instances of abbreviation: chelovechiy, zveriy, zaplesnevshiy, stisn' (instead of stisni), vskhlip (instead of vskhlipyvaniye), bukh pushki (instead of bykhan'ye), gud (instead of guden' ye), znamenosets, besshabash'ye, zhdan'ye.

If we compare these words with the usual forms: "chelovech-esk-iy, zver-in-iy, zaples-ne-vev-shiy, stisn-i, bukhan'ye, gud-eniye, znameno-nosets, besshabash-nost', ozhidani-ye", then we see that everything superfluous has been abandoned, everything that dilutes the word has gone. The word, reduced in this way, produces a condensed image, which in certain cases is transformed into a short blow (bukh, stisn').

By abbreviating the words, Mayakovsky gives the illusion of a blow delivered from a short distance, the illusion of a sudden deafening by means of a sound:

> "Chto ni zvuk—*bukh* pushki"
> "Sekunda eta stala nachalom neveroyatnogo *guda*".

And the artist's sensitivity does not betray him when immediately afterwards he says:

> "Ves' sever gudel,
> Gudeniya malo …"

A humming ("*gudel*") in the north—that is definitely somewhere very far away. And so here, the old elongated form ("*gudeniya*" instead of "*gud*") is more suitable.

In contrast to the shortened adjectives, such as chelovechiy and zveriy, we sometimes find in Mayakovsky elongated forms, such as tramvayskiy ("Yazyk tramvayskiy vy ponimayete"). The sense of this elongation is clear: since he is dealing with a talking tram then this form "tramvayskiy", whose ending brings it close to "chelovechesky" (human), could not be more appropriate.

Perhaps myopic critics will reproach Mayakovsky with mysticism because of this tram language. But placing Mayakovsky and mysticism together is the same as accusing Poincaré of communism. There is no mysticism whatsoever here, but rather Mayakovsky makes aesthetic a thing which was inacccessible or almost inaccessible to the old poets and to the generation which was raised on them, which knew only the aesthetic of nature (willows and meadows, roses and reveries).

In exactly the same way, Mayakovsky replaces the short word "bol'" (pain by the elongated form "boleniye" when no strong accent is required, but, on the contrary, he needs to emphasise the duration of the process: "v lyubovnom bolenie" ("in the pain of love").

Instead of the word "dal'" (distance), we find in Mayakovsky "dalekost'". Here again, elongation of the word changes its significance. "Dalekost'" fills the lacuna which has always existed in Russian when distance is indicated. "Dal'" is too far away, "otdaleniye" ("a certain distance") is too near, while Mayakovsky's "dalekost'" is between the two.

Mayakovsky says: "slezovaya tech'" ("a flood of tears"). Try to combine "tech'" with the usual sleznaya and you'll get something like the mixture of oil and water. He also has "likhoradyus" instead of the generally used "menya likhoradit". And here, as always, his method of word formation fully corresponds to the spirit of the language: the new word is formed by analogy with already existing formations: "muchit—muchayus'", so "likhoradit—likhoradyus'".

We also find a whole series of words which are vulgarised by their ending: gost'ye, dam'ye, dver'ye, (by analogy with familiar forms, kham'ye, muzhich'ye). Others are kvartiroshniy, bozhishche, bozhik, krylastiye, kul-turishka, zagrab', lyubovishki, lyubyata, and so on. Here the revolutionary, even class approach to the word is so obvious that any elucidation is superfluous.

In conclusion, I will quote some further examples which speak for themselves:

"Yele rasstalis', *razvidelis'* yele ... Tsely ostrov *rastsvetochen-nogo* kovra ... Kto dnam velel *iyulit'sa* ... *Vysaryu* v moyu poslednyuyu lyubov' ... Pevnost' metny v lozhi *mrushchim* glazom byka ... Strashnoye slovo na golovu *lav'* ... Voron'em *okarkan* ... Ulitsy rvushchiysa *vymakh* ..." and many more.

We have before us a genuinely revolutionary method of word formation.

The Revolution of Syntax

We find exactly the same processes in the field of word combination. Mayakovsky has not the least respect for the age-old, well established rules of syntax: without hesitation he breaks the old forms if he feels confined within them. He is sickened, as he is sickened by anything which has a whiff of the bourgeois spirit, by the generally accepted literary, salon language, with all its i's dotted, with all its copulae, prepositions and so on—this language which is sleeked down, punctilious and, in repose, "like the pulse of the deceased".

The revolutionary psyche of the poet cannot endure empty words— those idle verbal menials who throng the hall-way simply to take the fur-coats of the arriving guests. Mayakovsky does not need verbal parasites. He takes every word and sets it to work. That same scientific organisation of labour of which we are only beginning to talk, has already been realised in his work.

Mayakovsky's language is not the language of the salon or the bourgeois sitting-room, but that of the revolutionary street: it is daring, alive, energetic, accurate, condensed and trenchant. The street does not like long, smooth, sleek phrases. It does not need a word which resembles a sleepy rocking-chair. It needs a word which is like a punch.

The street says:
"E-ka nevidal'!" (Well, I never!)—no predicate.
"Idu i vizhu ... " (Go and see ...)—no subject.
"Nashe—vam ... " (Ours to you ...)—no subject.
"Chorta li v ney!" (The devil!)—no predicate or adjective.
"Skazal, tozhe!" (Said also!)—no object.
"Stupay, stupay!" (Go, go!)—no adverb of place—and so on.

We can observe exactly the same at a factory, during construction or any form of work. Here language is particularly laconic: not one unnecessary word.

Poetry for Mayakovsky is not an amusement, but work. For this reason, his language too is laconic. Without hesitation, he shortens sentences and restructures words, even if in the process he is obliged to comb not the hair, but the ears of the Russian language.

"Nel'zya sapozhishcha!" (No boots!)—no predicate.
"Rastopchu, chtob—bol'shaya" (I'll crush, so that—big)—no predicate.
"Starayetsa mimo" ("Tries past")—no object.
"Veselilis', tantsami mchas'" ("They enjoyed themselves, dashing by dances")—instead of "mchas' v tantse"—"dashing in dance".
"Oknu lechu" ("(To) the window I will fly")—the preposition 'k' (to) is omitted.

In the last instance, quite apart from the laconicism demanded by the sense (headlong movement), by omitting the preposition Mayakovsky avoids an extremely unpleasant phonetic displacement: koknu.

But is this going over the top? Perhaps all this is excessively revolutionary? Perhaps we are extending the Russian revolution too far when we take it into such a neutral area as Russian grammar, which would seem to have no point of contact with politics?

But this is only the way it seems.

I have already shown that the words of human speech can be divided into two armies: the old and the red. What is grammer after all? The regulations of the old army of words. Can these regulations be applied to the Red Army without any reworking?

The bourgeoisie considered its order to be eternal. After it had exhausted all its economic possibilities over the centuries, it became ideologically petrified. And, naturally, at the same time, it became formally petrified. To move onwards meant to move onwards to socialism.

To stop action one must stop consciousness, but to stop consciousness one must place a bridle on the external form of consciousness—the word.

Grammar in recent times was such a bridle.

Human language was able to develop precisely because, at first, it did not know the dictatorship of grammar. Grammar should serve the word, and not vice versa. But what happened to the human collective also happened to the verbal collective. The leaders who, to begin with, served the collective, took power in their own hands and forced it to serve them. The word, like man, found itself bound hand and foot.

Futurism has emancipated the word by casting off the absolute power of grammar. It has destroyed the petrified form of the word which had bound thought. It has refashioned the old "military regulations" in a revolutionary manner. The red army of words is now free of the discipline of the rod, and in the person of Mayakovsky has found its first revolutionary leader.

The Rhythm of the Revolution

Alongside the phonetic and verbal revolutions, Mayakovsky has also carried through a revolution of rhythm, that is, of the music of word and sound. His rhythm is what is most incomprehensible and intolerable for bourgeois and philistine readers. No regularity or measure. At each step unexpected jolts and interruptions. But, surely—this in the very heart of revolution! How is one to accommodate its immense soul, its mighty dynamism, its elemental upsurges, its frantic and changing tempi, its zig-zags of lighting in the tiny, quietly rocking cradle of the old rhythm? How is one to hail a world-wide rebellion with the same cadences which were used to hail the "whispering, the gentle breathing and warble of the nightingale"? Only old songs sound good in the old rhythms. Even the most nimble of them—the trotting iamb—sounds funny now, like Esenin's foal which tries to outstrip the steel horse.

In Mayakovsky's most recent piece *About This*, there is the fine image—the marching of the line. His line began to march in gigantic steps even before the revolution, and so it now steps at its pace, at one tempo with it, one rhythm:

"Budilas' prizyvom
iz lesov
sprosonok
Lezla sila sverey i zveryat,
Vizzhal pridavlenniy slonom porosyonok,
Shchenki vystraivalis' v shchenyachiy ryad".
(*It awoke, to the call
From the forests
half-asleep
The strength of beasts and their offspring climbed,
The piglet, crushed by the elephant, squealed,
The puppies arrayed themselves in ranks.*)

What measure could one use for this restless, broken rhythm, this mounting wave of sounds which bursts forth at the end in a short, powerful blow?

You will find nothing like this in old textbooks on literature. And the poet has not rummaged among these textbooks: he found this rhythm in the rhythm of our life.

"Svoyo zhivotnoye gore kin'te im!
Dosyta nayest'sa khot' raz by yeshcho!
K chrevatym sazhennymi travami Indiyam,
K amerikanskim idemte pastbishcham!..."
(*Throw them your animal grief!
To eat one's fill just one more time!
Let us go to the fraught Indies, sewn with grasses,
To the American pastures!...*)

And this scream of hunger which seems to be fired out in the words—kin'te im, raz by yeshcho—would surely be perverted into a false, tedious moan if we tried to squeeze it into the smooth, measured strophes, according to all the rules of the old nursery and salon poetry.

"Skore-ye-ye-ye-ye-ye-ye-ye!
Skorey, skorey.
Ey

Gubernii
snimaytes' s yakorey!''
(*More qui-i-i-i-i-i-i-ckly!*
More quickly, more quickly.
Hey
Provinces
Anchors away!)

How could one possibly think here about regular music of the
line? The poetry of the revolution knows but one correct rhythm,
and this is the rhythm which organises the strike-forces of the
revolution:

"Mimo barov i ban'
Bey baraban!
Baraban, baraban!
Byli raby
net raba"
(*Past bars and bath-houses*
Beat the drum!
The drum, the drum!
There were slaves
There is no slave).

The rhythm of the poet of the revolution is his heart beating in
unison with it.

What is characteristic of Mayakovsky is his sensitivity to the sounds
of life. For this reason he is incapable of talking falsely about it,
incapable of talking through his nose about the revolution with the
motif "Lord, have mercy" as the Bryusovs, Gorodetskys and thousands of others do.

One should also point out the close link between the revolution in
rhythm and the phonetic revolution. The new rhythm—the phonetic
image of the revolution—is organically fused with the new rhyme—
the phonetic images of the revolutionary word. And indeed, take such
rhymes as:

asfal'tom/pospali tam,
prozhektory/na nozhe kotoriy,
seyat'be/Odisseya tebe etc.

and it will become clear that the old, even, smooth and fluent rhythms
are completely useless here.

The Destruction of The Old Aesthetic

I now move on to ideology.

Even when I was elucidating the essence of futurism and the formal side of its poetry I had to touch on many aspects of its ideology, if only in general terms. I defined the ideological essence of futurism as a rebellion against the everyday life of the old regime. Now, with a concrete instance, that is, the poetry of Mayakovsky, I wish to show how this rebellion becomes a revolution.

Three stages can be clearly seen in the process of Mayakovsky's creativity: rejection of the taste of the old world—rejection of its everyday life—rejection of the old order as such.

I have already said and once more emphasise that we political communists are moving in exactly the opposite direction: we began with a rejection of the old order, we're only now beginning to talk of everyday life, and we will reach taste only when we cease to rummage through the old aesthetic trash and go to take lessons from the futurists.

What, then, is taste? It is what we usually call aesthetics (in the narrow sense of this word), in other words, that which defines our image of beauty. The proletariat is the economic antipodes of the bourgeoisie (i.e. an individualistic versus a collective economy). Ideologically, too, it is its opposite. But what is aesthetics? A part of ideology. The great fissure which has split the world in two must also produce a split in aesthetics. The proletariat cannot have the same aesthetic perception of the world that the bourgeoisie had.

Let us turn to Mayakovsky's aesthetics.

> "People are scared—out of my mouth
> A badly chewed cry shakes its legs".

Mayakovsky's very first poems were a cry which the old literature was unable to chew properly. It was clear that entering the gates of literature was someone alien, large and coarse, who had not the slightest respect either for its contemporary idols or for its relics and remains: he came and began to throw out all these "holies" as unnecessary rubbish:

> "The sheets of the waters were under the *belly* ... The street collapsed, like the nose of a *syphilitic* ... The river is like voluptuousness which spreads out into *saliva* ... Having cast away the linen to the last leaf, the gardens *obscenely* fell into ruins in

June ... And the *drooping lips* thrust stone dummies into the skies ... Some sort of *dirty scoundrel* looked down from the sky, like Lev Tolstoy ... I will sew for myself some black *breeches* ... And beyond the sins of the streets, somewhere, a flabby moon that no-one needed was *hobbling* ... Let us throw the feathers of the *fading angels* on to the hats of our loved ones ... '' etc. etc.

"Belly, syphilitic, saliva, obscenely, dirty scoundrel, angels fade, the moon hobbles—this isn't poetry, but bombs, this is a shock to every aesthetic fundamental!''—such were the wails with which bourgeois criticism greeted Mayakovsky. And quite correctly: his poetry was indeed a shock to the fundamentals of the old aesthetics.

But all the same, this belly, saliva and breeches, what are they for? Could he not have shaken the fundamentals without them?

Mayakovsky's coarse, cynical word was a blow against bourgeois aesthetics.

The bourgeoisie, as the ruling class, created its own aesthetics, its own "ideal" of beauty, which corresponded completely to its shop-keeper mentality. Its essence lay in the slogan: "show something to good advantage" or to put it more simply "not beauty, but prettiness". The Greeks admired the naked Venus de Milo. This won't do: if one undresses Vanderbilt's daughter, then she won't be any different from a farmer's or worker's daughter. And so, down with naked beauty, long live half-naked beauty! The delicate soul of the bourgeois aesthete cannot abide naked reality, he needs tinted reality. Art for him is a buffer between life and his soul.

"We do not need powerful jolts, we do not need the cruel truth, or coarse, truthful words. Rather give us illusion, fairy-tales, give us 'the deception which elevates us' ", this is what the bourgeoisie demanded of its poets. And the poets gave satisfaction in the best possible form:

"I have captured the fleeting shadows in my reverie
The fleeting shadows of the extinguished day,
I ascended to the tower and the steps trembled
And the steps trembled beneath my foot".

Or:

"I have a twelve-storey palace,
I have a princess on every floor ... "

Princess, palace, tower, reverie, shadows, steps—such is the lexicon of the old poetry. And it is understandable that when, amid this decorous and euphorious verbal aristocracy, there appeared the rough, coarse, plebeian words—*belly*, *saliva*, *breeches* and *spittle*—it was like some devastating pogrom.

Indeed, it was a pogrom, but a revolutionary pogrom. It was a formal cleansing of the Augean stables of poetry.

Down with the verbal aristocracy! In the new society of words, just as in the new society of men, everyone has his right to freedom, as long as he is not a counter-revolutionary, not a criminal nor a parasite. And the poet, as the herald of the new society, prefers belly and saliva to princesses and reveries as the former are useful objects, while the latter have long since merely idled their lives away.

Mayakovsky turns God into a caricature and declares war on all mysticism: "Let us throw the feathers of the fading angels on to the hats of our loved ones...".

At the same time he uncrowns nature as well: the river becomes saliva, night is obscene, the sky has drooping lips, some sort of dirty scoundrel looks down from it, the earth has become like an old woman, the moon hobbles, and so on.

What has nature done to Mayakovsky? It has done nothing, but the poets had made of it the new idol, they had placed it on a throne in place of the decrepit and doddery Lord God. The inoffensive word, nature, did not deceive the poet of the revolution. His keen sensitivity showed him that there, beyond the deserted clouds, a new religious mystery was beginning, with its incense, worship and all the other attributes of slavish boot-licking. For bourgeois ideologues (philosophers and poets), nature was the last entrenchment into which they attempted to drive mysticism as it retreated before materialism. God, as the creator of the world, as the being who stood over nature, had already lost all credibility. And, to re-establish his tottering patrimony, they decided to join him in marriage with a rich fiancée. God became nature, and nature became God. Such is the entire essence of philosophical idealism. Its aim was to rejuvenate God and to put him back in circulation, under a new identity (God is the Idea for Hegel, the Will for Schopenhauer and Love for Tolstoy, and so on).

The same thing happened in poetry. Incense had been burned before God, and now they started burning it before the cosmos. They grovelled before psalms and hymns and now it was the turn of sonnets and triolets. Balmont sang hymns to fire, water, the moon and all the elements. Bryusov lit wax candles and played the part of the priest at the sex act, Sologub told fortunes by the stars, while Andreev cursed the town with the oath of a wild beast, and so on. Nature, which is so simple, guileless and in no way terrifying, if one approaches it with a sober, materialistic mind, was first clouded by all these "prophetic charms", and then transformed into something mysterious, into a force "equal to God in magnitude". When the poet begins to talk of nature he inevitably gets on his poetic stilts: each epithet is like a word from a prayer and each artistic image icon-like.

Inevitably, night is *sovereign*. Stars twinkle *mysteriously*. The sky is a silver *chasuble*. And the poet himself has come into this world exclusively to see the sun and the mountain summits.

The old poets were unable to talk of nature in any other way. But even in contemporary poetry we constantly hear the same servile, prayer-like notes:

> "The moon is in the abyss of the world
> It is the *wizard* of familiar fields,
> A real *prince*.
> It is the master of all heights."   (Oreshin).

> "Oh, why *am I singled out by you*.
> Boundless, snowy heights."   (Aleksandrovsky).

> "The world breathes the breath of peace,
> The world *has come to rest* in sunlit radiance."   (Panovsky).

> "My soul takes wing in dumb *supplication*
> Beneath the quiet flame of starry tears,
> While my heart, like a migratory bird,
> Strives to the polar azure".   (Gerasimov).

> "I love the arrival of *regal* spring"   (Nechayev).

Nature is not at all terrifying for the new man who is coming into the world, for the proletarian materialist. For him, in essence, there is no difference at all between the forests and skies on the one hand, and the factories and machines which he has created with his own hands, on the other. The immense magnitude of all these skies, seas and lands do not frighten him. What is terrible in the fact the sea is large? Fedora is large, but stupid, while he is small but intelligent. Just because something is large, that does not at all mean that it is magnificent. And if one is going to talk of the magnificent then he, the little man, is, if you like, much more magnificent than the large sea. Has he not subdued it, explored its depths, has he not overcome the immense extent of the land with his trains, telephones and telegraphs, has he not colonised the sky itself? So why should he seek miracles in some kind of "cloudy jelly" and in the "sleek mirror of the water" when he, man, is the greatest and finest miracle in the world? How ridiculous it all is!

> "Go round both sides,
> On each be amazed by the five rays.
> It is called 'Hands'.
> A pair of fine hands!
> Note: I can move from right to left
> And from left to right.
> Note:
> I can choose the best neck
> And wind myself around ...
> Open up the box of the skull—
> The most precious mind will flash.
> Is there
> Anything I could not be! ... "

Elsewhere in Mayakovsky this re-evaluation of the great and small is expressed even more acutely:

> "Oh, if only I were as quiet as thunder ...
> Oh, if only I were as dim as the sun ...
> If only I could be as inarticulate as Dante or Petrarch.
> Oh, if only I were as poor as a multi-millionaire ... ".

Alongside the aesthetic re-evaluation we also see here a social re-evaluation (poor as a multi-millionaire) but of that, more later.

The new man looks at nature not from below upwards, but vice versa. He has no cause to quarrel with it, just as he has no reason to quarrel with the walls of his factory. But he needs to uncrown it, to tear from it, and roughly, all these regal mantles and holy chasubles, in which it was dressed by the old clergy, the poets and ideologues of the bourgeoisie. Mayakovsky does precisely this. He drags nature from its divine throne, he pokes stone dummies into the drooping lips of the sky, he smokes out of the "cloudy jelly" all the armies of mysticism that have dug in there, right to the last soldier.

In the new poetry, the poetry of the proletariat, which is reconstructing the world and turning nature into its factory, a much more modest place will be allotted to the aesthetic of nature, to the admiration of what it has created, to its image which has not been formed by human hand. What though, will replace all this in the new aesthetic? That which man has created: the town, the house, the factory, the machine and, in general, the thing. And this is fully comprehensible: after all, it is already the case that the life of man in the contemporary town is 90 per cent concerned with things and only 10 per cent with natural phenomena.

The aesthetic of the town, of the thing, as the weapon of man's power and authority over nature was exalted (as I have already said) even by the Italian futurists. But in their work there was only the programme for an aesthetic revolution. In Mayakovsky this revolution is brought to life. In the course of this, Mayakovsky, as an authentic revolutionary builder, did not stop at the uncrowning of nature, at the tearing away of its mystical garb (the mantles and chasubles), just as we communists did not stop at the tearing away of epaulettes and decorations in the construction of the army. Having removed the mystical aureole from nature, he uses it as a simple, down-to-earth subject, just as we make use of all the former "thunderers" who have lost their thunder and lightning along with their epaulettes, decorations and trouser-stripes.

Mayakovsky has not destroyed the aesthetic of nature but simply brought it closer to man, making it one with the aesthetic of the thing.

In aesthetic terms, the old poets grovelled before nature and despised the thing. Their aesthetic was like a three-barrelled gun: 1) nature, 2) man, 3) the thing.

Mayakovsky has no three-barrelled aesthetic: his aesthetic is one: man —the thing—nature. In this system all three do not have equal distinction, but their respective values are quantitative not qualitative. Man, as a part of the aesthetic, stands in first place because he has the greatest value as part of the world. The thing pushes nature to the background because, in the life of man, it has been materially placed in this position.

The aesthetic of the town, the aesthetic of the thing emerges clearly even in Mayakovsky's earliest work:

> "The crowd, a multi-coloured swift cat,
> Flowed and twisted, drawn through the doors...
> While the burning yellow cards rang
> Against the black palms of the flashing windows... "
> "The boats in the cradles of the entrances
> Pressed against the nipples of the iron mothers.
> The earrings of the anchors burned
> In the ears of the deaf steamers".
> "The trams, wearied by their march,
> Crossed glinting spears... "

"Little girls carry past tiny noises,
A freight-carrier will carry through crates of din,
A trotter will rustle in the tunic of the retina
A tram will spill peals of thunder..."
"We climb the earth under the eyelashes of descended palms
To catch the smiles of the dreadnoughts
On the shrivelled lips of the canals".
"The road—the horn of hell—intoxicate the snores of the
                                       freight-carriers".

In one of his poems the poet hurls the slogan:

"Read iron books!" (i.e. signs).

In another he reads a whole lesson from the new aesthetic, ending
with the question:

"And could you
Play a nocturne
On the flute
Of the drain-pipes?"

In these early poems Mayakovsky is still defaming nature: he cannot
forgive it its recent union with God:

"And beyond the suns of the streets somewhere hobbled
A flabby moon that no-one needed".
"For our boas we will chop off the tails from the comets
                          which hobble into the void".

But, once he has uncrowned nature, has dashed it from its throne
and chased it from the palace into the back yard, Mayakovsky forgets
the old accounts. Now he relates to it like a master, calmly and simply:

"The universe sleeps,
Having placed its enormous ear
On the pincered paw of the stars".   (*A Cloud in Trousers*).

Here nature fulfils its allotted function, like a good watch-dog. And
further on:

"I carry to you the strength of boundless America
The power of machines...
I present warm nights of Naples...
Freezing in the cold of the north
The sun of Africa to you!

Burned by the sun of Africa
Tibet descended from the mountains
To you
With its snows''.

Here the thing and nature side by side serve man both as material and as aesthetic values. But the thing pushes nature aside in the new poetry, just as it does in the new life:

"Our legs
Are the lightning-bearing passages of trains.
Our arms
Are the fans which blow the dust from the glades.
Our fins are the steamers.
Our wings—the aeroplane''.

One of the most characteristic features of Mayakovsky's poetry is his use of imagery. Here too, the poet remains true to himself: with his particular sensitivity he unearths the image which is harmonious with the revolution, an image which copies the revolution itself.

This is not a naturalistic image (i.e. a copy), nor a realistic one (i.e. a typification) nor symbolic (i.e. an idea turned into reality) but, as comrade Chuzhak has correctly defined it, an *ultra-realistic* image. It is that unverisimilar truth which our life, raised up by the revolution, has now become: it is a reality which has outstripped the richest fantasy, indeed, it is "the earth on its hind-legs".

The revolution converts hyperbole into fact. How, then, could the poet of the revolution not turn facts into hyperbole? Hyperbole and caricature are the only two extremes which are capable of representing the conflicts of our life, which have been intensified to the level of open hostilities. Our life has become the arena for the struggle between two gigantic forces, two world-wide collectives. In what sort of concrete images should one embody this struggle? No single one can accommodate its enormous content, can convey the immense dynamism contained within the headlong flow of life. Every such image will be false. The naturalistic approach to contemporary life is none other than a small old lie about a new great truth. The old images are impotent before the new reality which has been revealed to us. Take the first Red Army soldier you meet on the street and draw him with precise exactitude, as most of our artists do, only draw a forage-cap with a Tsarist cockade instead of a helmet and you won't make him seem any different from a soldier of the Tsarist army. But where then is the Red Army soldier who took Perekop? He doesn't exist, because Perekop was not taken by the Red Army soldier Petrov but by the collective of the Red Army.

Try then to embody in an image this most real of real forces from our contemporary life and you will get a hyperbolic image like Ivan in "150 Million", whose arm is the Neva and whose heels are the Caspian steppes. And it's the same with the image of Wilson who is Ivan's polar opposite. For Mayakovsky, Wilson is not an individual but a collective—namely, worldwide capital. Wilson's name is merely appended to it, like a good nickname. In order to create this image, Mayakovsky piles hyperbole on hyperbole, caricature on caricature and only as a result of this Cyclopean labour does he achieve a convincing, genuinely real image of a man who, in the course of three years, oppressed and all but finished off one-sixth of the world.

A Blow Against Everyday Life

The rejection of the old aesthetic was, as I have already said, the first step of the poetic revolution.

The second step was the rejection of the everyday life of the old world. Mayakovsky achieved the transition from the first step to the second very quickly.

Even in one of his early poems we find lines such as the following:

"People are scared—out of my mouth
A badly chewed cry shakes its legs
But I will not be judged nor berated,
As for a prophet, my track will be strewn with flowers.
All those with crumbled noses know:
I am your poet.
Your terrible court scares me, like a tavern.
I alone, through burning buildings
Like a holy treasure will be carried aloft by prostitutes".

This poem is, indeed, a badly chewed cry, but it is also a challenging cry, which makes "people" scared. Here the poet already places himself in sharp contrast to all of contemporary "society". His words are a slap in the face for this society.

Many poets and writers have felt pity for prostitutes. They have pitied them, and repented as people repent before the Holy Eucharist so that, having purged their soul of sins, as they would clean out a bag, they once more can have the chance of filling it to the brim with more sins. Some writers have even tried to make an icon of prostitutes, as Dostoevsky did in *Crime and Punishment*. But an icon exists simply so that one may believe in it during prayer.

Mayakovsky does not pity prostitutes, nor does he make an icon of them:

> "But the ruin of street-lamps, the tsars in a crown of gas, has made the hateful bouquet of boulevard prostitutes even more painful to the eyes. And the pecking laughter of their jokes is eerie … ".

Here there are no poetic illusions, no aesthetic buffers: it is man as he is, or rather, as contemporary society has made him.

When the good writer tried to assure the good bourgeois that the prostitute is better than him and for this purpose made a Madonna of the prostitute, this was not only not frightening but even comforting for the good bourgeois. He even envied the prostitute a little:

"Well, well, they're alright, these prostitutes: they can even be Madonnas!"

And, of course, he was merely flattered by the comparison: he—a simple bourgeois, and suddenly only a little bit worse than the Madonna.

But now along comes not a good writer, but a malicious poet and, furiously flinging in the face of the good bourgeois the stinking bouquet of boulevard prostitutes with their crumbled noses, their eerie jokes and pecking laughter, he hurls at him a cry which is still young, not properly chewed, but a cry that is already as roaring as thunder:

"Do you see this human filth, this rotting prostitute? You, good, sweet-smelling bourgeois are ten times as filthy and rotten!"

And this, for the good bourgeois, was not only no longer flattering, but frightening …

Rejecting bourgeois society with immense energy, Mayakovsky at first, with all his might, crossed every boundary and ends up where there is no longer any society at all but only the putrefying refuse of society. As yet, he cannot see the proletariat, the young, healthy force that is growing within the bosom of the bourgeois order. He is still alone. He has no support and, as yet, fails to look for it where he should and hurls himself around like a beast in a cage:

> "I am alone, like the last eye
> of a man walking towards the blind!"

But he does not submit and flings into the crowd which has come to look at the wild beast words which are like a snarl:

"In an hour your flabby fat will flow out
From here over a man into a clean alley-way ...
Here you are, men; you have cabbage in your moustaches
From some left-over cabbage soup;
Here you are, woman, with your thick white powder,
You watch like an oyster from the shells of things ...
... I will laugh out loud and joyfully spit,
Spit in your face,
I—the wastrel and spendthrift of worthless words".

The poet, like any other mortal, seeks love. But his love stumbles on a woman who watches like an oyster from the shells of things. Alas!— the poet has few things. He tries to convince the woman:

"It doesn't matter,
If for a while
I dress you in tobacco smoke
Instead of the chic of Parisian gowns".

But tobacco smoke is too insubstantial and cheap a shell for the woman-oyster. And she leaves the poet for someone who can make her "fancy clothes" and hang "necklaces of pearls" "like a stone on her neck".

And another:

"You did not stain your hands in vulgar murder.
You
Only let fall:
In a soft bed
He put
Fruits
And wine on the palm of a night-table".

A soft bed, a night-table, fruits and wine—these are not tobacco smoke but *things* ... .

And a third (the third found the very best shell):

"And in the middle,
Surrounded by an imperturbable border,
There is a whole island of many-coloured carpets.
Here lives

The Master of All
my rival
my invincible enemy.
The most tender peas are on his fine stockings.
The ravishing stripes of his dandy's trousers.
His tie,
hopelessly patterned
has crawled down from his fat neck
over the globe of his paunch''.

Through woman, the slave of things, the poet confronts, face to face, the Master of the Thing.

"Along the curve of the equator
from Chicagos
through Tambovs
roubles roll.
Stretching out their hands
Everyone chases around,
crushing with their bodies
  mountains,
    seas,
      roadways.
The same bald,
unseen one leads them,
The Chief dance-master of the earthly can-can
Now in the form of an idea,
Now like a devil.
Now hiding behind a cloud he shines like God''.

This, now, is a picture of the whole contemporary world, which is sketched in broad strokes, with the simplicity and succinctness of genius.

And the last stroke suggests itself:

"Revolutions shake up the bodies of kingdoms,
the human herd changes its drivers,
but you
the uncrowned master of hearts,
not a single rebellion touches you!''

And from here, there is but one step, one movement for the poet to pass to the third step.

The Approach to Communism

I do not know how Vladimir Vladimirovich Mayakovsky came to revolution—but the poet Mayakovsky came to it through love. In almost all his long poems there was the same chain: love—woman—the thing—the uncrowned master of things, and through them of hearts, and, finally, the idea of rebellion against this uncrowned master.

Love, like a battering-ram, flung the poet-intellectual into revolution, just as hunger and poverty impel the worker. For us materialists, love is the same hunger and the move from love to revolution should not surprise us, just as we are not surprised by the transition from hunger to revolution.

Mayakovsky does not pretend. Neither in his first pieces where he had still not perceived his ties with the proletariat, nor in the most recent works, written after the revolution does he try to masquerade as a proletarian (as many poets now do in the hope of re-establishing their shaky credit—both spiritual and material). He always writes about his own personal experiences, but they are the experiences of the man who fights, the man who "has raised his heart like a flag". And, because of this, his individual experiences are, in their essence, profoundly social. He is not afraid that the proletarian will not understand him, writing as he does about himself, saying *I* and not *we*. The word *I* which is in harmony with millions of men and is repeated in every echo, becomes by itself the word *we*, whereas the latter word, even if shouted out a hundred times, remains as empty as the soul of the very person who shouts it. And so "we" will always sound alone like the smallest possible *I*.

Mayakovsky talks of his love, but the path followed by his love is the *path to revolution*, and the proletarian who has come to revolution by a different, but related path will understand Mayakovsky and value him as a poet when ... he discovers that, apart from Pushkin, Koltsov, Nikitin and Nekrasov, another such poet also exists (that is, when we communists stop guarding the worker against "pernicious futurism").

In this period of his creativity, love in Mayakovsky is nothing other than rebellion. And it is understandable that in his work love harmoniously combines with the great rebellion—the last decisive storming of heaven and earth, which he, as early as 1914, anticipated with inspired insight in his poem *A Cloud in Trousers*. This poem is a chunk of revolutionary ideology, compressed virtually to the dimensions of a slogan. It is a rejection of the old aesthetic, the everyday life of the old world and of the old order—a rejection which is virtually condensed into one cry, one grenade:

"Your thought, dreaming on a softened brain,
like a fattened-out lackey on a greasy couch
I taunt with the bloodied scrap of my heart,
Insolent and sarcastic I'll jeer my fill.
I have not a single grey hair in my soul,
and in it there's no senile tenderness.
Smashing the world with the power of my voice,
I go on—beautiful,
twenty-two years old".

So this poem begins. Further on, the poet begins to taunt and jeer:

"Tender ones,
You place your love on violins.
The coarse one places his love on kettle-drums...
...Come and learn—
from the drawing room comes a cambric
prim clerk from the angelic league
And who calmly leafs through her lips,
like a cook browsing through the pages of a cookery-book".

The stagnation of a thought, dreaming on a softened brain, and the stagnation of a feeling that has gone dead in a decorous salon—these are the first obstacles which the young, newly arrived poet encounters in his path (and the same for a young class, I would add).

"If you like, I'll be irreproachably tender,
not a man, but a cloud in trousers".

And suddenly, breaking off his calm, mocking tone, the poet hurls words in the face of this decorous, salon world, which hit as hard as slaps:

"I do not believe that blossoming Nice exists!
Once more I glorify
men, as stale as a hospital,
and women, as ragged as a proverb".

But love comes to the poet in the form of a cambric, prim clerk. It comes and it leaves. She leaves because she is a "Giaconda who should be stolen", while he is a "simple man, spat out by the consumptive night into the dirty hand of Presnya". The prim clerk is frightened by

this love which she cannot calmly leaf through and "place on violins",
is afraid because this love does not lie, because it is a genuine love and
not amorous window-dressing:

> "Maria!
> The poet sings sonnets to Tiana,
>   while I,
> made entirely of meat,
> I simply ask for your body,
> as Christians ask
> 'give us this day
> our daily bread' ".

For the first time since poets began to sing of love, truthful words
have been spoken about it.

Yes, when man loves he asks for a body. We all know this. We know
that the basis of love is sexual feeling and, that in the sexual act,
bodies merge, and not souls. We know that it is possible to love a
person without loving their soul, and impossible to love without
loving their body.

And all the same:

> "And my song is holy incense
> Before the altar of the goddess of beauty..."

Our poet does not produce altars and incense, but the clerk from
the angelic league cannot do without them: altars and incense are
essential aspects of her amorous practice. The poet-revolutionary fails
to produce a revolution in the heart of the woman he loves.

A great love can bring with it great anguish. But he does not whine,
does not "wallow in his love", does not torment himself with sorrow
as has been the age-old custom, and one which has been sacredly
observed by all poets. He writhes in pain, curses and threatens. He is
entirely "pain and bruising", but the pain is active, and the bruising
charges his soul, like a cannon, with revolutionary buck-shot.

And in the second, third and fourth parts we see how this shot
dashes against all the values and holies of the old world.

The first part ends with the personal catastrophe. The poet's heart,
like a bonfire, is aflame with awful suffering. The poet wishes to leap
out of his own heart. His whole being burns and:

> "a hundred-eyed glow dashes from the quay
> towards shaking people in the quiet of their flats..."

And so the fire in his heart turns into the fire of revolution.

His burning heart throws the poet from the quiet, from the woman's house, from the shell of things onto the street, to the place where:

> "Krupps and Krupplets make up the city
> with the bristling of ominous brows,
> while the bodies of dead words decompose
> in my mouth—
> only two live on, and grow fat,
> 'scum'
> and one other,
> it seems to be 'borshch' ".

But what of the great, free etc. Russian language? The word of the poet? This word is not for the street, but for certain select souls. Indeed, the poet's word exists to cut these souls off from the street. Poetry is the new obstacle, as long as poets:

> "boil up, while scraping at their rhymes,
> some sort of broth from loves and nightingales,
> the tongueless street writhes—
> it has nothing with which to shout and talk".

Hearing these two words ringing out from the street—"scum" and "borshch",

> "The poets, drenched in tears and sobs,
> Rushed from the street, ruffling their hair
> And behind the poets the street hordes:
> students,
> prostitutes,
> contractors".

Here, with inspired force, in three words the line of the great class divide is drawn, the line which, in just over three years divided our country into two hostile camps. The intelligentsia (students), the petty bourgeoisie (contractors) and the déclassé elements (prostitutes)—all these parasites of the bourgeoisie gathered on the other side of the barricades.

All those who had interceded on behalf of the people—the poets and writers—in the course of fifty years have been transformed beyond recognition. Domesticated by the bourgeoisie, nourished and groomed by their charitable hand-outs, they had long since restrung their lyres to a new tune, abandoning the uncouth baritone of

Nekrasov, which had hammered out "Go to the Volga, whose moans ring out", for the heart-rending puny tenor of Balmont, who sings of "ladies, love and a flower beneath the dew". Now they fastidiously avert their noses from:

> "people like us,
> pock-marked with soot".

They run from the street to the quiet of their flats, taking their admirers with them. And suddenly the word of the poet, cast onto the street from the quiet of flats by the fire in his heart, crashes down on this fleeing crowd, in a bellowing, blacksmith's bass:

> "Gentleman!
> Stop!
> You are not beggars,
> you do not dare to ask for hand-outs!
> We muscular ones,
> with our huge stride
> must not listen, but tear them apart,
> they,
> who cling like a special supplement to every double-bed!
> Should we humbly ask them:
> 'Help me!'
> And pray for a hymn,
> for an oratorio.
> We ourselves are the creators in a burning hymn—
> the noise of the factory and laboratory".

Here the poet is moving to a new aesthetic—an aesthetic which is born amid the noise of the factory and laboratory. He moves towards the beauty of the human collective, to its great power, which transforms every speck of dust which enters its whirlwind into something alive:

> "We
> with a face, like a crumpled sheet,
> with lips, drooping, like a chandelier—
> we
> convicts from the leper colony,
> where gold and dirt have ulcerated leprosy—
> we are purer than Venetian azure,
> washed clean by both the seas and the suns".

The old beauty, coddled by the ages, fades before this new beauty:

> "I don't give a damn that
> the Homers and Ovids have
> no people like us
> pock-marked with soot.
> I know—
> that the sun would grow dim seeing
> the gold fields of our souls!"

The poet has found his support in the masses, in the collective, and the challenge he throws to all the age-old junk already rings out with confidence, like the blow of a worker's hammer:

> "Sinews and muscles are more reliable than prayers
> Is it for us to beg for the charity of the times
> We—
> each of us
> holds in our fists
> the driving belts of the worlds".

And now, when each of us has in our hand the driving belts of the worlds and when we can subjugate time itself to ourselves, not by any mystical prophecy but by the most real roar of the machine which forges tomorrow, these words of the poet ring out:

> "I, the laughing-stock of today's tribe
> like a long
> obscene anecdote,
> can see one who crosses the mountains of time,
> whom no one sees.
> Where men's limited eye stops short,
> at the head of the hungry hordes
> in the crown of thorns of revolutions
> 1916 approaches".

And, together with tomorrow's day, the poet also forges the soul of the man of tomorrow, the warrior man, the man who will be a "knuckle-duster to slash the skull of the world".

> "Nothing can any longer be forgiven
> I have burned out the souls where tenderness was grown.
> That is harder than taking
> a thousand thousand Bastilles".

The time has come for a moral re-evaluation of man—a time when tenderness becomes a crime, meekness—treachery and goodness—murder. The age-old edifice of human morality, resting on the "Lord Jesus" himself, is already cracking, rocked by the slave chained to it. Who will be victorious—those who feast behind the walls of this building together with the God that has crossed over to their side, or the slave of yesterday, who today has found new strength?

The poet knows: man now has only a few slaves devoted to him, although there are still many devoted to God. The poet knows that God will aid those who feast in the building. After all, God is only the third hypostasis of the one—the master of all—the chief dance-master of the earthly can-can, and he no longer benignly shines behind the clouds:

> "Suddenly the clouds and all the rest
> have raised an incredible storm in the sky,
> as if some workers in white have lost control
> after declaring an embittered strike against the heavens.
> Thunder has come out from behind the clouds like a wild beast,
> has provocatively blown its huge nostrils,
> and the face of the heavens for a second was twisted
> in the severe grimace of an iron Bismarck…"

And, scenting this new enemy descending from the skies, the poet sounds the alarm:

> "General Gallifet is coming once more
> to shoot down the insurgents!"

And his battle slogan now rings out in an animal, rather than a human voice:

> "Take your idle hands from your trousers—
> take a stone, a knife or a bomb
> and if there is anyone with no hands—
> let him come to strike with his forehead!"

Those who no longer believe in God will go, but how is one to raise in battle against "the Holy Trinity" those who are poor in spirit, the meek, those who live with a side-long glance at heaven, the ones softened up by the Gospel? Let the Holy Trinity itself help the poet:

> "Come unto me all those who labour and are burdened…"

And the poet begins his gamut with the sweet tone of the Gospel, and raises the tone with every line:

"Go, hungry ones,
perspiring ones
the humble ones,
those who are stagnating in flea-ridden filth!
Go! [it is no longer a call but an order—N.G.]
We will make our Mondays and Tuesdays
festivals of blood [no longer an order but a shout—N.G.]
Let the earth remember beneath our knives
whom it wished to debase!
The fattened earth, like the mistress
whom Rothschild loved!
So that the flags might flutter in the fever of gunfire,
like on any decent festival—
raise higher, you street-lamps,
the bloodied carcasses of corn-dealers! ... "

These are not just shouts but the blows of the knuckle-duster man,
who slashes the skull of the world. The challenge goes out not only to
the direct assassins of the working class—the Gallifets, but to the
indirect murderers too: the Christians, the Tolstoyans, the non-
resisters, the democratising souls who would like the revolution to take
place like an orderly procession and, refusing "to dirty their hands" in
the blood of the enemies of the revolution, wallow up to their necks in
the blood of the working class, together with the generals and oppres-
sors.

The poet senses that the divine commandment "thou shalt not
kill" has been used to justify murder, that this eructation of God may
ruin everything. And this is how it happens in reality:

"and some-one, entangled in the chains of the sky,
stretched out his hands to a café,
seemingly like a woman,
tender somehow
and somehow like a gun carriage".

The cannons of the Lord God help those of man:

"Night will come,
will bite in two
and eat you up.
Do you see—
is the sky playing Judas again
with a handful of stars spattered with treachery?
Night came.

Feasted like Mamay,
Squatting with its backside on the city.
Our eyes cannot break this night
black as Azef!''

And from here the storming of the sky, with which the poem ends, logically ensues—the prototype of the coming great revolution.

"I will crawl out
dirty (from spending nights in gutters)
I will stand side by side
will lean over
and say in his ear
'Listen, mister God!
How is it you're not bored
dipping your benevolent eyes every day
into a jelly of cloud?
Let's—you know—
Construct a carousel
on the tree of knowledge of good and evil' ''.

The Lord God (exactly like the lord man—his image and copy) has fenced himself off from worldly nastiness with his jelly of clouds. He does not wish to see the order which he himself has constructed on this earth. He hides from life like a coward, finding for himself a quiet, cosy nook behind the clouds (and it's the same as behind the quiet of the flats). And the poet takes him by the ear, like a puppy, and sticks his nose in the mess he has made.

"Omnipresent one, you will be in every cupboard,
and we'll spread out such wines on the table,
that sullen Apostle Peter
will want to step out in the ki-ka-pou.
Again we'll settle some little Eves in paradise
Give the order—
This very night
I'll drag to you
the most beautiful little girls from all the boulevards.
Do you want me to?''

A carousel on the tree of knowledge of good and evil, wines, the ki-ka-pou, the bourgeois' cupboard and ... little girls of the streets—such are the delights created on earth by the Lord God, this is it—the much vaunted divine world.

The poet suggests transferring this earthly carousel to heaven. Like a coward, the Lord God refuses. The battle preparations are completed and the poet finishes his poem with a furious attack on the heavenly forces.

> "Almighty, you have invented a pair of hands,
> you've made it
> so that everyone has a head—
> why didn't you see to it that
> one could kiss, kiss, kiss
> without the suffering?!
> I thought that you were an all-powerful Deity,
> but you're a dim-wit, a minute tin-god.
> Can you see, I'm bending down,
> I get a shoe-maker's knife
> from the top of my boot!
> Winged scoundrels!
> Rush into heaven
> Ruffle your feathers in terrified flight:
> I'll cut you, stinking of incense,
> wide open from here to Alaska''.

In the final, furiously thundering chords there clearly rings out the same theme as at the beginning of the poem—love. And so ends this first authentic song of the great revolution. Love, the eternal theme of poetry, is not avoided by the revolutionary poet. But the old poets, while glorifying love, deserted the surrounding world for the shell of their own hearts, while the new poet, engulfed by the flames of love, breaks the walls of his shell, his own small heart, to find a new, large heart—the heart of the collective.

Before, love was the nursemaid of the everyday life of the old world. Now, love is the dynamite which blows this world apart. Before, it was the arrow of God which pierced the heart of man, now it is the arrows of the human heart, which kills stone dead all the gods.

Futurism, the Art of the Revolution

I have only dealt with the works from Mayakovsky's first period of poetic creativity, because I thought it important to show how much revolutionary fire was inherent in the poet's ideology even in his first pieces, ideologically unformed as they are. As concerns his more recent pieces, with a very few exceptions, they arouse no dispute from the ideological point of view. However, a detailed artistic evaluation would have filled a whole book.

My aim was to reveal the revolutionary movement in the process of Mayakovsky's creativity through three stages: aesthetics—everyday life—social order. And I consider that I have completed this task.

To elucidate the social nature of Russian futurism, I took its two extreme ends, the two poets Kruchenykh and Mayakovsky, of whom one least of all, and the other the most of all, advanced along the path of revolutionary art. I will not speak here about the other futurist poets who occupy intermediary positions (such as Khlebnikov, Kamensky, Aseyev, Tretyakov), as this would only complicate my task, without changing anything in my conclusions.

In concluding my sketch, I think it not superfluous to emphasise, by means of an obvious comparison, the dependent relationship between Russian and Italian futurism which I established in theory—a relationship which confirms my basic idea that there are not various futurisms but only one futurism: that is, futurism viewed as the revolutionary art of a great social watershed.

Here is a series of extracts from Marinetti's programme, placed side by side with extracts from Mayakovsky's poetry from the first period, when the influence of the Italian futurists on the Russians was still very strong:

"We have listened to the exhausted prayer of the old canal and the grinding of bones of the dying palaces with their nature fashioned from greenery". (Marinetti).

"Surely you must be completely bored by the pages, palaces, love and lilac bushes". (Mayakovsky).

"And suddenly voracious automobiles have begun to bellow beneath our window". (Marinetti).

"Red-haired devils, automobiles have arisen, blowing their horns right into our ears". (Mayakovsky).

"We glorify the destructive gesture of the anarchists". (Marinetti).

"And I will burn up like a bloody vision in the black souls of murderers and anarchists". (Mayakovsky).

"We glorify the huge crowds, motivated by work, pleasure or rebellion". (Marinetti).

"The crowd, a multi-coloured swift cat,
Flowed and twisted, drawn through the doors". (Mayakovsky).

"We wish to destroy the museums, the libraries...". (Marinetti).

"I place 'nihil' over everything that has been done

I never
want to read anything". (Mayakovsky).

"Lust is understood outside my moral conception and, as an essential element of the dynamism of life, is a force. The flesh creates just as the spirit does: their creativity is equal in the face of the universe. One is not higher than the other and spiritual creativity depends on the carnal". (Marinetti).

"Beautiful males, covered with wool,
we will feed the desires of the hungry females ... " (Mayakovsky).

"We hail the nocturnal vibration of the arsenals and shipyards beneath their powerful electric moons, the voracious stations which gulp down the smoking serpents ... the adventuristic packet-boats which sniff the horizon". (Marinetti).

"We climb the earth under the eyelashes of descended palms
To put out the wall-eyes of the deserts,
To catch the smiles of the dreadnoughts
On the shrivelled lips of the canals". (Mayakovsky).

Here we see a whole series of conjunctures at which the paths of Russian and Italian "futurisms" overlap. This coincidence is not, of course, by chance. Seeing "two paths" is simply a defect of vision on the part of myopic critics, who are incapable of seeing things in their historical perspective. The two paths are, in reality, the beginning and continuation of the single path of revolutionary art.

Futurism and Proletarian Poetry

One more question remains: what is the relationship between futurism and contemporary, so-called proletarian poetry?

By proletarian poetry we understand poetry which is now being written by poets of working-class origin. But can we consider this poetry genuinely proletarian?

Of course, we cannot. The proletariat has not yet had time or favourable conditions to gather strength in the field of verbal creativity. Many of our contemporary proletarian poets began writing even before the revolution. What came of this? Having begun publication in newspapers and journals, the proletarian poets, for the most part, became estranged from the working milieu, were infected by the petty-bourgeois atmosphere and, in the end, turned into typical intellectuals. But, if they did not become estranged from this milieu, then they preserved the integrity of their proletarian mentality (and this integrity is highly relative, since, in pre-revolutionary conditions, the proletariat, as a class, was under strong ideological pressure from the bourgeoisie) at the cost of narrowness of horizon and paucity of spiritual baggage.

This was the situation before the revolution.

But the revolution demanded from every one of us primarily deeds and not words, and the word itself became a deed, which forced it to serve the interests of the present day. It used art as propaganda, as a slogan or placard (Down with Kolchak, down with Denikin etc.). Moreover, all the most energetic, gifted, vigorous forces that existed in the proletariat were directed to the struggle itself, to the creation of life itself. (The best illustration is the major poet and genuine proletarian Gastev, who left poetry for production.) The mentality of the genuine proletarian, the mentality of the communist was entirely captured by the single slogan, "to arms".

At this time, "creating for the future" became the lot of the weak, the ailing and the feeble. Such people gathered and worked at this task under the sign, "The Forge".

It is extremely characteristic that these proletarian poets stubbornly refused to have anything to do with agitation, they did not wish to squander their talents on "trifles".

But at that time "these trifles" were the very destiny of the proletarian republic.

In those severe years genuinely proletarian poetry could only be one thing—the sword and shield raised against the real enemy.

Everything that was above this came from a petty bourgeois spirit. But above this was, as I have already said, almost all proletarian poetry. Instead of lending all their strength to the defence of the man of today, the proletarian poets occupied themselves with a truly divine affair—the creation of the new man. They began to "forge" his ideology, but with what tools? The word of the worker? Such a thing did not yet exist. With the word of the futurist? Such a word had already been spoken, but the light (indeed, a very light) hand of the most responsible leaders of our cultural front ostracised this word from the party, as "the product of the break-down of bourgeois culture".

This was how comrade Lunacharsky christened futurism in his speeches and articles. Comrade Bukharin, in his book *The Theory of Historical Materialism*, approached futurism with exactly the same "lightness":

"And now, by way of contrast, let us look at the art of the moribund bourgeoisie. This art has been given a particularly striking expression *in Germany* (my italics N.G.) where, after the defeat and the treaty of Versailles, on the one hand, and because of the constant threat of a proletarian uprising, on the other, the general tenor of the life of bourgeois circles is at its gloomiest, where the capitalist mechanism is breaking down more quickly, where, consequently, there is an acceleration in the process of declassment, of the transformation of the bourgeois intelligentsia into "human dust", into isolated individuals, who lose their heads at the moment of large events. This state of disorder is expressed in the growth of individualism and mysticism. *An anguished search is conducted for a new 'style', new generalising forms which cannot be found: every day there emerges a new 'ism' which soon grows old; after impressionism came neo-impressionism, futurism, expressionism and so on*". (My italics, N.G.).

We scarcely need to offer a serious rebuttal to this confused muddle. Comrade Bukharin lumps together everything that ends in *ism* (although, of course, communism also ends in *ism*) and everything is gathered under the sign of individualism and mysticism. The declassment of the bourgeois intelligentsia, its estrangement from its own class and the search for a new "style", new generalising forms, that is, the ideological process which has already been directed against bourgeois ideology, and, consequently, is naturally split into two currents—one reactionary (individualism, mysticism) and one revolutionary, which feels for points of contact with the proletariat—all this complex situation of our contemporary culture is schematised by comrade Bukharin in two words: *mysticism triumphs*.

Comrade Bukharin fails to notice the elephant of the new art—Russian futurism. In general, contemporary Russian art is, for some reason, invisible to him. If it were visible, then the difference between the "isms" would also be visible (futurism, on the one hand, and acmeism, imaginism, neo-classicism, parnassianism and so on, on the other). There is not a single word about contemporary Russian art in the book. Comrade Bukharin does not wish to waste time on the study of such a "trifle" and, in order to complete the task he has set himself (that is, to carry through the whole programme of his work according to the theory of historical materialism), he undertakes a fleeting visit to Germany with a suitcase crammed full of various guide-books and

Baedekers, like Max Dessoir and Max Martechteig (bourgeois theorists of art). It is understandable that, given the almost immaterial transience of our materialist, when not only the *isms* but the telegraph poles as well merge into a single whole, all that remains clearly distinct is what was written in the guide-books and Baedekers.

Hence the glaringly confused muddle I have already noted. If the leaders of our party can get so confused, then it's hardly likely that the proletarian poets won't. Warned off futurism by Lunacharsky and Bukharin, they went to learn from ... the mastodons and ichthyosauruses of the pre-flood (pre-revolutionary) epoch, from the old, inveterate singer-poets of the past.

As a result, we have an almost all-pervasive eructation:

> "There is a purity in iron.
> A seductiveness, a luminosity
> Of mimosa—soft eyelashes.
> There are the trills of flutes,
> They caught fire and burned up
> In the smiles of rapturous faces.
> In iron there is a tenderness
> A playful snowiness..." etc.

Who is this—Balmont pretending to be a "proletarian"? ... No, it's worse: the proletarian poet Gerasimov writing "in the style of Balmont".

In the ears of a real proletarian who puts iron into life, this flowery treatment of iron, this lullaby lisping—purity, luminosity, tenderness, snowiness—cannot but sound like irritating falsity.

Another example:

> "It was an evening like the others. The engines were shouting
> And the stars were completing their ancient march.
> People were walking. They were laughing, conversing.
> The month was June, the year 1919 (!) ...
> All was so clear, solutions are superfluous—
> The sky and the stars, the crowd and the poet:
> All was correct, all was in order.
> So will it be *one thousand years hence!*"   (V. Kirilov).

The poet is wrong: not everything is clear and solutions are not superfluous. Where is the solution to the fact that this poem was written not a thousand years ago, but in 1919, in the days when the proletarian revolution was at its height, and was written by a poet who calls himself proletarian?

Which of the past centuries has presented us with this mouldy bouquet of impenetrable philistinism? We will find the answer in the speeches, articles and books of our learned Marxists.

Another example:

> "By the old hearth we will
> Listen to the moans of the wind outside,
> Sadness will be the sole sovereign,
> The pain in our hearts a beautiful dream.
> The night is dark. You and I are forgotten
> In this wild, northern corner...
> Long will the wind beyond the wall
> Sing the psalm of a languishing soul".

And what is this—an unpublished tear-jerker by Apukhtin? No, it is a poem by Alexandrovsky, published in 1921. And there is plenty more of such examples of "proletarian poetry".

The conclusion is clear. The flight from the revolutionary art of today, i.e. futurism, and prostration at the feet of bourgeois mastodons has destroyed the first poets to emerge from the proletariat. After the old (alas, already old) proletarian poets come new, young ones.

May this be a lesson for them. Let them remember that the dead snatch the living, and not cling so closely to dead poets (even if they be classics, since in the face of the new life classical poetry is nothing but classical carrion), but to living poets, the futurists.

Proletarian poetry will gain strength when it passes through futurism and masters all its not inconsiderable revolutionary gains. At the same time it will bring fresh life to futurism with its own strong, healthy workers' spirit by weeding out the remnants of intellectualism which are still embedded here and there in its cracks and pores. The revolutionary experience achieved by futurism over the last ten years ought to be used by the young, workers' poetry. This is necessary, if only in terms of simple economising of effort, so as not to break down open doors or to discover Americas which have already been discovered.

As regards further experience, everything depends on whether the progressive inertia of Russian futurism has been exhausted in the first stage of the revolution.

If not, then proletarian poetry will go on further together with it; if it has been exhausted, then proletarian poetry will advance through it.

1   The reference is to a book by the critic Shapirshtein-Lers published in 1922 under the title: *The Social Meaning of Russian Futurism*. Shapirshtein-Lers is better-known today by the name of Jacob Efimovich Elsberg and for his studies of Herzen. In the 1920s he belonged to a group of proletarian writers formed around the journal *Na Postu* (On Guard).

2   The Lena shootings: on April 4, 1912, in the gold-mining district of Lena, in Northern Siberia, troops opened fire without warning on workers gathered to demand the release of their arrested delegates. This massacre sparked off a wave of strikes and demonstrations throughout Russia.

3   NEP: New Economic Policy introduced by Lenin in 1920 in an attempt to extricate the new regime from the appalling difficulties then besetting it. It represented a return to a certain form of capitalism: restoration of private trade, of the wage system and of peasants' rights to ownership of their produce.

G. CONIO

Afterword—
Towards a Proletarian Literature

Nicolas Gorlov sought to justify futurism in Marxist eyes by showing that this was the highroad to proletarian poetry. Osip Brik,[1] for his part, held that the sole aim of Opoyaz[2] was to promote an authentically proletarian creativity. Formalists and futurists alike, then, disputed the Associations of Proletarian Writers and Poets their title, to which they also laid claim; throughout the 1920s there was no title more irrefutable, more sought after or more coveted among those groups that had sided with the Revolution than that of "proletarian literature". Besides, the relative importance attached to "literature." in this pairing was determined directly by that accorded to the word "proletarian", depending on whether one was talking about literature "by" or "for" the people. People who wished to go on according some weight to literary values rejected a restriction which, in their view, could only result in an absurdity. The Rappists,[3] for example, denied that anybody not of proletarian origin was entitled to write at all, and they conceived of literature as being made by the proletariat or not at all. This, paradoxically, was to serve as the pretext for the dissolution of the Proletarian Writers' organisation in 1932 and for the vesting of control over culture and literary affairs in the Party. It was in the name of literature that Stalin, in founding the Writers' Union, dealt literature its death blow. It is therefore essential, if we are to see our way clearly in this business, to examine the concept of "proletarian literature" in the light of its evolution as expressed in the different groups and factions, taking us right to the nub of the question of the relations between writers, literature, and power.

Just before the October Revolution, from the 16th to the 19th of that month, Lunacharsky and Bogdanov[4] organised a conference on proletarian culture in Petrograd, and this conference gave birth to the association known as Proletkult. The aim of this association was to stimulate the growth of proletarian culture, destined to replace bourgeois culture. It played a dominant role in the early years of the Soviet

Union, but came under growing criticism for its "leftist" positions and finally disappeared, its place being taken by new proletarian organisations (V.A.P.P. and R.A.P.P.).

In the aftermath of the 1905 Revolution, Lunacharsky and Bogdanov had already founded a movement ("Forwards") in émigré circles, whose theories were subsequently to underpin Proletkult. We know that, philosophically-speaking, Bogdanov (an early Marxist) was an exponent of the ideas of Mach and Avenerius, which had been refuted by Lenin in one of his most celebrated works, *Materialism and Empirio-criticism*. An expanded editorial committee of the newspaper *The Proletarian*[5] met in Paris, from 21 to 30 June 1909, in order to pass judgment on the errors of Bogdanov, one of the newspaper's correspondents and a prominent member of the Bolshevik Party. Bogdanov was expelled first from the paper and then from the Party. Lunacharsky, on the other hand, soon mended his ways and regained Lenin's favour; he was appointed *Narkompros*[6] after October. He was criticised in particular for heresies expounded in his book *Religion and Socialism*, in which he had attempted to reconcile and merge socialism with religion, socialism being, in his view, the best approach to "God-building". This is how he presented his errors, many years afterwards:

"Although I did not share Bogdanov's empirio-monistic philosophy, I was close to it nevertheless and in any case, so far as philosophy was concerned, I stood no closer to the party than Bogdanov, inasmuch as I attempted to introduce into Marxism elements of Machism and empirio-criticism which were alien to it. Together with this (and there was, of course, a profound connection here) my political views also coincided with those of Bogdanov, in that I, too, espoused the erroneous policy of ultimatism.

But the greatest mistake which I made at that time was my creation of an original philosophical theory, that of so-called 'God-building'.

At the time of the defeat of the revolutionary movement of 1905 I, like everyone else, witnessed the religious tensions and searchings which were prevalent then. The term 'God-seeking' concealed at that time every kind of mysticism which did not wish to be compromised by connection with the already revealed god of the official religions, but sought in nature and history this god who undoubtedly ruled the world.

I had the following thought: of course, we Marxists deny the existence of any kind of god and consequently believe that there is no point in seeking god, because it is impossible to find what does not exist.

Nevertheless we are surrounded by a vast number of people, who find themselves under the particular spell of religious inquiry. Among them are certain circles (particularly, as I thought, among the peasantry) who find it easier to approach the truths of socialism through their religious and philosophical thought than in any other way.

At the same time, I reasoned, scientific socialism conceals within itself colossal ethical value; its exterior is somewhat cold and severe, but it contains gigantic treasures of practical idealism. So one would need only to reveal in a special kind of semi-poetic journalism the internal content of the teaching of Marx and Engels, for it to acquire a new force of attraction for such elements.

Guided by this false attitude, I produced a number of works (among them the large, two-volume *Religion and Socialism*), in which I treated scientific socialism as the progress of man through social conflict, science and technology towards a constantly expanding power over nature. God, I explained, did not have to be sought, he had to be given to the world. He does not exist in the world, but he could. The path of the struggle for socialism, i.e. for the triumph of man in nature—this was God-building.

While it is true that I was very careful in my books to indicate that socialism, which I interpreted as the highest form of religion, was a religion without a god and without mysticism, in fact the entire conception constitutes something in the nature of an over-simplified Fichteanism, adapted to a semi-materialistic means of expression.

The control of the party soon made itself felt. Subjectively, it was quite unexpected so far as I was concerned. When the article 'Not on the road' appeared in *The Proletarian*, I was profoundly indignant and angry.

Subjectively, I considered that I was doing the party a useful service and for some time I continued to resist, insisting that my conception was the same Marxism as that of the party, simply in a special guise designed to be effective in a particular sphere, and that my definitions of socialism, my expression 'God-building' did not in any way diminish that most consistent atheism which characterised my conception.

When a party man attempts to defend what he knows to be an erroneous point of view, he tumbles down, one step after another. My article in the second book of *The literary collapse* was a complete failure from all points of view. It was full of anger and attempts to appeal to 'the freedom of opinion and creation' in the party, to a 'broad' understanding of Marxism as opposed to a 'narrow' one and similar flabby, dangerous tendencies of a struggle against the exact and clear boundaries of the party, a struggle for rotten liberalism for myself and for other such 'wandering seekers'."

This self-criticism by a faithful and close companion of Lenin, made towards the end of his life, contains the confession of a deviation which, although it had been condemned and was undoubtedly open to condemnation from a Marxist standpoint, is nonetheless highly significant from our own point of view. His attempt was a strange mixture of cynicism (although this may have more to do with self-justification after the event), and of socialism contaminated by the then-fashionable notions of mysticism and messianic inspiration inherited from nineteenth-century Russian populism. This populist messianism was later to be found among most of the poets and thinkers who hailed the October Revolution, and in particular it heavily impregnated Alexander Blok's *The Twelve* and *The Scythians*; Lunacharsky transformed it into a proletarian messianism, substituting, in place of the people as a whole, the idea of a chosen class containing within it the seeds of the future and carving out a passage for "God-building". One finds here too an eschatological element characteristic, as Berdyaev has pointed out, of Russian philosophy; but at the time it was more widespread than that, emerging in the work of Rilke, for example, this proletarian messianism later inspired urbanist and constructivist poetry, just as populism and the values of the countryside were to inspire Klyuev and Esenin. In any case, we subsequently encounter most of the aspirations expressed here—including the desire for emancipation from the power of the party—in Proletkult, at a time when Lunacharsky, as Commissar for Education, was obliged to act as interpreter and executant of Lenin's will and was thereby forced to seek to reconcile the aspirations of the rank and file with the leadership's directives. *Narkompros* though he was, Lunacharsky was never a vulgar *apparatchik* such as were later to take his place (Zhdanov), and he never abandoned his dreams for the future of an authentic proletarian culture.

In 1920, Lunacharsky was elected Chairman of the International Proletkult Bureau. On 8 October 1920, he was sharply reprimanded by Lenin for the speech delivered to the First Proletkult Congress, which *Izvestia* had reprinted:

"In the 8 October 1920 issue of *Izvestia* I read that Comrade Lunacharsky told the Proletkult Congress exactly the opposite of what we had agreed on the previous day. Comrade Lunacharsky says he has been misrepresented ... Yet the resolution is nonetheless utterly useless".

Lenin then sketched out a draft resolution which he got the Congress to adopt:

"1° No particular ideas, but Marxism.

2° No inventions on the subject of a new proletarian culture, but the development of the best traditional models, of the outcome of existing culture from the point of view of the Marxist world-vision and of the conditions of life and struggle of the proletariat during the phase of its dictatorship.

3° No breaking of links with Narkompros, but rather merging with it, because R.K.P. (Party Central Committee) + Narkompros = Proletkult.

4° Proletkult's narrow dependence on Narkompros".[7]

Lenin took a dim view of Proletkult's independence from the Party and of its pronounced separatist tendencies. In addition, he was sceptical as to the advent of a *new* proletarian culture founded on the ruins of tradition. The members of Proletkult shared the futurists' hatred of the past, their desire to wipe the slate clean, their nihilism in connection with everything and anything inherited from bourgeois culture, i.e. from culture, period, or as Lenin put it "existing culture".

Furthermore, Proletkult still counted amongst its members a number of Bogdanov's followers, and Lenin was afraid they might start spreading heretical ideas liable to undermine the hegemony of Marxism; it was this concern which underlay the first article of his draft resolution. As can be seen from this, the guiding principle behind Lenin's cultural policy was the desire to maintain control over organisations which bridled at or even rejected Party domination. He distrusted Proletkult's radicalism or nihilism as much as he did that of the futurists. Nowadays we tend to look at these two conflicting movements less in terms of their differences than of their similarities: a certain measure of autonomy vis-à-vis the rulers and a determination to destroy their artistic and literary heritage in order to clear the way for an entirely new era, the era of proletarian culture (which each movement imagined in its own particular manner).

Thus, in a recent book on Lunacharsky we find:

"Contrary to Proletkult, the Futurists formed only a small group. They even squabbled amongst themselves (Futurists and Proletkult). On most of the main questions of literary and political principle, however, they frequently concurred. Thus it was no accident that the Central Committee's letter (*Pravda* 1/12/1920) on Proletkult referred to Proletkult and Futurists in the same terms..." (Terekhov, p. 523).[8]

In his book on formalism Victor Erlich makes the same comparison:

> "The poet-innovators, whether of the Futurist, Imaginist or Constructivist persuasion, incessantly harped on the theme that revolutionary form is as essential a prerequisite of truly proletarian art as revolutionary content. These declarations were echoed by some *bona fide* Marxist theoreticians. A. Gastev, a spokesman of the Proletkult group, maintained that 'the notion of proletarian art implies an overwhelming revolution in the sphere of artistic devices'."[9]

But respect for and preservation of the literary and artistic masterpieces of the past was one of the mainstays of Lenin's cultural policy and one of the principal reasons for his criticisms of Proletkult and the Futurists; their anarchistic extremism exasperated him. Lunacharsky was known to have been the architect of this policy, and he shared Lenin's ideas on this subject. His conception of proletarian culture in no way entailed hostility to "existing" culture inherited from the past. Quite the contrary: had he not resigned from the Party right in the middle of the civil war on the strength of a (false) rumour that the Cathedral of St. Basil the Blessed had been destroyed by Bolshevik troops (resignation withdrawn, needless to say, on receipt of evidence that the rumour was indeed false)? Even so, his "liberalism", his "soft-heartedness" and the tolerance that he manifested towards the "leftist" iconoclastic tendencies continued to earn him reproaches from Lenin. When the latter visited the Higher School of Fine Arts, called Vkhutemas, on 25 February 1921, he observed the popularity of Mayakovsky among these young revolutionaries destined to become the future artistic cadres of the Soviet Union. But he was disappointed at their ignorance of the Russian classics. Nadezhda Krupskaya relates how he bitterly remarked to Lunacharsky: "They're a fine bunch, a very fine bunch, these youths—but what are you teaching them?"[20]

As *Narkompros*, and on Lenin's instructions, Lunacharsky sought to emphasise not the break with the past, but rather continuity with it, and, while lending the weight of his authority to Proletkult, he sought to temper its line. In his directives and speeches, he denounced deviations in the direction of a cultural revolution: his book *Proletarian Culture and Bourgeois Culture* (1923) roundly attacks the "paradoxicalists of proletarian culture who, in the name of pseudo-leftist slogans, seek to persuade the proletariat to break the natural links that bind its future to the cultural past of humanity".

He took up a middle-of-the-road stance between the left and the right currents which then divided the intelligentsia and threatened to disrupt its unity. He explained his position thus:

"If Sosnovsky were Narkom instead of me and if he were free to do as he pleased, he would crush the Left Front once and for all, while if it were Meyerhold who was in my shoes, he wouldn't think twice before smashing the Right Front. And if, after Lunacharsky, you were to get first Sosnovsky then Meyerhold, you'd get successive pogroms against the left and then against the right. The fact that there are differences of opinion means that a Narkom must not allow his tastes—no matter what those tastes may be—to govern the land".[11]

During his period of office Lunacharsky upheld his role as referee, never yielding to excesses of administrative arbitrariness. This is what accounts for the cultural flowering of the 1920s and the coexistence of opposing, antagonistic movements inspired by contradictory ideologies and aesthetics. Futurists, formalists, imaginists, constructivists, parnassians, neo-classicists, acmeists, negativists, and a host of others thus enjoyed the right (and the means) of expression. Lenin and the other Bolshevik leaders (Trotsky, Bukharin), while concerned to establish Party control in every sphere, never dreamt of interfering with the writers' and artists' freedom of creation and expression, as evidenced by Lenin's remark to Clara Zetkin:

"Every artist, whoever he may be, has the right to create *freely, in accordance with his ideals, and independently* of all interference. But it goes without saying that as communists we cannot remain passive and allow things to develop chaotically in all directions. We are absolutely bound to direct the process methodically, and to shape its outcome".[12]

This apparently contradictory state of affairs well illustrates the cultural situation in Lenin's Soviet Union. The individual rights of artists and writers were respected, but firm organisation was regarded as vital in order to prevent the dynamic of the existing antagonisms from degenerating into disorder and anarchy. While tolerating, accepting, and sometimes even protecting the most extreme of tendencies (Lenin reproached him his indulgence towards Mayakovsky and the futurists), Lunacharsky nonetheless saw as his chief task the propagation of "already existing" culture, in order to enlighten the proletariat; his task was to instruct and educate hitherto under-privileged classes in popular culture (rather than "proletarian" in the revolutionary and quasi-messianic sense still advocated by some). His achievement in this respect was considerable, and his great merit was that he eschewed dogmatism and rigidity along with *a priori* planning from above, preferring an open-ended approach that sorted well with his humanism, his intellectual curiosity, his vast learning, his love for literature, poetry and the theatre.

His record was positive in as much as he held sectarianism at bay and prevented the triumph of any one tendency at the expense of the others. His activity amounted to a programme of conservation and diffusion of the literary and artistic works of the past which was launched in the very first days of Soviet power. It demonstrates firstly the importance (contrary to what has often been claimed) that the Bolsheviks attached to cultural questions, and secondly that right from the outset their policy tended in a direction utterly opposed to the one hoped for and demanded by the futurist and proletkult avant-garde. The Russian classics were reprinted by the million; measures were taken to safeguard and restore historic monuments and works of art; in particular, a gigantic publishing and translating venture, the "Universal Library" was embarked on, partly in order to secure the allegiance of intellectuals to the new regime by providing them with work, and partly to bring the literatures and cultures of the world within easy reach of the masses. This wonderful, grandiose project unfortunately ground to a halt before it could be completed, but it does stand to the credit of the Soviet Union of the 1920s when, in the midst of famine and civil war, the government gave evidence of such generosity and determination to build a brighter future for all—and from every point of view: material, intellectual and moral.

Such was the "proletarian culture" Lenin had in mind. He aimed at providing the proletariat with access to a culture of which it had until then been deprived and isolated—this culture being, moreover, the very one inherited from Tsarist imperialism and the capitalist bour-geoisie (Russian and western).

The policy was plainly one of preservation and conquest of the past, founded upon a deep mistrust of "modernism" and the "avant

garde'', and primarily concerned with a widely and easily communic-.
able art and literature, that would be accessible to the broadest
possible public. Although he continued to pin his hopes on the future
of a "new" culture, Lunacharsky, out of loyalty to Lenin and swayed
by a certain humanist sagacity, threw his heart into the job of carrying out this policy. He was particularly successful in his efforts to open
up the Soviet Union to the outside world, projecting a more reassuring
image of the country and winning over growing numbers of sympathi-
sers. It was essential to break out of the isolation and the intellectual
blockade that had been thrown up around the new regime, and hence
to adopt a policy of compromise. It was Lunacharsky who coined the
term "fellow traveller", and expended an enormous amount of
energy in establishing vast international organisations in which these
"fellow travellers" could play a role. To this end he made use of his
personal connections with leading European writers such as Romain
Rolland, Stefan Zweig, H.G. Wells, George Bernard Shaw, Feucht-
wanger, Jules Romain, Henri Barbusse, etc. His aim was to win over
ever-broader sections of the European intelligentsia. He realised that
in order to achieve this he would have to avoid setting impossible
political demands. He issued a great many appeals and undertook a
number of initiatives with this end in view. In 1920, for instance, he
sent friendly greetings to a group of "left-wing" French writers and
artists. In an article published in *Clarté* in 1921 he remarked with
satisfaction that "the proletariat exercises a more powerful attraction
over the young intelligentsia than does capital, and this despite all the
resources at the latter's disposal to buy it off''.

Resolutely internationalist, fluent in several languages and curious
about cultures other than his own, Lunacharsky fought against the
nationalist tendencies which were ultimately to triumph. His efforts to
re-establish contact with western intellectuals presupposed a free flow
of information, and one can only admire the objectivity with which,
under his auspices, even such "bourgeois" (or positively reactionary)
playwrights, writers and poets as Marcel Proust, Jean Giraudoux, Paul
Morand and Paul Claudel (*L'Annonce faite à Marie*) were introduced
into the Soviet Union, translated and performed during the 1920s.
Aesthetic and political objectivity went hand in hand, as can be seen
from the fact that Joyce's *Ulysses* was translated into Russian and
received with a chorus of praise.

Lunacharsky pursued the same line on the home front as abroad,
with the same open-mindedness, the same freedom from sectarianism
and dogmatism; he rallied a great many intellectuals by recruiting and

encouraging "fellow travellers", tirelessly defending them, moreover, from attacks by certain factions hostile to them in the name of ideological purity.

The "fellow travellers" were indeed the favourite targets of the proletarian writers gathered around such journals as *October*, *The Forge*, and above all *On Guard* (*Na Postu*), which formed the core of the "Association of Proletarian Writers". For a while the latter managed to virtually monopolise Soviet literature. A resolution published in *October* in 1925 declared that "the commonest variety of 'fellow traveller' is the writer who disfigures the revolution and who frequently besmirches it; who is impregnated with the spirit of nationalism, great power chauvinism and mysticism...We may say with a great deal of justification that the literature of the 'fellow travellers' is essentially directed against the proletarian revolution" (No. 1, p. 11).

These words were directed as much against left-wing western writers who sympathised with the new regime as against Soviet literary groups such as "Pereval" or the group gathered around the Marxist journal *Krasnaya Nov* run by Voronsky, which had preferred cautious collaboration to unconditional adhesion and which also counted themselves among the "fellow travellers'". The latter included the "Serapion Brothers". Such was the name adopted, in memory of Hoffman, by a group of young writers seeking to renew the aesthetic of the novel. Most of them were former students of the Institute of Art History, which in 1920 had become one of the leading centres of formalism in Petrograd. These young writers, Kaverin, Lunts, Vsevolyod Ivanov, Nikitin, Slonimsky, Fedin, sought to apply the teachings of their masters Eykhenbaum, Tynyanov and Shklovsky in their novels. While they felt close to the Revolution, they claimed that literature was entirely autonomous vis-à-vis political ideology, and they were profoundly hostile to propagandist or circumstantial art. The fact that they took Zamyatin as their model but also received advice and encouragement from Gorky suffices to demonstrate how ambiguous their position was. Their work, and especially that of Kaverin, may be viewed as an extension of formal aesthetics, an attempt—sometimes fruitful, sometimes less so—to build the literature of the future on the foundations of formalism.

The very existence of this group (whose members subsequently experienced very different fates: Zoshchenko was condemned by Zhdanov, while Konstantin Fedin was to become Secretary-General of the Writers' Union) is evidence of just how complex cultural life in the Soviet Union in the 1920s was.

Some movements tried to reconcile the most contradictory tendencies, and often died as a result. Yet between 1925 and 1932 the
Proletarian Writers strove, with growing obstinacy and success, to
identify literature with the Party line. From this disparate confusion of
slogans and tendencies there gradually emerged an order that was
ultimately to establish itself unshakeably. The R.A.P.P. had
managed, little by little, to eliminate its rivals and, under the arch-
bureaucrat Averbach's direction, instituted a veritable reign of ideological terror in the world of letters. This reached a peak in 1930, at the
Congress held in Kharkov, where its line triumphed utterly and
succeeded in having all the other tendencies condemned, especially
those that aspired to harmonise their "modernist" and formalist
conception of art with revolutionary faith. Mayakovsky's battles with
these proletarian poets towards the end of his life are well-known;
having spent himself struggling against them in vain, he finally went
over to them shortly before his death.

To be sure, he shared with the "October" and "On Guard"
proletarians their hostility to the culture of the past and their ardour in
rooting out the petty-bourgeois mentality awakened and fostered by
the NEP, as well as their preoccupation with ideological commitment.
But proletarians and lefists clashed violently on the question of form
in literature, for this problem bore directly on the work's power of
communication and accessibility to the masses. This indeed was one of
the main criticisms levelled at Mayakovsky's poetry.

The formalists and futurists, for their part, took issue with the
proletarians over the contradictions between their theory and their
practice—between revolutionary content and the forms inherited from
the past (which negated the content).

In *Futurism and Revolution*, Gorlov reiterates most of the LEF's
objections to proletarian poetry, accusing it of failing its revolutionary
vocation by taking inspiration from such outdated models as the
romances of Balmont and Bryusov: an epigones' poetry devoid of the
least vestige of innovation, content to transfer the clichés of the lyric
poetry of the past onto proletarian themes.

For LEF, the revolution now occurring in the economic and social
structures of society had inevitably to be accompanied by an aesthetic
revolution: the task before them was as much to transform people's
habits and mentalities as to change their class relations, and poetry was
meant to help promote a new kind of man.

This naturally implied a poetry and an art diametrically opposed to
the gratuitous, non-committal, aestheticising conception that had
characterised the heyday of symbolism and decadentism. The LEF

constructivists claimed to be seeking a fresh definition of poetic language, one capable of inventing words with the full force of the emotion, conviction and necessity truly consonant with the era then emerging: such a definition would flow from an intimate, profound and total harmony between the poet and his age, between the poet and the spirit and demands of the society of his time. It was with this intention that the lefists issued their first battle-cry "social command", which was immediately taken up by the Rappists, although in a very different register. The triumph of this slogan towards the end of the 1920s was to assure the Organisation of Proletarian Writers virtually absolute domination over Soviet literature, subjecting it to a set of ideological criteria which, little by little, came to take the form of a vigilant Party control. Condemnation was not restricted to such tendencies as could justifiably be said to deviate from or actually oppose Marxism; even writers and critics who had shortly before been regarded as leading figures of the Marxist school, such as Voronsky or Perverzev, were ruthlessly denounced and purged for deviationism, on the grounds that they did not wholeheartedly subscribe to the Rappist line.

Thus the RAPP embarked on a process which it was not long in falling victim to itself, crushed by a logic by now familiar to us all. Its liquidation in 1932 was merely the regime's appropriation of a policy the efficiency of which it had admired before determining to apply it directly, for its own ends. The "line", henceforward, would no longer be laid down by a group of writer-ideologists, even in "uniform", but would emanate directly from the Supreme Organs. This monolithism was to result in the banishing of any aesthetic that conflicted with the ground-rules laid down once and for all; one could even say, in the last analysis, that it contrived to freeze all literary and artistic life, almost totally stifling critical and creative activity.

Following the dissolution of the RAPP, all reference to proletarian culture, literature or poetry vanished, to be replaced by the canons of "socialist realism". As pointed out earlier, though, the Writers' Union proved a worthy successor to the spirit and methods of the RAPP, and the prevailing aesthetic under its reign was no less restrictive or sterile than the one dictated by the RAPP in the name of "social command".

The period of apparent liberalism and relative thaw that accompanied the First Congress of Soviet Writers, held in Moscow in 1934 under Gorky's chairmanship (at which a certain Zhdanov was to make his first public appearance) was illusory, for the dice had already been cast. The RAPP's proclaimed hatred of intellectuals in the name of the interests of the proletariat and of proletarian culture engendered a long-lasting revulsion from anything that smacked of intelligence. It lasted, to be precise, until destalinisation and the revival of Russian letters that ensued. Add to this the fear of imagination that accompanied this bureaucratisation of culture and of life in general, which Mayakovsky had already attacked in his *The Bedbug* and *The Baths* and which for Russian letters was to replace the myth of Pugachev with the sinister shades of Nechayev, and his "barracks socialism". Formalism became an apithet of shame, attached to any and every innovative tendency, whether in literature, poetry, literary criticism, the plastic arts, music or the sciences.

In this way, though hardly in the form they had anticipated, were accomplished the dreams of destruction which, since the end of the last century, had haunted Russian thinkers and poets alike. This great populist myth of destruction and purification which, with its sources laying in Bakumin, was embodied in the sagas of Pugachev and Stenka Razin, never did produce a revival in which poetry would become identified with the people in the blossoming of a wild, untrammeled liberty, with Russia turning its back on the West to return to its Asiatic roots, as Blok, Esenin, Khlebnikov and many others had dreamt. Indeed it was to work the other way round, in a tragic and total misunderstanding which mistook the proletariat for the people and indeed confused the minority that led the proletariat for the proletariat itself, producing the fossilisation of traditional forms, immersion into the grinding monotony of the *byt*, and the sinister and familiar sound of dykes, barriers and gates clanging shut.

The seeds of all this had been contained in the direction taken by proletarian culture at the decisive turning point of the middle nineteen-twenties, when Lenin's death had left the field wide open to the rival factions.

1924, the year of publication of most of the articles reprinted here, was therefore a crucial year in every respect. The formalists were at their apogee, and the LEF, to whom they were very close, looked like having every chance of triumphing, under the leadership of Mayakovsky and Osip Brik. The Marxists, fearing this success, sought by every means to check it, seeking first to persuade by reason, later by intimidation; their aim was to convince the formalists of the error of their ways, to isolate them from their public (from youth) and, having isolated them, to oblige them to surrender (Shklovsky), or to shut up (Eykhenbaum).

By lumping formalism, futurism and every form of ''modernism'' together with the old idealism of the believers in ''art for art's sake'' (the symbolist and decadent sects), the way was paved for the realism—or rather the utilitarianism—of a Pisarev, which in turn prepared the ground for the massive return of bourgeois academicism.

The public debate organised by *Press and Revolution* served as a focal point for the campaign being mounted by the spokesmen of Marxism (Kogan, Lunacharsky, Polyansky and Trotsky) against formalism, to which the rest of the avant-garde was not yet assimilated. This campaign waxed increasingly virulent until 1930, the year of Mayakovsky's death and of Victor Shklovsky's self-criticism, putting an end to hopes people might have placed in formalist criticism and in futurist poetry as the forerunners of a new culture and of a new life. It is worth noting, in this respect, that the adversaries of both the formalists and the futurists concentrated their criticisms on two essential principles, which they sought to present as latter-day versions of the old art for art's sake theories: the specificity of literary facts and language facts, and the refusal to dissociate form from content in a work, which was to be apprehended as an indissoluble whole. In fact these principles lay at the heart of a current of thought which, far from seeking to cut art and literature off from life, actually conceived of them in terms of profound unity with it.

This specificity of verbal and literary creation claimed by the formalists in their works as critics, and by the futurists in their poetry is conceivable solely through the freedom that it derives from the necessity of its own internal laws and its autonomy; but it is immediately deformed and misconstrued if we try to consider it in a biographical, ideological, political, religious or some other light—which is not to deny its obvious links with all these other series but merely, on the contrary, to accord them their full weight and meaning. Separation into categories, the independence of series, specialisation (''specification''), are a necessary condition—if not a sufficient one—of the progress in every sphere of a creative invention that is only capable of being exercised if subjected to competent, knowledgeable criticism, but which dies out or else ossifies if reduced to a single all-powerful guiding idea, to a single ''line'' or dogma. The pluralism of that period contrasts with the monolithism of the succeeding one. Which is why formalists, futurists and constructivists all conceived of their activities not as being in opposition to Marxism but as complementary to it.

This refusal to artificially distinguish form from content equally upset the hollow rules, the conventions and the facile schemas of the old dualist mentality.

The futurists' "new word" was supposed spontaneously and naturally to express the new society, the modern era. The rupture with "psychologism" here went hand in hand with the revolt against the academic tradition.

The importance accorded to words, to verbal matter, and to the organisation of this matter conceived as an organic whole in which to attempt to dissociate form from substance would be fruitless, brought them far closer to materialist positions than to the idealism or spiritualism imputed to them. The views put forward by Arvatov in LEF on literary production, however schematic they may have been, were significant of this tendency to merge formalism, futurism and Marxism.

A literary work, then, is on the one hand a system of signs constituting an indivisible organic whole: it is impossible to dissociate, wrote Zhirmunsky, the emotions and ideas of a poem from the words which express them; on the other hand, it is a product, a manufactured object, and it would be just as absurd, the same Zhirmunsky went on, to try to separate out the form from the content in a work of literature as it would be in a "ready-made".[13] Art is a series of processes of manufacture, of techniques which need above all to be understood and described. The "how" must precede the "why", and exact knowledge the final judgement. This scientific premise ought to be sufficient to head off the kind of misunderstanding which, either through ignorance or malevolence, is always the first step in the direction of the rejection of truth and negation of the spirit.

"The literary work of art", wrote Eykhenbaum, "is always something made, shaped, invented—not just artful, but also artificial, in the best sense of the term". (B. Eykhenbaum, Poetica-Petrograd, 1919, p. 161).

Note in passing the bonds this assumes between the critical and the creative spirits, between industry, skill, talent and science, between taste and knowledge.

The functional beauty of the constructivists flowed from this formalist notion of a rigorous, coherent and necessary composition which overthrew all those luxurious, ostentatious, superfluous and—precisely—formal aspects of the traditional bourgeois way of life which corresponded to a gratuitous, decorative idea of beauty for which economic and social conditions were able to supply an adequate explanation. The aims and the experiments of the Russian literary and artistic avant-garde, of what was termed at the time "left-wing art", at the turn of the twenties, thus sought to replace the aesthetics of bourgeois culture and life-styles (which were then tending to seep back via the NEP) with a new, "modern", functional aesthetic, one that accorded with the transformation of society taking place and that aimed at changing, organically and at one and the same time, people's tastes, mentalities, and life-styles.

As opposed to the conception of culture which consisted simply in making the classical heritage available to the proletariat, in order to educate it, which is more or less what Lenin, Trotsky and Lunacharsky wanted (although the first two were fairly sceptical about any chances of a "proletarian culture" coming about); opposed, on the other hand, to those in the Proletkult and later in the RAPP who thought that culture should be the work of the proletariat alone, and who, acting on this belief, merely ended up with a ridiculous parody, a sterile repetition and a copy of the past, the formalists and the futurists advocated a "modern" literature and art that was not only intended to answer the aspirations of the rising class but also to affect its future. Their art and their literature were to mobilise the intelligence and the imagination of each and every one of us in the process of permanent creativity.

It was not enough merely to change the economy and society: it was also vital to change man himself, on pain of being drawn remorselessly back into the past. Lenin understood this when, shortly before his death, he insisted on the need to transform the Russian peasant morally, if anything was to be achieved, rather than use force on him; it was Lenin too who, his repugnance for avant-garde poetry notwithstanding, praised the political usefulness of one of Mayakovsky's satirical poems aimed at the bureaucracy.

And yet, gradually, between 1924 and 1930, the positions of the formalist and futurist avant-garde disintegrated and, through a succession of recantations and abandonments, finally sank for good, yielding their place to an academicism that, by a perversion of that same language onto which these poets and critics had sought to impress coherence and rigour, was hailed as the aesthetic of the Revolution.

1   Brik: see note 6 p. 96.
2   *Opoyaz*: see note 2 p. 95.
3   Rappists: members of the R.A.P.P. (Association of Russian Proletarian Poets).

4   Bogdanov (pseudonym of Alexander Alexandrovich Malinowsky((1873-1928), philosopher, sociologist, economist, doctor; one of the founders of Russian social-democracy, he was also one of the leaders and theoreticians of Proletkult.
5   *The Proletarian* was the name of the newspaper founded by Lenin in 1904 after *Iskra* had passed into the hands of the Mensheviks.
6   *Narkompros*: abbreviated form of People's Commisar for Education.
7   Lenin, *Collected Works*.
8   *Lunacharsky, Articles on Soviet Literature*, Moscow 1971 (presented by Terekhov).
9   Victor Erlich, *Russian Formalism, History, Doctrine*, Mouton, The Hague 1955, (p. 63).
10 Recollections of Inès Armand's daughter, quoted in *Lunacharsky, op. cit.* p. 540.
11 *Ibid.* p. 525.
12 *Ibid.* p. 540.
13 Victor Zhirmunsky, *Voprosy Teorii Literatury*, Leningrad 1928, pp. 20-22.